The Blind Man

Thinking from Elsewhere

The Blind Man

A Phantasmography

Robert Desjarlais

FORDHAM UNIVERSITY PRESS

New York 2019

Fordham University Press gratefully acknowledges financial assistance and support provided for the publication of this book by Sarah Lawrence College.

Fordham University Press also publishes its books in a variety of electronic formats. Some content that appears in print may not be available in electronic books.

Visit us online at www.fordhampress.com.

Library of Congress Cataloging-in-Publication Data available online at https://catalog.loc.gov.

Printed in the United States of America

21 20 19 5 4 3 2 1

First edition

CONTENTS

PREFACE

Imagine a man, a scholar, say, or a writer, in midlife, who, unsure of his aims, becomes interested in photography. This work becomes a passion of his. He learns of photographic desire and regret. He takes photos most when he is traveling, which in these years means Europe. In his spare time, while on train journeys or in hotel rooms, in random cafés, he looks closely at the images involved. He makes a study of these apparitions and their phantom forms. Along the way he becomes interested in one of the subjects of the photographs. He travels to Paris and tries to meet this person. In perceiving this stranger and the images his appearance projects, he begins to imagine what this man's life is like and how he perceives the world around him. Eventually, the scholar-writer becomes unsure as to what he sees, hears, or remembers. Through these interpretive dilemmas he senses the complexities of perception, where all is multiple, shifting, spectral, a surge of phantasms in which the actual and the imagined are endlessly blurred and intertwined. His mind shifts from thinking about photographs and images to being fixed on the visceral force of apparitions. His own vision is affected in a troubling way. In the end, the man comes to realize that he, too, is phantomic, that everything in life, and in the lives of others, is phantasmal.

This happened, more or less, to the author of the text that follows, through a series of encounters and events chronicled in these pages. One of the main narrative strands of the book attends to the sensate fact of several photographs that I took of a man who frequents the Basilica of Sacré-Coeur in Montmartre, Paris, in the hope of receiving donations from those who visit the basilica. I took the first photographs in October 2012, in the final days of a seven-week journey through France, in which I was collecting material—observations, memories, words, images—for a "photographic memoir" I was then composing of my life as a student in France years earlier. While standing on the steps of the basilica one chilly autumn morning I photographed this man as he was being photographed by two other men. As I was working with black-and-white digital photography then, I converted the image into a monochrome photo and included it in the memoir I was writing. (That memoir, "Photos in My Lost Hours," remains unpublished. It got lost along the way.)

Only much later did the intricacies of the photographic image come to intrigue me, particularly in terms of the perceptions, motives, and understandings of those apparent in the image. While traveling in the South of France in the summer of 2014 I carried with me the unfinished memoir, one page of which held a print of the photograph. I found myself trying to grasp the complexities of a picture that attended to the rich and polyvalent moment of a complicated encounter. I began to write out a series of reflections on what appeared to be taking place within the space of the image. I kept these tentative reflections in a notebook, with each entry dated. I did not necessarily have any sort of book project in mind, then; I was simply writing out my thoughts. In time, these interpretive endeavors led to a wide-ranging inquiry into processes of vision, blindness, and imaginative phantasms as they take form in people's lives. I returned to Paris in 2015, to undertake informal ethnographic research at the Basilica of Sacré-Coeur and in Paris more generally. This work in part entailed "hanging out" at the basilica and observing much of what took place there, including the engagements of tourists, musicians, beggars, sellers, and police who frequent the place. Through the course of these visits I encountered the man on several occasions; I took additional photographs of him, observed his modes of interacting at the basilica, and exchanged a few words with him. As the first photographs were in black-and-white, I stayed with that monochromatic method. These engagements and the reflections they generated form the core of this book, which attends to the fraught, ambivalent dimensions of photographic capture; encounters with others and alterity; modalities of vision and blindness; the politics of looking; forms of voyeurism and surveillance; the unsettling powers of the gaze; media images of violence and abjection; and the nature of fantasy and imaginative construal. In effect, the book is an inquiry into intersubjective knowing in its many modalities in contemporary life.

Questions of image and fabulation lie at the heart of the text. How do images circulate in the world, be it in a person's life, or between strangers, or through collective representations and global forms of media? What is the play between imaginative fancy and actual circumstances in life? The book explores these concerns by attending to a plethora of images encountered during my engagements in France and elsewhere (simulations, doubles, delirium, fantasies, specters, hauntings, projections, memories) and their media modalities (perceptions, the body, dreams, prosthetic devices, films, videos, speech, the Internet, fables, storytelling, books, architecture, paintings and drawings, graffiti) in order to attend to the imaginative dimensions of a life and to stress the central role that fabulation plays in the lives of human beings. Such inquiries, as conveyed in these pages, lead not so much to any clear and direct ethnography, to the writing of a people's way of life, than they do to a "phantasmography," a writing of phantasms, a graphic inscription of the flows and currents of fantasy and fabulation. "Phantasm" is considered here in the variable sense of an apparition or illusion; a ghost or phantom; an imaginary construct; a fantastical image or vision; a haunting memory; a fanciful idea; or a cohering fantasy, momentary or lifelong, conscious or unconscious. This book, then, is a compendium of phantasms. To paraphrase one passage, so much in life is imagined, not concretely real, and an anthropology attuned to the imaginary—a fantastical anthropology, an anthropology of the phantasmal—needs to account for the force and tenor of the imagined, the possible, the conjectured, the feared and dreamed of, specters of memory and perception, within the phantasmal flow of its thought and expression. It's not enough to stick with empirical studies of apparently real things, for life is much more than that. Nor can one contend that there is a strict divide between what is taken as the perceived and the imagined, or the actual and the virtual, for these forces are closely intertwined. At stake is a *phanomenology* of perception and imagination, of life itself.

A narrative approach to the material at hand—rather than a systematic analytic approach, for instance—makes good sense. For one, the material is rooted in a temporal framework; each passage in the book appears as a dated entry in a journal kept for over a year's time. The engagements noted in the text took place in time, and thus writing about all of this in a récit-like manner reflects well the emergence of thought and imagined actualities. Perception itself occurs, and transforms, in time. The perceptions recounted hold a multitude of singularities, baroque looks and second looks in a delirium of looking. No singular thesis or argument is advanced in the book, nor is there any clear and coherent conclusion to be found. The text is marked, rather, by shifting forms of sensory perception, the instability and mutability of vision, the impossibility of certainty, the limitations of language, thought, and logical reasoning, and the haunting powers of imaginative vision.

The book is composed of a weave of words and images—photographs and drawings, especially. The combination of texts and images is in itself of some significance, as much of photographic art is coming to explore how text and photographs might work together to say something new and telling about people's experiences in the world. Through these engagements in photographic practices—fieldwork in photography, as it were—I have been trying to understand what is involved in such practices, from the politics of looking to the global circulation of visual imagery. This inquiry explores the many, sometimes vexed ways that photography can serve as a means of anthropological inquiry. It also touches on themes of voyeurism implicit in social science research and the possible exploitative use of the images and lives of others as well as the violence implicit in forms of surveillance, profiling, and perceptual interpretation.

I realize that, in circulating photographs taken of a man unknown to me, I risk being at fault for voyeuristic exploitation. Some readers I imagine will find this to be the case. I have doubts myself about the integrity of this project, and I remain ambivalent about the publication of this book. But perhaps there is value in writing about such matters in direct, attentive—and ambivalent—ways, such that others might also come to perceive the concerns at hand.

Imagine a man who encounters another through the fantastical medium of photography. In picturing this man, and others, envisioning what their lives are like, how they sense and know an angled world, spiders included, he gets caught up in the force of imaginative fancy.

Take care: in playing with phantoms, one becomes a phantom.

And if seeing was fire, I required the plenitude of fire,
and if seeing would infect me with madness,
I madly wanted that madness.

—Maurice Blanchot, *The Madness of the Day*

Prends garde: à jouer au fantôme, on le deviant.

—Roger Caillois, *Mimétisme et la psychasthénie légendaire*

Photography tears the subject from itself

July 6. Paris. I cannot see this man. I cannot perceive or know him. There is no mark of truth to him, no pure sign of light.

July 7. How does perception work in the contemporary world? What is involved in any act of seeing? How do images pulse through life or seed within a tremulous brain?

July 8. Arles. I am looking at a photograph. I have been looking at it for days now. The photo keeps calling me to take another look, and another after that. The image has taken possession of me like a restless spirit from elsewhere seizing hold of an unknowing mortal. I find myself swooning into the picture much as I have fallen into deep afternoon sleeps after arriving jet-lagged in Paris: when I wake hours later into a funk of grogginess, unsure where or who I am in the world or what day or hour it is, the sleep rears up and pulls me into the depth of dreams and murmured voices.

I took the photograph two years ago, in October 2012, while standing on the steps leading up to the Basilica of Sacré-Coeur in Paris, on the Butte Montmartre, mount of the martyr, the highest point in the city.

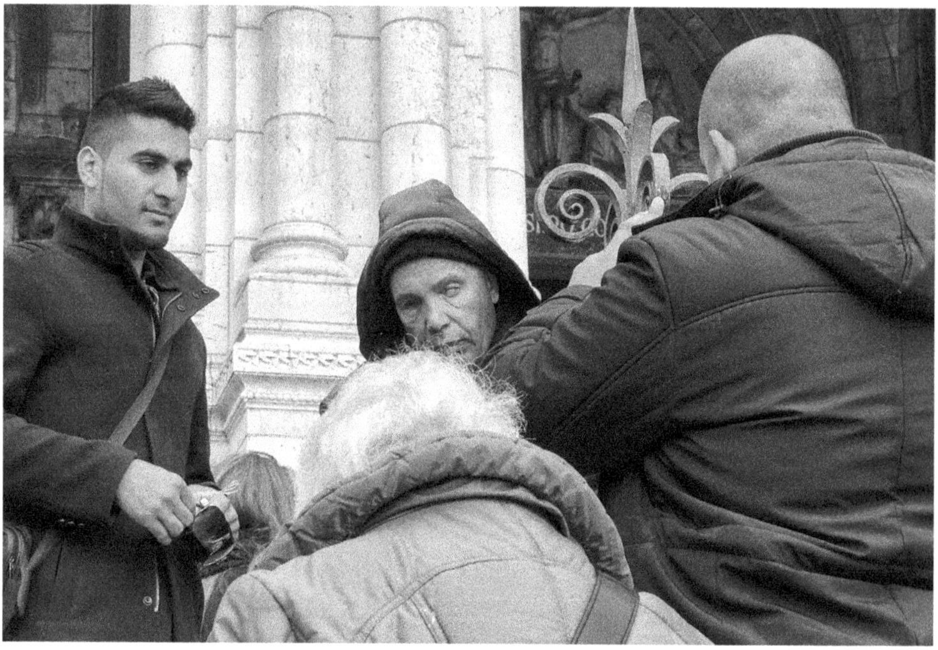

At first glance it's a simple story, once you know something of the photograph's production in time and space. The man to the left had asked the man in the center if they could be photographed with each other. His friend, the man to the right, is taking the photograph. I photographed the three of them in the act of photographing, in a moment just before, while, or after the camera clicked an image.

The man between them had been standing about the steps for some time, for as long as I had been there that day. He was asking for money—begging, panhandling, *mendier*, to beg, solicit charity, call it what you will—in a quiet, understated way. He stood out among the others because of his appearance, his silent stillness. He had positioned himself by the steps, embraced by a dark winter coat, with his hand held out, softly, close to his waist, not assertive. He did not want to be there, his stance suggested, but he was there within the elements to earn a keep for the day.

Police were roaming about in those midday hours, asking beggars and street sellers to move on. They did not ask him to leave, he was not drawing attention to himself. He did not thrust out an empty hand, beseeching passing tourists, as other beggars had been doing, until the police swept them away. He stood quietly, hands close to his sides.

The man did not look like the alms-askers who wait outside the entrances to churches in France and elsewhere, *le priant*, the praying, who hope to receive charity from devout souls leaving or entering a church. He looked unsure of how to plead for money at this site of reverence and attraction.

I had come to Sacré-Coeur that day to revisit a place I had encountered years ago. The cloying rush of tourists, hovering about the scrub of land like ants treading a sand hill, was displeasing to me. Yet the scene made for easy photographs. Just about everyone had a camera. Friends and families were clicking high and low, making pictures of the basilica straight on, they held their iPads aloft, they peered into cell phones, they crafted snapshots of themselves among friends or family with the church as a majestic relief and the hazy arrondissements of Paris far below. I simulated joining in on the visual frenzy in seeking to photograph all that moved about. I was a wolf among sheep, plucking images from the flock. I took photographs of children spinning about the ponies fixed into a carousel at the edge of Montmartre, of the miniature, glow-in-the-dark Eiffel Towers sold by men from Africa, of people relaxing in lunchtime sunlight, and of a woman seated by its entrance, asking for alms.

Camera in hand, I stepped inside the cool of the church. I returned to the sunlight near the steps. At some point I saw the blind man standing next to another man, about to have a photograph taken. I must have acted quickly. It was easier that the man was not looking my way. I raised the lens and triggered the shutter, which sparked the twenty-three million image sensors in the camera's cortex to ink their photographic work. I held onto the picture that now lies close to these words.

I now have this image with me, along with a few other photographs, as I travel about in France. The image lies below my retina when I sleep at night.

July 10. I now have a decent read on the photograph, after considering it for hours, walking about this city of images. Better and far more pleasing photographs are to be viewed at the photography festival taking place this summer, and yet my thoughts circle back to an image taken two years earlier.

Four figures stand most apparent in the photograph, or five if one counts what appears to be a girl on the periphery; her image is fragmented, supplemental, easily overlooked. The four figures form a quartet of bodies: the man, potentially blind; the man standing next to him; the man taking the photograph; and the woman below those three, walking into the frame of my own secondary photograph. Whenever I look at the image my eyes move from figure to figure apparent in the image, the two faces visible and the two others present. The perceptions are dispersed, moving from face to face, to stone column, metal post, to the camera held in one man's hand. I keep coming back to the man in the middle of the image. The energy of the vision centers centrifugally on that central figure, his face especially. There is a gravitational force to his dark sun presence. The photograph as a whole is a rustle, a disturbance. Some experts speak of photography as a medium of death. For me, this photograph comes from a tumult far before death, or in the ferment before a birth.

The man on the left is posing for the photograph. Apparently. In dim light I thought at first that this youngish man was holding another camera in his hands; the object now appears to be a pair of stylish, glare-resistant sunglasses. Sunglasses can enhance vision by diminishing hazy sunlight; they can also hide the eyes and obscure the soul that sees through the eyes, and so better to take the glasses off when posing for a photograph. Is this young man visiting Paris? He is probably not from France, or so I suspect. He hails from another land. He is traveling with his friend, the man taking his image. Or his friend lives in Paris and he is visiting him there. They are going about the town, seeing the sights, nightclubs, riding the Métro, snacking on crêpes smoldering with chocolate Nutella. The image is rife with possibilities, you see, there are many lines of probability, suggested by the imagery involved. Of nothing can we be certain. We tell ourselves stories. It's a cold day in Paris.

My thoughts go to this young man, to his face and eyes and the branch of veins and knuckles in his hands. I try to imagine what his life is like, what brought him to Paris and to the basilica that day. Will he send the image to a girlfriend or a sister back home? Much of his life lies ahead of him, his minor history is behind him. I am in that vague uncertain terrain that lies indefinitely in the interface between one person and another. We know so little about others. A flatness defines my comprehension of this man. My perceptions hit a wall as dense as the dark, rain-resistant fabric of his coat.

This youngish man is holding the faint line of a clipped smile, just a thin line, no beaming for the folks back home. Self-conscious before the camera, he is holding himself still and stable for the picture. In this one instant he is there, standing on the steps of the basilica, he is in Paris on this fine sunny cold day in October. He wishes a photo to mark the occasion, a record of that concrete fact. There may have been other pictures taken of him before this moment, and others after that. They might have surfaced on Facebook, or Tumblr, or Instagram. You have to wonder about this, where the images get to, one way or another. Images travel. They disperse like pollen in an April breeze, particles petering out or emerging into new and vital formations. When I consider their many possible destinations, time opens up before me, present, past, and future, I get lost within those swirls of time. I am taken outside of myself, once again. I am far from singular or finite. I try to come back to the present. It's not easy holding onto a single moment. Each moment skips off into other moments, like stones skimming across ocean waters.

The younger man is standing next to the man apparently blind. I was stunned when I saw that sudden pairing. He had asked the blind man to pose with him. How outrageous, I said to myself, to put the man on the spot in that way. The photographers wanted to have him become a freakish sideshow, to be a dramatic figure within a photo at a tourist attraction, a selfie with a twist: a man stands by the entrance to the basilica, a blind man by his side. Passion and suffering on the Mount. The blind man of Sacré-Coeur. We know of the photoerotic pleasure of coming close to the ground of suffering, of witnessing its presence, vicariously living the tale of it, of seeing and being seen close to its presence, but not too close.

The two subjects of that brief instant are standing side by side, a good foot apart from one another. There are no bodies leaning into one another, no arms embracing, there is no trace of a touch or sensate contact. I see no shared looks, no real connection. They are others to each other.

The blind man appears to be looking down, away from the view of the camera, with no smile or glint of joy on his face. He looks alone among others, head bowed.

Why did they think this would make for a decent photograph, *un bon souvenir*? We are left to wonder if the two visitors had some particular notion in mind, unfamiliar to me, to the effect that it's an auspicious matter to be photographed while standing next to a blind man. Would the image serve as a lucky charm down the road? Or was there something in the culture of the two visitors that encouraged them to enact a record of standing alongside a figure of abjection? The interpretations run rampant, you see, we can barely hold on. We are left to wonder.

And yet the blind man went along with the arrangement. He agreed to be included within the frame, for a few centimes. Evidently. I cannot recall observing the two men's request, their pitch to the blind man to be included in their photograph. What I do recall remembering, or imagine remembering, or remember imagining, is that once the photo was taken there was a release of the still pause, a dissipation of the tension of bodies held taut. Their worlds ticked on, the young man retrieved a coin and handed it to the blind man apparent. That older man held the coin in his hand, he looked down, checking its value. He looked up and nodded his head, signing off on the deal. The young man nodded in turn. Transaction completed, they parted ways. I cannot say that they looked each other in the eyes. I don't know about that. You see I cannot say if the blind man could see, or not.

There was a careless, casual meanness to their intent, I thought. I was no better, perhaps. No worse, perhaps. I was prepared to picture the man's unseeing presence in another form of visuality, when we were not standing face to face, no words involved.

July 12. The photograph has been transporting me to an imaginary realm between the actual and the phantasmal. My eyes are drawn to the man in the center of the photograph, the blind or semi-blind man. He is looking down. His visage is one of humility, graveness, and, perhaps, shame; or so I read his downcast expression. I do not think he is simply performing that humility, making a show of his abjection, better to make a buck. He is not pleased about being photographed with his visual deformation on display, because of that deformity, but he's gotten used to it, it comes with the territory. He is required to sell his deformity, display himself, convert poor vision into hard cash. He needs the looks of others while dismayed by those looks. This is how I imagine him without knowing him at all. Such is my sympathetic leaning toward him. I have only his appearance to go by and what my imagination weaves out of the silk of those fine details. The man's face appears weathered, folds of surface skin moon-circled below his eyes. I have at times wondered if this man was Moroccan in origin, in proscribed or proclaimed identity, for in the photo he is wearing clothes that remind me of the djellaba that Berber men wear. That perception sets off a sea of possibilities, histories of fantasy and simulation. That perception appears to be a mirage. The man's coat looks as though it could come from a bargain store in France. The thought occurs now that the man might have acquired that particular coat because it reminded him, subliminally or overtly, of the clothing he and other men wore back home, and he found comfort in that enveloping resemblance. Perhaps.

My fancy goes to this unknown man, if fancy is the right word for the imaginative inquiry I seem to be on. If the man is blind or semi-blind, how did he come to be this way? At what age did he sense something was wrong in how he pieced together the world? Has he tried to have his vision repaired? Where does he bed down at night? Does he have a family, any sons or daughters who worry about his welfare? Would he be back at the basilica the next day, or the day after that? Would I be able to find him there again, two years since? We tell ourselves stories. We can be voyeuristic in imagining the features of another's life. He served in the military. He is transcendently spiritual, beyond the means of this current life. He lives with a roommate, a hobbled, unshaven man. He dreams on a mattress of cardboard. See how easily thoughts venture half-blindly into the province of his subjectivity, the tragedy of his blindness, and ours, without stubbing a toe on anything real or certain. I cannot be sure of anything, nor can you, dear perceivers. A photograph can be at once crystal clear in its substance and terrifically uncertain in its implications. Photography is a tangled play of surface appearances and infinite, uncertain depths.

I believe the man was blind. Or, at the least, his vision was impaired. It appeared as though a cataract, an opacity in the lens of the eye, seemingly pure white in its waxy substance, had come to cover over the pupil of one eye, the left eye at least, the one most visible in the image. With that sightless eye the occluding matter is *flowing down*, like the white foam of a waterfall, to use words that reach back to the etymology of the word for this optical disorder. Cataract, from the early fifteenth century, stems from the Latin *cataracta*, "waterfall," and from the Greek *katarhaktes*, "waterfall, broken water; a kind of portcullis." The water is "swooping, down-rushing" (from *kata*, "down"). The second element of the word has been traced either to *arhattein*, "to strike hard," or to *rhattein*, "to dash, break." The hard white foam of a downrushing waterfall resembles the hard white stone clouding the lens.

He must be able to see a little, this apparent blind man, at least a little. Otherwise, he would not be able to get his bearings. He would not know if, when, or how he is being photographed. He needs to know where the camera lies, doesn't he? He needs to see when he is being seen. I would like to zoom in on the quadrant of his eye with any photographs I have of him. I would like to focus in on the pixels that reflect a trace of his eye, disturbing as that action sounds, and try to assess the damage, to unravel what disease disturbance came to impale his eye. I would like to ask an ophthalmologist, a physician wearing white, to pin the question down. I have looked at images of cataracts online to see if there's a resemblance to the marred eye in the photograph. It's difficult to keep looking at those pained orbs of yellow white looking back at me. I look away. I shut down the screen, a pair of eyes closing their lids. A diseased unseeing eye is disturbingly other to what we take an eye to be.

The younger man is looking down as well. I can see that now, in the photograph, theirs or mine. His eyes are aligned with the sturdy midriff of his friend. Perhaps this too the young man finds appropriate, not to look directly at the camera, be it because of convention, deference, humility, or shyness. I would like to think his lowered eyes indicate he felt some discomfort, if only unconsciously, in having asked the blind man to pose with him within the frame of the photograph. I wonder if with him was some sense of the morally fraught, double-edged fact of the arrangement. Of this interpretation I cannot be sure.

There's the bulky, partial presence of the man preparing the photograph. He might have his photo image taken, in turn. With the lunar globescape of his head tilted toward the viewfinder, it's clear he is concentrating within the long moment of focusing the lens. He is inching to press on the release trigger at just the right, well-formed instance. I say "he is concentrating" in the present tense, and I know you think within that timing too, even though that present moment is now two years past and counting. Photography implies a grammar of multiple tenses, past, present, future. The photograph is multitemporal. It carries the trace of a once ago present. It's as though we are in that moment, too. We are in many times at once, you see. It's difficult to hold onto just one.

We see so little of the photographer's camera. I wonder if he's using a simple point-and-shoot device or something more sophisticated. I doubt he is using it in manual mode, adjusting the aperture and shutter speed for a finely tuned balance of light and time. Still, there is a sense of delicate care in this man's photographic technique. Presumably. The photographer cares for his friend, for any images he might take of him. He knows the pictures are important. Others will see them. They might last a good while. His name will be inscribed invisibly on them. His sense of care in that moment is, perhaps, more for the character and quality of the anticipated photograph than for the condition of the blind man. A good photograph counts for something.

And what do I care for, in all of this? Do I care more for images of the blind man, or for his welfare?

It's conceivable that when the friend, pictured in the photograph, looked at the image later that night, or the next day, or a year or two after that, he was disappointed with his actions that day, for having asking the blind man to pose within him. Or a friend or a cousin asked him, *What the fuck?!* The young man felt a tinge of shame. He took down the photograph from Facebook. He tore up glossy prints. Perhaps. He tried to forget the moment. Perhaps. Nietzsche wrote of the arrival of what he called "philosophers of the dangerous Perhaps."[1]

I have the photograph, still.

Just now I am carrying a copy of this image, and a few others, while I am traveling. The original digital files, the RAW color versions of all the photographs I took that October day, are on the hard drive of my computer in my home in New York, some six thousand kilometers away. I'll have to wait until I return there at the end of the month to see where the greater story lies.

July 13. His eye is motionless instability. A white, silent eye, errant unkempt seeing.

July 13. Aix-en-Provence. I am staying for a few days with a friend and her husband on the outskirts of Aix, in a fine provincial house set along a road that leads to the abandoned Bibemus quarries where Cezanne once painted. A. is an anthropologist. She also studies people. This afternoon I told her about the photograph that has come to interest me. She looked closely at a copy of it. She told me that, when she first saw the image, after I had sent a digital copy to her months before, she took the figure in the center to be an inanimate part of the statuary of the basilica, a stone figure from medieval times. "It was so immobile, so sculpted," she said. "Right there are the strong bones, and sculpted face, down to the pools of the eyes."

I can see how the man's head could be perceived as one of those *grotesques*, those fantastic human and animal forms that look down from the heights of stonework built into facades of many churches in Paris (grotesque, as from *grotto*, "small cave," the hidden "crypts" of rooms and corridors of an unfinished palace complex of Roman times, which had become overgrown and buried, until they were broken into again, mostly from above). "And sculptures like that do not have eyes," my friend added. A medieval gargoyle, a blind man from Morocco. So many glances stir up images from the vast, unruly optical unconscious that lies within the sediment of our perceptual memories.

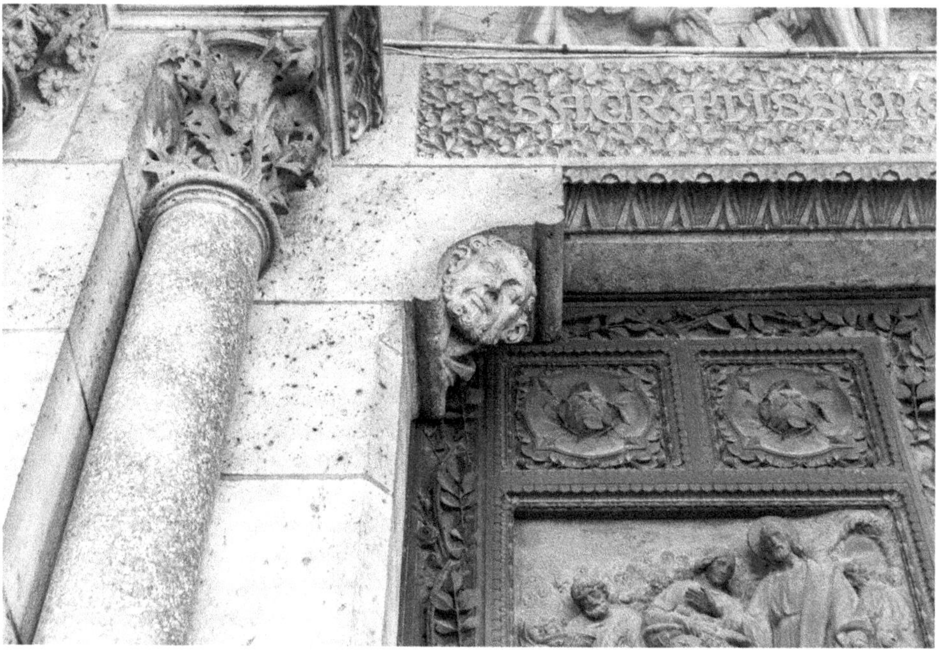

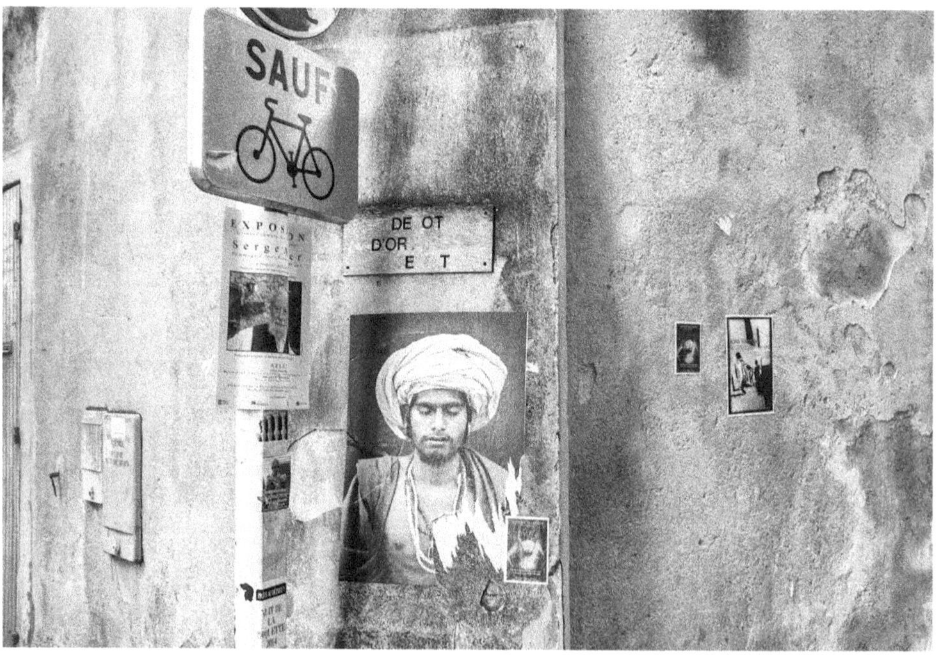
SAUF
DE OT
D'OR
E T

July 14. This afternoon I read to A. what I have written to date concerning my tentative understanding of the photograph. We sat at a patio outside her home on a fine summer day, cups of espresso set on the small table between us, and she listened to the lines of interpretation while looking at the image. Once I had finished, she introduced another sensible reading, counter to the one I had put together. "The three men in the photo are probably Maghreb," she said, "from either Morocco or Algeria." It's possible, she proposed, that they are from the same village or the same region, and they wanted a photograph to mark the occasion of meeting in this faraway town. Perhaps they recognized him from somewhere else. And even if they had no known connection with him, it must have been interesting to encounter another Maghreb standing on the steps of Sacré-Coeur. The two men might have wanted a souvenir of that chance occurrence. It's also important for Muslims to do good works and to give alms to those in need. The two men might have combined a donation with the request of a photograph. The man standing between them might have also had that idea in mind when coming to the basilica, but he was unsure how to go about asking for alms in a Christian setting, and so he stood uncertainly along the steps leading up to the church. This all could well be true. There's no way to know, for sure. We tell ourselves stories.

So went our speculation in that hour, in which we saw or imagined the three men perceived as belonging to a certain culture, once colonized by the French. We gave the man a form and a profile, a religion and a life, drawn from our own cultural imaginings.

July 14. While stepping about the patio in the heat of afternoon sun I noticed a small fury of activity on the top surface of a stone wall, among the pine needles fallen there. I came closer and thought I saw a couple of ants seizing an insect, caterpillar, or inchworm, trying to drag their prey while that poor creature put up fierce resistance to its capture. Once my eyes had gained better focus I was surprised to see that a small beady spider was spinning rapidly about a single ant, encasing its prey within a coffin of gray silk.

July 15. We have yet to consider the fourth figure, the woman passing through the frame of the secondary photograph, perhaps because she seems incidental to the main action. Her presence in the image is apparently accidental. The accidental, the aleatory of chance, characterizes so many photographs. She is stepping into the frame of that moment.

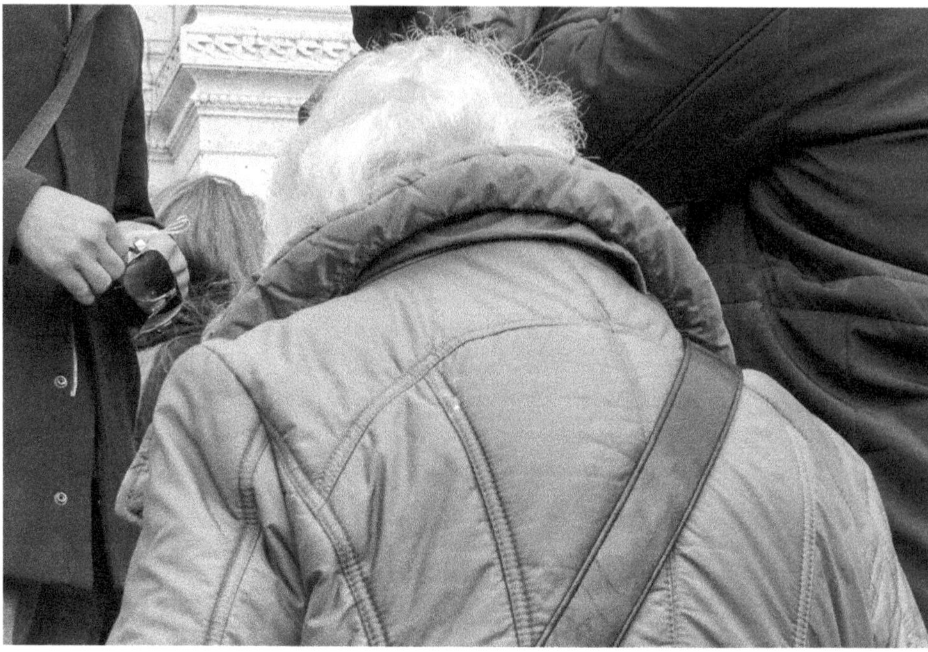

She is climbing up the stairs, apparently, beelining it toward the interiors of the basilica. The lofty ascent is fatiguing her, her feet are tired, the bag held by her right shoulder grows heavy, and yet she is determined to witness the majestic beauty that lies ahead. This is the line of desire she is on, alongside the trajectories of those around her. What does she see and think in this moment, or in the brief instances after that? Has she noticed the photograph being taken just before her? Did she know she was within the path of my optics? Would she remember that moment, at all, if asked about it again? That day at Sacré-Coeur. Her face is not visible in the photograph. There is no clear persona or identity apparent. Perhaps she is with others, a daughter, young grandchildren, together for one last intercontinental trip before she's too old for it, she can't get about like she once did. I do not count on a husband being with her in these years. Visions of my grandmother, my mother's mother, her hair white and frail in her final, dignified years, slow frail movements about the house, reach me now.

The woman's gray winter coat is an agent of sorts; it obscures and enhances. The coat blocks any clear view. It continues a slashing line, right to left, which begins with the photographer's coat. The blind man's look seems to follow that downsloping line toward a lower ground, be it earth, rest, death, or damnation. And then the line veers upward, following the line of the young man's coat. The face of the man who appears to be blind is set within the virtual *V* that appears to a viewer's eye. This arrangement helps, in this present viewing, to make the hood about his head look like a dusky halo, profane and nonecstatic. The arching crescent of that half halo is echoed by the wrinkled curve crowning the top of the woman's coat, which appears just below the incandescent glow of white in the space between. It's almost as if the silent, unspeaking affinity between those forms points to the ways in which there can be instances of likeness and connection among different forms of life. It's almost as if the straggly luminance in the between suggests the possibility of quiet beauty, transcendence even, within the knockabout arrangements of everyday life. Almost. There is no angelic transcendence here. It's just a Monday afternoon on the steps of Sacré-Coeur.

For some time I disliked the woman's incidental presence in the secondary photograph. Not that I had anything against her. I thought this blank dull whitewash of a figure obscured any clear perception of the relations between the three men half-visible. In waking dreams I have tried to reach the image with my hand and scratch it from the camera's line of sight, to see more openly what lies beyond.

I once showed the image to a friend of mine, a photographer. It's a shame, I said, that all that stuff is there, in the foreground, the gray-white coat and the white hair. She said she liked this blotchy disturbance. It made the picture less clear, less ordinary. I trust her judgment. It strikes me now that the occlusion caused by the woman's presence fits well with what I have come to perceive within the elements of this picture. To photograph is to be partially blind. A photograph is hobbled perception. Like a cataract eye the filmy substance lies obstructed, occluded. A photograph implies a hallucinatory phantasm of half perceptions and partial, surface knowings. We see what is there, before us, at that moment, in that particular configuration of time and place, and the implications of this are what linger in time. We see so little, and we envision much more than that. A photograph stands as a combination of sure apparent surface and infinite uncertain depth.

Beyond the man taking the photograph, past the camera held in his hand, stands an upper part of the cast-iron gate. Our eyes can make out the graceful swirls of the solid metal apparent in the picture, while the tip of the lance, the punctum that could prick a heart, lies unseen and

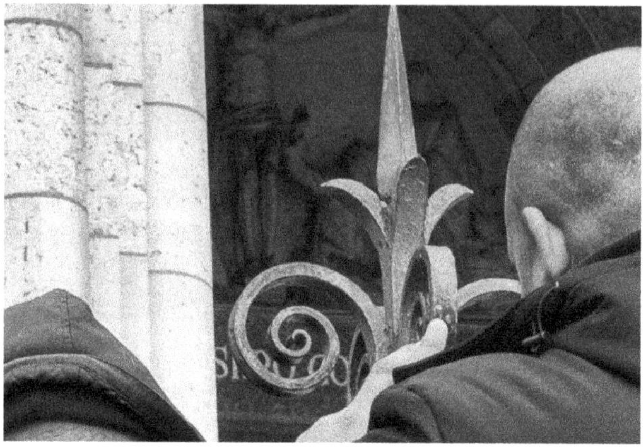

unapparent. The rest of the metal remains to be seen. We sense a substance there and its incomplete, uncertain continuation. Much the same could be said of any given photograph.

July 16. The picture keeps looking back at me. It brushes against me like that man in the streets of Arles the other night. Four figures animate the photograph, five if you count the hint of the girl. Six, if you include the person who took the secondary image. Countless other figures lie beyond the scene of the photograph, all the potential viewers of it, all the eyes and imaginative sensoriums that might chance a look at it, the many possible viewings of it, theirs, yours, or mine. The moment and look of the image has the potential to expand infinitely into space. The photograph can be found on a website on the Internet. It has reached Seattle. It has rested on a kitchen table in Bucharest, and on an oak table in a restaurant in New York City. The image has bounced about Massachusetts. I've had the visuals on my laptop while in Paris and Besançon. They've been close to the waters of the Mediterranean coast, along the Calanques near Marseille. One place it probably has not appeared is in the home of the blind man or of the two men who photographed him.

July 16. I wrote that the blind man is looking down, toward the ground or toward the vague space the woman occupies. Now that I have looked closely at the print I'm not sure about this observation. I can see now that it's possible that the man is looking at me, at the remote figure behind the camera taking the secondary photograph. He might have noticed, in the act of being photographed, another camera pointed his way, and he glanced toward that second optical presence. I cannot be sure of this.

Looking close, I can see that the pupil in his left eye is completely covered over by a milky-white cataract, the size of a small fingernail. There's no mercy in that. It's as if that cataract eye is looking at me, though I know that can't be the case. It would be crazy of me to really think that, wouldn't it? A blind eye cannot see. It's a lookless look. Still, that eye appears as if chastising me, scolding me for my photographic yearnings. Shame on me for wanting to take a picture of a blind man on the steps of Sacré-Coeur, and for free, no less. His right eye is seen unclearly. There is a dim dulled squint to that vision. Perhaps that eye, too, is affected by cataracts, not as much as the left. This makes me think the man could see partially from that eye. His vision might have worsened by now. I feel for him, infinitely so.

He is looking at me, the man in the photograph, and he is not looking at me. I did not see that in the time of photographing. Now, I can piece together a timeline of events, tentative, relevant looks and motives included. He was on to me, I can see that now. He knew I wanted his image. Perhaps I had gathered that, if the two men could take his image, then another picture from me would not hurt matters more. I stayed close, waiting for a decisive moment. He must have seen me, if palely and obscurely. He was not sure, either, what he was seeing. His look toward me was an interrogative.

Between people lies ruptured space.

July 16. The white eye is neutral. There is no meaning there, no subject history, no biography. It's beyond the self, contrary to it. The biology of protein crystals hindered a distraught eye.

July 17. The more I look at the photograph, the more I doubt what I know or could possibly know for sure. The "I" of myself and of others is undermined. There is a dissolution of a stable self. I am taken outside of myself, into a field of partial bodies and obscured consciousnesses. There are no bounded, neatly packaged forms of perception, no coherent selves to speak of. We are brought into a coarse, dense, intricate mosaic of sociality composed of an infinite dynamic patchwork of precepts and sensations within the image.

That uncertain, ever-changing mosaic is point-blank within everyday life as well. It's as if the photograph slows time to a charged pause, so

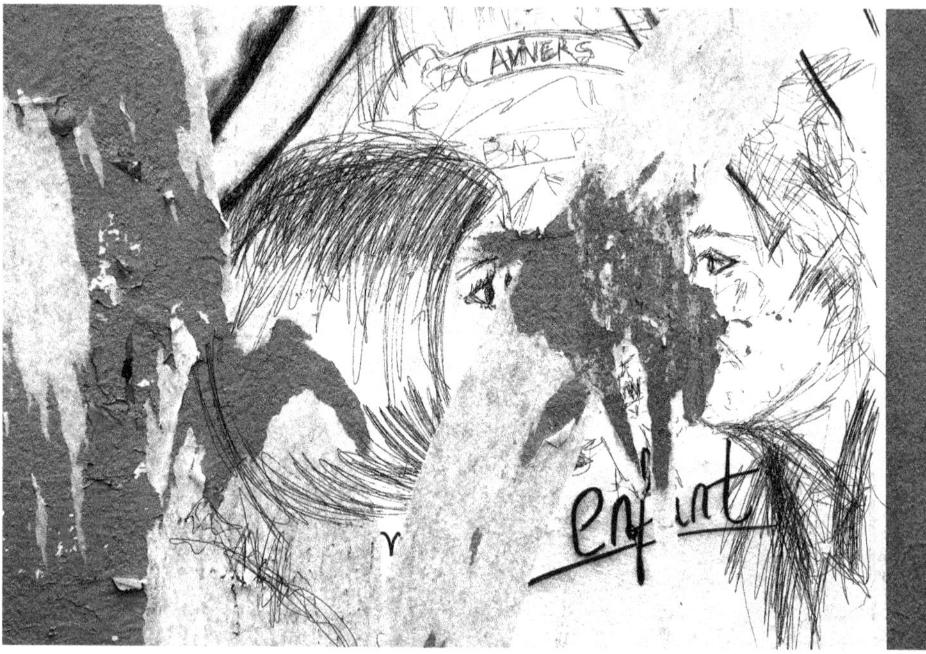

slow, gradual, and a careful regard of its composition unravels elements that we often take for granted, like a sure sense of what is going on in this moment or that, or who we take ourselves to be, how we regard others close to us. Once we've stepped into that space of perception and adopted a certain optics of attentiveness, the world emerges increasingly complicated; it becomes multiple, ambiguous, uncertain, and, at times, illuminated. The tangled interplay of otherness and sameness in everyday life becomes evident. Every detail matters, each wrinkle in time.

Looking at a photograph can offer a vexed phenomenology of perception. The closer we look, the more appearances grow strange, uncertain. I am thrown here and there. I try to grab hold of something near me.

The photograph leaves me uncalmed, unsettled. It tears me from myself.

July 17. In invoking the idea that a photograph can tear a person from himself I have in mind something Michel Foucault said in a 1979 interview with an Italian journalist named Duccio Trombadori. "You speak of phenomenology," Trombadori asked Foucault, "but all phenomenological thought is centered on the problem of experience and depends on it for tracing its own theoretical horizon. What sets you apart from it, then?" To which Foucault responded:

> The phenomenologist's experience is basically a certain way of bringing a reflective gaze to bear on some object of "lived experience," on the everyday in its transitory form, in order to grasp its meaning. For Nietzsche, Bataille, and Blanchot, on the other hand, experience is trying to reach a certain point of life that is as close as possible to the "unlivable," to that which can't be lived through. What is required is the maximum of intensity and the maximum of impossibility at the same time. By contrast, phenomenological work consists in unfolding the field of possibilities related to everyday experience.
>
> Moreover, phenomenology attempts to recapture the meaning of everyday experience in order to rediscover the sense in which the subject that I am is indeed responsible, in its transcendental functions, founding that experience together with its meanings. On the other hand, in Nietzsche, Bataille, and Blanchot, experience has the function of wrenching the subject from itself, of seeing to it that the subject is no longer itself, or that it is brought to its annihilation or its dissolution. This is a project of desubjectification.
>
> The idea of a limit-experience that wrenches the subject from itself is what is important to me in my reading of Nietzsche, Bataille, and Blanchot, and what explains the fact that however boring, however erudite my books may be, I've always conceived of them as direct experiences aimed at pulling myself free of myself, at preventing me from being the same.[2]

Classical phenomenology tends to affirm the status and stability of selfhood by attending to the significance of everyday experiences of perception, language, and body. What draws Foucault to thinkers like Nietzsche, Blanchot, and Bataille is that they engage in a kind of negative phenomenology in which they explore situations of intensity, impossibility, and limit which have the effect of undermining the self, dissolving or annihilating the subject, more or less "tearing" or "wrenching" the subject from itself. "Can't there be experiences," Foucault asks, "in the course of which the subject is no longer posited, in its constitutive relations, as what makes it identical with itself? Might there not be experiences in which the subject might be able to dissociate from itself, sever the relation with itself, lose its identity?"[3]

Seen in a similar, desubjectifying light, photography tears the perceiver from itself in such a way that she or he is no longer a stable, coherent, integrated seer as such. Look at a photograph. Notice how the mind's eye moves from scene to scene and takes in the many matters at hand. Consider how it's easy to fall into a certain kind of reverie, one that takes a consciousness outside of itself, which dissolves into imaginative and empathic possibilities. Keep in mind the ways in which a photographic image can affect bodies and minds in all sorts of ways that go beyond conscious forms of thought or coherent modes of perception. Notice how a person can very much swoon into a photograph and drown within a sea of imagery. Think of the way that a photograph is as real as ink marks on paper and as ephemeral and immaterial as ink marks on paper.

All of this ties into certain disconcertations of perception and consciousness. For once you start to engage with photography in any in-depth way, once you start to take pictures or consider them in late hours of a night, once you are caught up in the magic of them and get lost within the heady vertigo of memory and imaginative fancy that they so often induce, then the more you realize that photographs are much more complicated and phantasmal than we often take them to be. And once you realize that, then it's just a quick leap into grasping that everyday life is itself altogether more perplexing and phantasmal than we take it to be.

Photography tears the subject from itself. Photography disrupts conventional notions of experience, as photographs so often involve complex foldings of past, present, and future, self and other, the actual and the imagined. Photographs upend set ideas of selfhood, temporal clarity, and steady, continuous streams of experience. They often involve a double temporality (it not triple or multiple temporalities) of past moments and present scenes of looking. A photograph can entail a "limit experience," to use that philosophical term, in the sense that an engagement with its content or material pushes us into a fault line in our understanding of how we think the world works, or should work. As with other limit experiences, such as abandonment, suffering, madness, illness, death, and literature, photography comes close to pointing out the near impossibility of living. Photographs throw into question commonplace ideas about perception, consciousness, time, and memory. A photograph can lead a viewer of an image to inhabit different subject positions and different planes of experience all the while suspended in a vertigo stretch of past, present, and future times. A peculiar madness lies at the heart of photography.

Yet what is perhaps most unsettling about photographs is not that they show us that these forces are at work in any given moment of life.

The eventualities of life, like photography, disrupt things in such a way that the person is no longer a person as such, perception is no longer perception as such, and time is no longer time as such.

July 17. Here is another statement of Foucault's, from that same interview:

> I don't regard myself as a philosopher. What I do is neither a way of doing philosophy nor a way of discouraging others from doing philosophy. The most important authors who—I won't say shaped my thinking but enabled me to deviate from my university training—were people like Georges Bataille, Friedrich Nietzsche, Maurice Blanchot, and Pierre Klossowski, who were not philosophers in the institutional sense of the term. There were also a certain number of personal experiences, of course. What struck me and fascinated me about those authors, and what gave them their capital importance for me, was that their problem was not the construction of a system but the construction of a personal experience.[4]

Foucault found that each book he wrote—an experience in its own right—transformed him and transformed what he was thinking: "What I think is never quite the same, because for me my books are experiences, in a sense, that I would like to be as full as possible. An experience is something that one comes out transformed. . . . I'm an experimenter in the sense that I write in order to change myself and in order not to think the same thing as before."[5] For this historian, the experimental method of excavating the past, examining its archives, statements, and forms of thought and power, brought new understandings that altered the grounds of life and consciousness.

I am in favor of a similar undertaking, though here the method, however errant it might be, is to happen upon encounters with others—strangers, friends, photographic images, ways of looking—within the tumultuous grain of everyday life. Through these encounters, the subject might be transformed, the subject loses its identity, is no longer the same, and the presumed grounds of perception and relationality come into question.

Could a writer concern himself not with the problem of constructing systems or theories but rather with direct, personal experiences that speak intensively to certain possibilities and impossibilities in life? Could he construct a singular book around encounters in the world? Could he write within a flow of image and thought that follows the thin line of a razor's edge?

July 18. I am now in Besançon, where I once lived and studied at the university in town. I've returned to this city to continue with the photographic memoir I've been working on. I am staying for the week in an apartment rented through airbnb.com. It appears that the owner of the place, a young woman, usually resides in the apartment and stays elsewhere when she has a short-time tenant. We haven't met in person, having communicated only by messages online. Books, file folders, and a diploma hanging from a wall suggest she is a nutritionist, and she meets with clients at a desk centered in one of the rooms. It's odd to use the utensils in her kitchen and sleep on the mattress in her bed, a red blanket wrapped across my shoulder. Walking about the rooms of the place, looking at posters on the walls and reading the titles of the books lining the few bookshelves, it occurred to me that one could conceive a singular portrait of a person's life and circumstances by photographing, alone, the many surfaces of that person's home—the icon held by magnets on the kitchen fridge, the lavender soap in the bathroom, DVDs stored along the mantel in the living room—without touching anything at all, no drawers dug into, no closets opened, no papers or letters leafed through by curious hands and eyes, surface shallows no greater than the thinness of a photograph. For a few moments I thought of making a project of it through the week. My brain began to foresee where that voyeuristic endeavor could lead, what flat intrigues the photographs would show to others. That idea was creeping me out, and I decided against it.

July 18. He cannot see well. He sees with hands and stick, taps along the wall and stairwells that descend into the streets of Montmartre.

July 19. Doubtless it's one matter to conceptualize blindness, to imagine its phenomenal feel in abstract words and images, and another altogether to inhabit a space of blindness, sensing one's way in an obscurity of light.

To reach the apartment where I am staying I have to unlock the heavy wood door at the ground level of the building, walk down a corridor lined with mailboxes, trash bins, and rusting bicycles, and climb up a flight of stairs until I reach the entrance to the apartment. When stepping into the building at night I have to press a light switch near the entrance and then walk toward the end of the corridor and hit another switch, which serves to light up the area around the stairs; each of these lights is set to a clicking timer that runs for twenty seconds until the urgent clicking stops and there is a cessation of light from bulbs hung from walls and ceilings. Last night, in leaving the apartment to walk

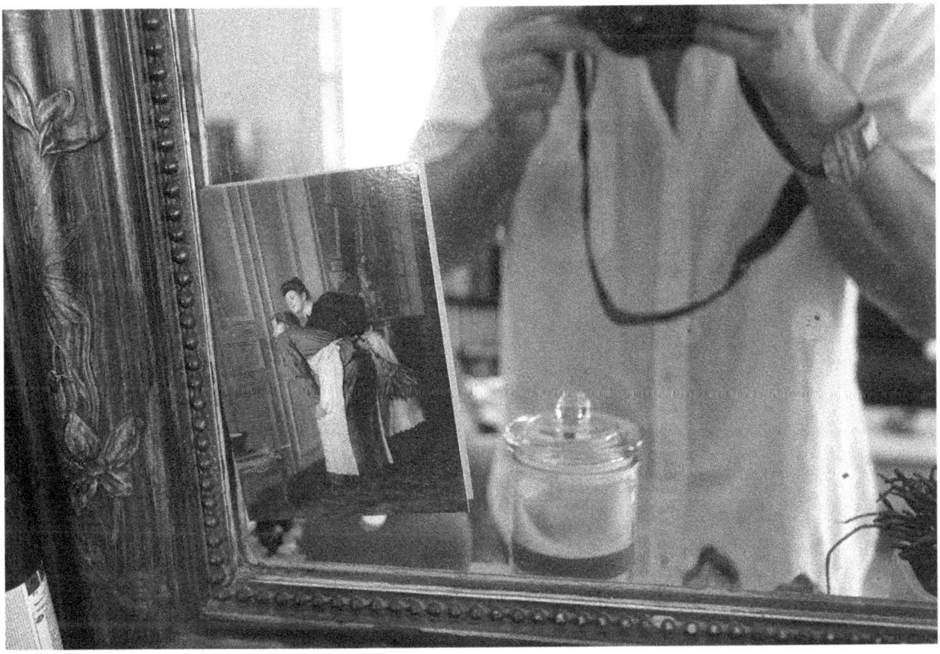

about and take some photographs at night, I realized I would be standing in the dark once I shut the apartment door and stood by the stairs leading down to the corridor to the outer door of the building. I did not know where any second light switch was on the first floor; I looked around but saw no signs of one or of any neighbors who could help me out. I figured it would not be too difficult to navigate the stairs downward in the dark until I reached the light switch by the entrance to the building and so I turned off the lights in the apartment and shut and locked that door. Darkness swarmed, I felt for the railing in the pitch dark and shuffled my feet along creaking level floorboards until I toed an empty absence, the drop of a step. My hands and feet made tentative movement around the turn of a railing, my eyes were wide open but unseeing in the darkness, no visual signs to decipher, everything touch and vague sense, the stairs mute and dark, no one to guide me, gravity a natural danger, the objects about the place stood neutral, uncaring, quiet. I could hear the sound of worried breath and heartbeat. I felt for each plank of the stairs, counting on a mental map of stairs and building, sensing each inch of matter or its absence, hands and feet worked as stabilizers to keep the body balanced, each step meant a potential fall onto hard stone. Half-bound toward my goal, I realized I risked real bodily harm, broken wrists, kneecaps, jaw exposed, with no eyes to see. I retreated back up the stairs. Hands grabbed hold of the railings known to be there, patching together a flow of movement until I found the frame of the apartment door, felt for the keyhole, felt for the key to unlock it, opened the door, and turned on the light switch in the first room there. I left the door open and used that welcome stream of light to see my way down the stairs until I reached the light switch set on the wall by the corridor. I ran up the stairs again and reached the apartment, turned off the light in the first room, shut and locked the apartment door, and made my way down the stairs, reaching the switch moments before darkness immersed the stairwell.

Venturing into the dark, a real chance of bodily harm, stumbling against lone matter, darkness an uncertainty, no guiding force but guesswork strivings, hands reaching into empty air hesitantly seeking contact; all of this was a pale facsimile, no doubt, of what it's like to be blind within the dark of night.

July 19. Another scene of encounter keeps returning to me. The image of it is right there, in the mind, it's there in the spaces beyond, hovering like a substanceless ghost. It's from those finite hours that I wandered about the steps of the basilica that October day, though I cannot locate it in a specific time. I was looking at the apparent blind man looking back at me, ten to fifteen feet away, a few steps below the solid stone level step upon which he stood. I'm not sure when that moment occurred, there's no way to name the precise timing, though much depends on it. Others passed between the man and me. I looked his way, held the camera in my hand. He turned and looked in my direction as if he was looking back at me. *As if* is a tricky phrase, a trickster of a phenomenon. In English, the words are used to describe how a situation seems to be, whether true or not. It suggests a possibility, a scenario, which could be true or not so true, real or conjectured. *Like something was actually so*, as one grammarian puts it. A photograph is likewise an "as if, as though" phenomenon. A visual image is like something that is actually so.

I could not tell if the man saw me, at that point. I couldn't tell if he could see me, at all or a little, or not at all. If he could not see me, I wondered, then why was he looking directly at me? He had to have seen me, I thought, otherwise why would he hold his gaze steady in my direction for those long seconds?

Wonder lies at the root of a photographic image.

It's a disturbance to look into the eyes of a blind person. We often take the eyes of others to carry a glint of the soul revealed within. Plato, for one, insisted that it is not the eyes that see but rather our soul that sees by means of the eyes. When the eyes are impaired, gone, damaged, or blunted, something has been altered. "Their eyes, from which the divine spark has departed," wrote Baudelaire in his poem "The Blind." We're left unsure where to look. We face a disconcerting optical resistance. We cannot look into the eyes, in the same way, and we do not know where to glimpse the soul in relation to our own. We cannot rely on the conventional, time-tested means of communing with the living self of the other. If we do not know if the other can see, or not see, or to what degree, we are thrown off further. Everything comes into doubt. We proceed hesitantly, within unsteady hazards of time. This might help to explain the frequent use of shaded glasses over unseeing eyes, for those shiny obscurities can hide erratic vision.

I saw him seeing me seeing him. At least I think I did. He had me in his sights, or he did not. Or he saw me through an obscure and milky film and he was trying to glean what I was up to and gauge if or when I sought to photograph him. Perhaps. He was not sure himself. The situation was equivocal. Like so much of life, it was open to more than one interpretation. It could go either way or many ways at once. The ambiguity in his look was disturbing. His look back, and the uncertainty of what it entailed or did not entail, ruptured my steady gaze upon him. That he could see me, and could not see me, broke down my coordination. I lost my photographic rhythm, thrown off in the desire for a pure image. I could not take the easy shot. I couldn't photograph him at will, blissfully, blindly, with the complete freedom to spring one digital picture after another. Any clear turn of the camera his way risked a vigorous response from him. He might yell at me, or berate. Condemn. Cast a curse. Give me the evil eye, *l'oeil mauvais*. I couldn't be sure. I am always a bit unknowing in time and space.

If he can see me, I thought, he is looking at me to see if I am going to try to capture his image, for free. He would want to be compensated fairly, a euro piece placed in his hand or coins drawn from a side pants pocket. That was the exchange implied, economic and moral. He deserved remuneration for the lifting of his image. How much is a person's resemblance worth? He had me in his sights. He was impairing my movement, obstructing my vision. Contemplating the portraiture of a blind man looking uncertainly my way was not covered in any of the guides to photographic composition that I had picked up back in the

States. I am deadly aware of the irony: I wanted to have an unfettered regard of a blind man, much as we would like a clear view of a photographic image. His look my way disturbed that comprehension. Most often, the excitements of voyeurism, the pleasures of looking, imply that the looker is not seen or noticed by the subject of his gaze. A look back disturbs the purity of the equation. If you are going to peek through a keyhole, chances are you won't want to encounter another eye blinking back at you. A blind eye peeping back at you would be even more unnerving. A seeming blind eye countering one's gaze throws things off entirely.

I could not acquire the man's image just then. The encounter was too direct. His face was straight onto mine. It wouldn't be fair. I could only release the tension, relax the grip on the camera and walk away. I took a few steps down the stairs and turned my attention elsewhere. The man might have watched me for a while, his head swiveling in tune with my movements down and across a set of steps. I did not want to look back at him and find his eyes trailing me. I suspect he turned his attention elsewhere.

I do not have a photograph of that long, uncertain moment when the man was looking my way, or not, while I was looking his way, camera in hand. If I had a picture of that arrangement, I could study it closely and try to assess if he was in fact looking at me. I would tenderly survey the features of his face as they appeared just then and scan for any glint of recognition, I'd search for that moment shown in the eyes when a person realizes that someone, a creature he does not know, is staring straight at him—and that other person has a camera in his hands and looks primed to trip the aperture. Like seeing one's own reflection in a dark pupil, I'd see myself in his own way of looking. Without a steady, lasting visual picture of that sort, I have only a mental image. This is an abstract memory, vague and changeable. I lack the image in the concrete form of a semi-gloss print and yet the picture is still hauntingly there, in my mind, it lingers on those drifting steps of that moment; in lost reveries my eyes look at him possibly looking at me.

I'm not sure when this visual encounter or nonencounter with the man took place. I do not have the metadata, as it were, for that particular memory. There's no specific time or shutter speed recorded. I can only go back to the place where it occurred and try to reconstruct the situation.

July 19. Yes, that's it. I've decided to go to Sacré-Coeur next week, when I am in Paris again for a few days, before the flight home. I can revisit the place and try to piece together what occurred that October day. The rush of tourists will be tiresome, no doubt, shouts and antenna cravings on an anthill, but I need to be there and look about and learn if he is there still.

July 20. Walking the streets of the Centre Ville this weekend, taking photographs, I appreciated how much photographing in public is an occasion for anxiety for me. I worry that someone, anyone, will take offense to my visual captures, even if they are not the intended subject of the photo or anywhere close to the frame. My heart palpitates faster when the camera is in my hands, close to watchful eyes. A nervous energy releases once I have moved from the scene of interest—and then anxiously renews when the camera lights upon another tableaux of possibilities.

Whenever I look back at photographs I have taken while traveling in France my body grows nervous and I am reminded of the pressures of living among others.

I have taken to standing infrequently by the windows of the apartment and photographing the appearance of people on the streets below,

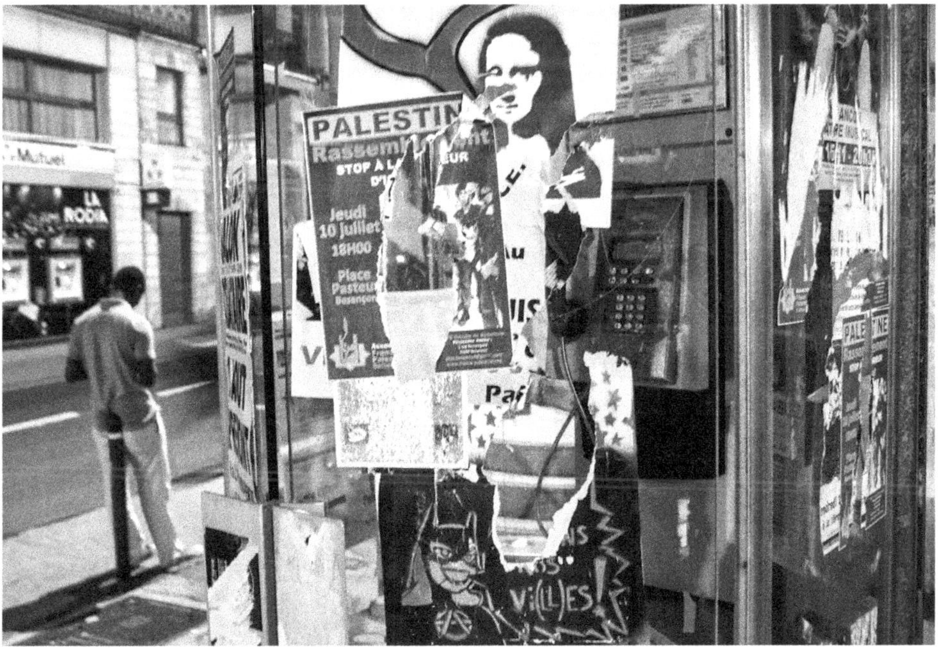

including those seated at the tables outside a café across the way. It's remarkable how quickly many of them pick up on my visual presence by the window and how vigilant they become once they notice the camera in my hand. Any quick movement catches their notice—they're like cats, in that way. They keep looking back, toward the windows, to see if someone is still there, possibly photographing them. One evening, I turned off the lights in the apartment and stood away from the windows to diminish the chance that anyone could pick up on my opaque presence. In this voyeuristic look onto voyeurism I have met with the curious sensation of observing myself, observing them. It's not a pleasant thrill on either side of the optics, watching or being watched, yet I feel compelled to taste the heated intersubjectivity of the encounter, even if someone is burned in the process.

One night I looked out from a darkened room and saw a gathering on the terrace at the restaurant across the street, a wedding reception, perhaps. I turned the camera toward people seated at a table. A young woman looked my way, she must have noticed the light of the camera. She spoke to those near her. They turned and looked in search of the camera that caught her eye. I stepped back into the darkened room.

Everyone is a little bit of a voyeur.

July 21. When I bring a camera to my eyes I cannot see well through the lens. There are smudges on it. I can't clear them away. I can make out some figures, details in the image, some children on bicycles on the street below, while other figures are obscured.

I photograph half-seeing, half-unseeing, due to my own tendencies in vision. With each step of the photographic process my vision is tentative, piecemeal, segmental, processual, half-knowing. When I hold the camera to my eyes I look through the eye-viewer, an ingenious pentaprism of mirroring glass, and try to size up the scene. I'm not sure what's there, not quite, or how those apparent elements will appear as a photograph, how the light will arrange itself, or the depth of field, or what disturbances will lie on the margins. I click the camera in a gesture of prayer, hoping for tangible results from the divinities of light, the photons hitting the twenty-four million image sensors in the camera's cortex. It's a process of guesswork; I'm not sure what's there until seconds or minutes later, and even then I'm unsure. I am nearsighted, myopic, too much curvature to the cornea causes refractive error, too much focusing power, which makes the light they transmit focus in front

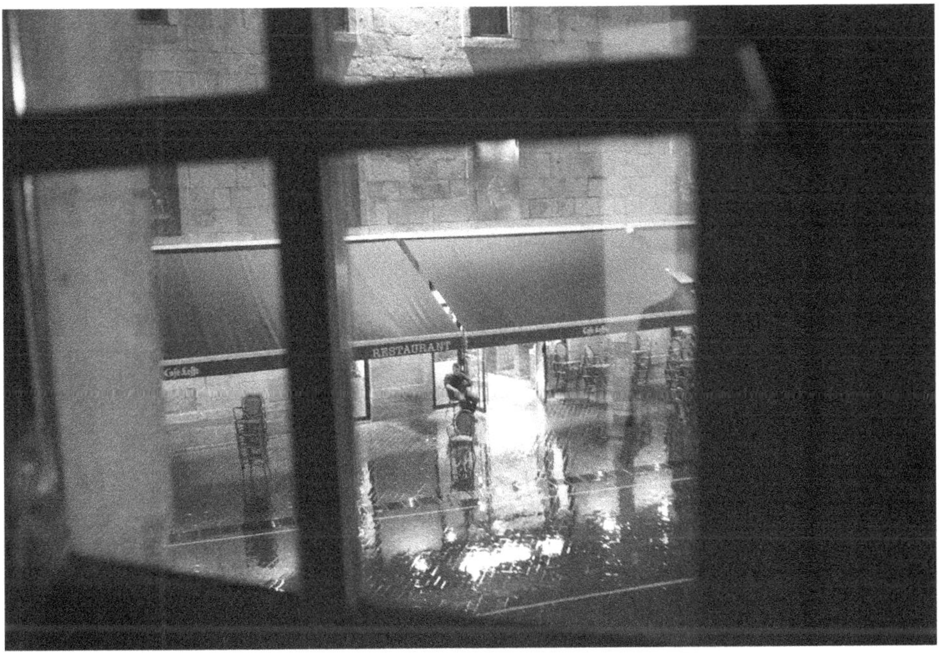

of the retina, undershooting its mark. I normally wear eyeglasses with corrective lenses to address this error. Without those lenses shaping the refraction of light reaching the retina my vision remains vague and diffuse, and I can easily get lost and confused. While in the act of photographing, I never know well whether to remove that pair of lenses, or keep them on. Lately I have opted for the latter, which means that once I snap a photograph I have to take off my glasses if I wish to look at the LCD screen at the back of the camera to see what image has appeared. This juggling back and forth between different optical lenses is awkward. If I wish to take another photograph I put my eyeglasses back on to look through the viewfinder again. And so on.

The LCD screen provides only a preliminary sense of the image, given its small size and its tendency to pick up any glare from surrounding light. I load any images taken that day onto the hard drive of my laptop, once I'm back at the hotel or apartment where I am residing. Here I don a pair of reading glasses, to counter the presbyopia, the "old eyes" that come with middle age, a loss of elasticity of the crystalline lens altered the refraction of light onto retina, which makes it difficult for the eye to focus close. With the reading glasses on I can then see each image more clearly and gain a sense of what's there. Still I cannot trust what I am seeing. Only when I am back home in New York and have use of a large LCD monitor screen do I have a secure grasp of what lies within any given image. And yet, as any good photographer will tell you, the image on a computer screen is different from what appears in print. A large quality print says more about the image—it becomes something other to what appears on a computer screen. Even then, I'd have to say I never have a thoroughly comprehensive understanding of an image, nor, I suspect, does anyone else.

All this is to say that our vision is tentative, delayed; constructed; a patchwork of optical impressions. Through time we come to see different aspects of an image. We never grasp a photograph completely. We never perceive any phenomenon through a single sensory event, even if we yearn to do so. We are always a little nearsighted, hesitantly groping our way.

It's not like the camera itself picks up on what is truly there in the world. While carrying great potential, any camera has its own limited optics.

July 22. My fear is of growing blind myself, of losing the trade of clear vision until I have to manage without, relying on sound and touch to make my way down trafficked streets or within the intimacy of a home.

"One day you'll be blind like me," runs a line in Beckett's *Endgame.* "You'll be sitting there, a speck in the void, in the dark, for ever, like me."[6]

I worry that, in photographing the man's blindness so cheaply and writing about him with sharp-edged words, I risk bringing a similar wound into the sockets of my own.

July 23. What is one to make of the fact that, soon after writing the above paragraph, my eyeglasses broke on me? This happened last night, in the apartment where I am staying for the week. I began to clean the lens of my eyeglasses with a piece of smooth, clean cloth, as I had done countless times before. On this occasion the force of the pressure from thumbs against the lens caused the frames of the eyeglasses to snap into two pieces, midway along the fine metal bridge linking the two lens. Broken, *cassé.*

This morning I brought the broken eye wire to an optician's shop in town and asked if there was any way to repair the damaged part.

A woman working there said that there was not, as the metal was "titanium," incapable of being glued back together. She was kind enough to try to mend the break by using tape and some glue to form a makeshift encasement holding the two stems together. For a few hours I walked around with the glasses held together that way; the cast lost its grip and the two halves fell apart, slipped from my face and fell to the ground.

July 24. Last night I woke into the darkness of an early hour and sleepily became aware that my hand was touching the eyelid of the right eye. The sharp, jagged edge of a fingernail was digging into the epidermis lid, behind which lay the ball of the eye. Perhaps in dreams or an unconscious state I was trying to clear out an irritating disturbance. This nonconscious action, undertaken while I was asleep, is alarming. I could have easily harmed that eye, or the other. Worse can happen. I've asked my body not to do any more damage while I rest. I nodded off with the prayer that I awake unharmed and clear-sighted. Sleep and dream should be safe havens, refuge from the onslaughts of the day, though dangers clearly lie there. "We surrender to sleep," wrote Blanchot, "but in the way that the master entrusts himself to the slave who serves him."[7] Strange to think that my body could have motives of its own, foreign to

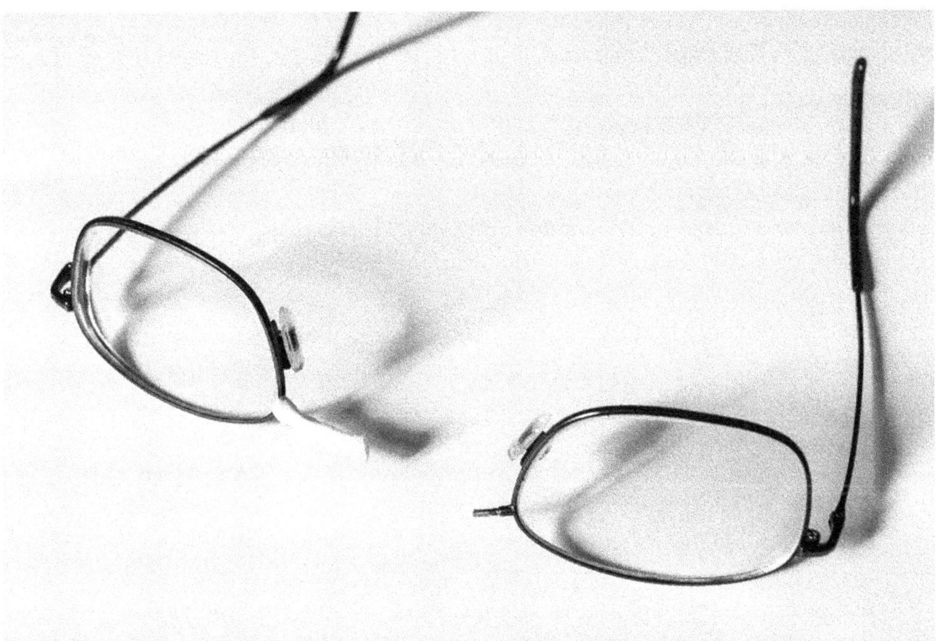

the conscious self, which could harm the organs on which this self so delicately relies.

I've taken to wearing a pair of prescription sunglasses that I have with me. These lenses work fine enough, though I worry that I appear a bit suspicious, "shady," *méchant*, when walking into cafés with the dark shades on, or when wearing them in twilight hours, or at night, walking about with the camera in my hands.

July 24. More curious still: I have just lost the sunglasses. I now have no intact optics with which to see the world clearly. This happened around nine tonight, in the dusky hour after the sun had set to the west of Besançon. Standing along the side of the Pont Battant I leaned over the railing there to photograph a linked series of buildings along the side of the Doubs. Below that seriation of form I saw a group of boys seated along the bank of the river. It looked like they were finishing up a quick meal. I could perceive one of the boys walk toward the river and come close to its side, to wash his hands. I tried to include that gesture within the frame of a photograph. By the time I had raised the camera and clicked the shutter the boy had moved away from the flowing waters. I took another photograph, and when I went to look at this last image on the LCD screen I took off the sunglasses to see well. I lost hold of the glasses. They fell down and away, jettisoned from the self, into that swirling river where the boy had just washed his hands. I heard the glasses hit against the metal edge of the bridge, and then silence after that. I looked down to see if I could spot them still on the bridge. Nowhere to be seen, the optics must have fallen into the opaque swirling depths of the river.

My first thought after losing the sunglasses was that I was close to blind. I worried I would face difficulties in finding my way back to the apartment building, climbing darkly lit stairs, stepping into a strange place, finding my footing on the creaking wood floors of the living room and kitchen. I soon realized I could still see much of the world, if vaguely so. I could not make out the details of signs set along the roadways, and I could not pick up the telling features on the faces of those walking past me. I entered a market to pick up some food for that night and the next day, and found, in walking about the store, looking for Comté cheese and Bonne Maman raspberry preserves, that I was as if half-blind, half-seeing—not far, perhaps, from how the apparent unsighted man perceives the world. Once home, I returned to using the regular eye-glasses, severed into two. While moving about the place, viewing words or materials up close, I held the right side close to the right eye, like a nineteenth-century monocle.

If need be tomorrow I could use the camera as a means of distanced vision. I can visualize my way through the labyrinth structures of Gare de Lyon, a 35mm lens fixed to my eye, reading the signs in the hallways and finding the right Métro to take.

Plastic intimacies

July 25. Just now I am on the train to Paris, seated in a window seat in second-class coach, looking out at passing towns and farmlands. This morning I realized I have a pair of contact lenses with me, lodged into a corner of a suitcase. I purchased a set of them back in March, before a trip to Morocco. Acuvue® Oasys® brand contact lenses, for astigmatism, with Hydraclear®plus lenses, "designed to keep your eyes moist and comfortable all day long." I have seldom used them, as they strain the eyes if worn for any length of time.

It took a while to fit the concave sides onto my cornea. My eyes are not used to such plastic intimacies; the cornea looked crystal pure, innocent of harm, before the contacts intervened. The lenses seem to be working well enough now. I'll have to rely on them during waking hours and trust they'll stay in place during the trip to Paris, while I'm carrying a suitcase and heavy bag. The lenses consist of flexible plastics that are pliable and hydrophilic, *water-loving*. This keeps the lenses soft and supple and allows oxygen to pass through to the cornea, enabling the eyes to "breathe" while blanketed in plastic.

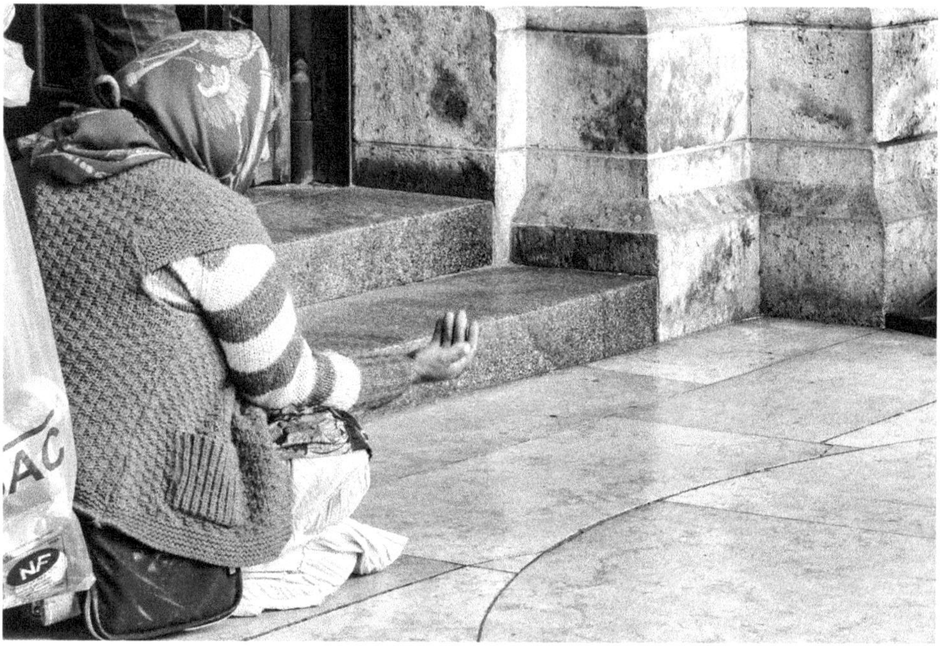

With the contact lenses on, my eyes cannot clearly see words or elements up close. And so I picked up a pair of inexpensive "reading glasses" off a rack at a pharmacy in Besançon, +1.50, to read texts, write with the laptop, and regard photographs on the screen. I'm using them now, as I write. Both eyes are adjusting to these new prosthetics of vision, one glare-resistant lens layered atop another, like lenses aligned in a telescope.

It's remarkable how many optical devices we rely on in this contemporary world. With each lens, vision is at once enhanced and partial.

July 26. Paris. A return is never a circling back to the same. I made my way to the basilica last night and again this afternoon. The scene before the church had changed with the alternate season and shifts in memory. The place was other to how I had remembered it. The uneven terrain before the church appeared smaller, scrunched together. It took a while to regain a sense of proportion.

A woman was seated close to the church, her hand held out toward the people passing by, her voice pleading for alms. I stepped inside the church, a site of "perpetual prayer." A guard stood by the entrance, telling people, "*pas des photos*"; a sign read, "Please respect the silence. No photos"; and yet people could not resist cramming icons into their cell phones while two priests performed a silent mass at the high altar. All was divine and hushed and somber, with the semblance of ants crawling about. I sat on a bench near the back of the church and watched a family scroll through smiling photos taken that day. I read a sign noting that the benches were reserved for those waiting for confession; "*Les bancs reserves pour les confessions.*" I jolted upright and left the church, into the open air.

Outside, men were selling water bottles. I heard them talking with each other in Hindi and learned they are from India. Other men were carrying boxes of Heineken beers with them, selling the bottles one by one to thirsty tourists while keeping an eye out for any police officers intent on fining or arresting them for selling wares without the appropriate permits.

I recognized one of the water sellers from when I had been in Montmartre two years before. He had been nabbed by a police officer while selling fresh, unopened water bottles by the gates of the basilica. I noticed the two of them soon after the encounter and watched as the officer walked farther up the steps while holding the young man by the back of his coat. This younger man, who held the bucket of waters in his hand, looked distressed. I took it that he had been selling the waters illegally, without a permit, and the officer nabbed him for that. Perhaps he had been caught doing the same at an earlier time. With the younger man firmly in his grip the police officer commenced a walking tour of the area by the entrance of the church, he was making a sweep of the place to clear out, as he saw it, anyone up to no good. That he was doing so while holding the man by the scruff of his neck, steering him this way or that, past the columns by the church, making a show of his control over him, was disturbing to me and, I think, to others who noticed the spectacle. The younger man could only walk in the way that the officer bodily directed him through the crowds mingling about. I followed in their wake, taking photographs of their passage through the active bodies there, within a thousand lines of sight. I don't think they noticed my shadowing presence; or the officer couldn't have cared less about me. I stood like a photojournalist capturing a scene of power and marginality, photos destined for a leftist weekly.

The policeman walked by a woman seated by the church. "I told you before to move on," he barked out. The woman turned in his direction without looking at him. She leaned against the ground, knees on stone marble, she collected herself, stood up, and stepped slowly down the stairs.

The policeman continued his sweep of the stairs and entranceways, eyeing the place for bodies foreign to this site of prayer and tourism. Only when he was satisfied with the current state of affairs did he bring the offending man in his grip to a police car parked in an area just below the stone steps. I stood on the terrace above and watched him and another officer use their phones to call into a station. They spoke with the young man, posed questions to him. The man answered quietly, reluctantly. I wondered if he was in France illegally, with an expired visa, and he would now face a harsh deportation. I saw this young man as being from Morocco or Algeria, living in an apartment building in a quadrant of the *banlieu* with his parents and siblings. He was trying to make a few bucks, there's no harm in quenching a tourist's thirst. He had hopes of going to college and becoming a documentary filmmaker, but he has a young wife and son to care for and so he needs to go for the quick money. See how easy it is to delve into a phantasmatical anthropology, where the forms and passions of a life are pictured for the reverie of

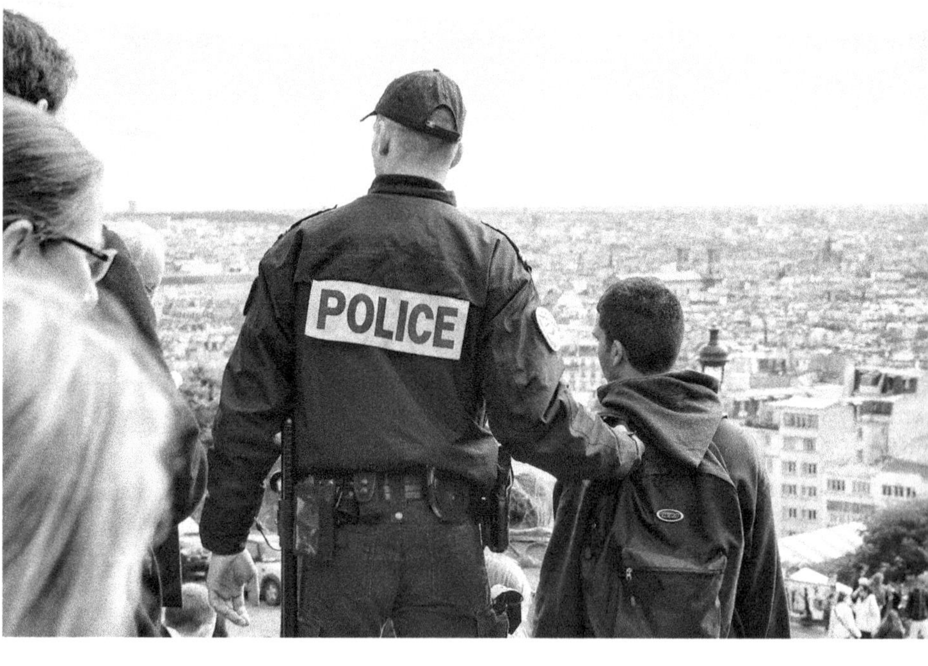

imagined knowledge? I told myself stories. I felt for him. I was there where he was. It looked like he was going to cry. I gave thought to photographing the scene further but I couldn't bear to record the young man's distress, it would have worsened his plight. He would have looked up and spotted me photographing him mercilessly. I saw that future mood as clear as day.

And now, twenty-one months later, the young man was standing close to the gate, a bottle of chilled water held out to those walking past. It was good to see him there and know he had survived the police and, apparently, had not been deported. I felt relief that my phantasmatics were for naught. An imaginative mind had plunked him down in a police station in Montmartre, on a boat bound for Tangiers or Algiers. This time round I bought a bottle of water from him for the fair market price of one euro.

No sign of the blind man.

July 27. This morning I returned to the basilica. When I arrived at the steps I noticed a man seated by the entrance to the church. Around my age, he sat facing the passing crowds, a box of hospital documents by his side, testifying to his medical needs. I walked close and gave him a one-euro coin, though my intent was directed less toward him than toward the man with the cataract I had encountered two years before. The present man was, to me, a surrogate, the recipient of alms virtually given to someone else, not there. The coin was a metal of symbolic compensation—or penance, perhaps.

In the afternoon I climbed the twisting stairs leading up to the Dome of the basilica, paying seven euros for the feat. Much of Paris could be seen from the open-air windows and walkway circling the Dome; the Cathedral of Notre Dame, the Eiffel Tower, the Louvre. Everyone was looking out, somewhere. What struck me most in those lofty heights were the many inscriptions engraved into stone by travelers passing through the place, nearly unreadable words scratched in English, French, Chinese, Spanish, Italian, Russian, Japanese, names, dates, initials, testaments to family vacations, existential claims, political manifestos, statements of undying love.

Billie was here.
Clay was here. Sonny was here 3/7/14
Alice e Paula. Now and again

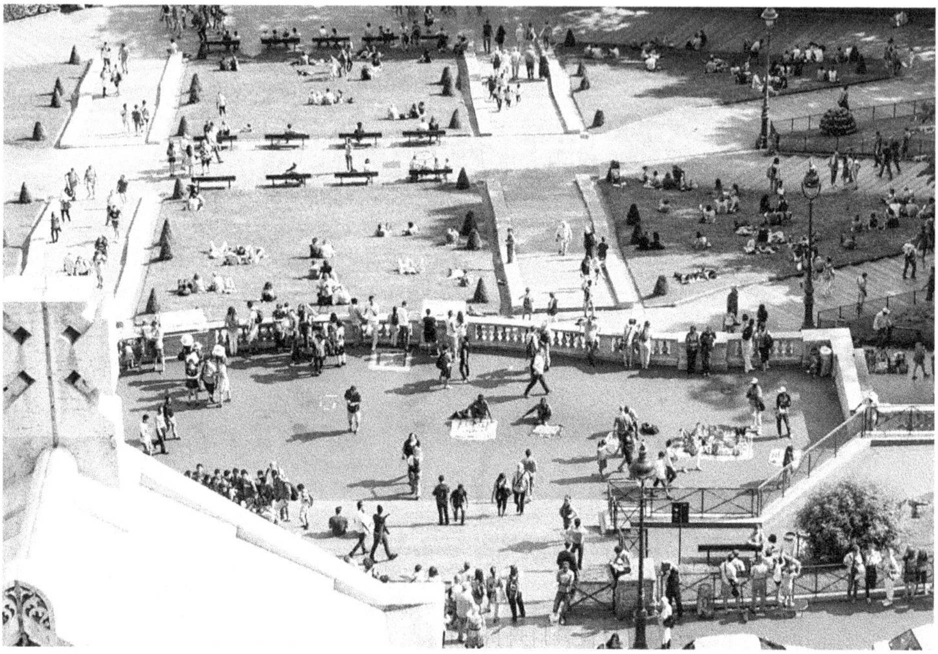

This need to leave a graphic mark, to attest to a onetime presence in a place or in a life.

While circling about the Dome I wondered what lay beyond its stone facade—whether there were secret chambers within, or a vacant, airless space laced with cobwebs, or the interior served as the crowning apex of the basilica. I looked down, toward the south, to see if I could spot the area by the steps leading up to the basilica; I could spy portions around it, the many people there, minuscule as ants; the steps themselves were blocked from view. Most of those circling about the Dome were taking pictures of themselves by the open-air windows, with white blue gray reliefs of Paris in the distance. A woman and her daughter, from Russia, I believe, asked me to take a photograph of them together with the camera built into their cell phone. Looking at the square box and finding no answers I had to ask them how to snap the image.

By the end of the day's excursions my eyes were sore and tired. There was so much looking to look at, many eyes were required to see all the eyes. I suffered an excess of vision. The cornea must have been adjusting to receiving slightly less oxygen from outside air. I went back to the apartment and dug out the lens from the glaze of my eyes, thirteen hours after layering them onto those watery orbs. The eyes breathed anew. I stumbled my way about the apartment with the use of the broken eyeglasses. The frames kept collapsing into two parts and so I resorted again to holding up one of the lens close to my right eye. I peered through that monocle while squinting the other eye shut. I went out to buy some groceries, carrying the single lens, held on its broken stick. Navigating poorly I bumped into a burly young man, our shoulders colliding near the yogurt section. We looked at one another, bothered by the disruption to our Saturday evenings. I returned his look of peeved annoyance.

July 27. The apartment is drab and poor of light, with the rank odor of a cleaning detergent stinking up the air. I can't stay there for long. Two bland windows overlook nothing but the cramped outer walls of brown white buildings nearby. A few windows above look down upon the window in the bedroom. When I lay on the bed at night, with a thin cotton sheet draped over my torso, I saw that anyone looking out from one of those windows could observe my prone body. It was too hot to keep the yellow curtains fully closed and so I left part of the blinds open.

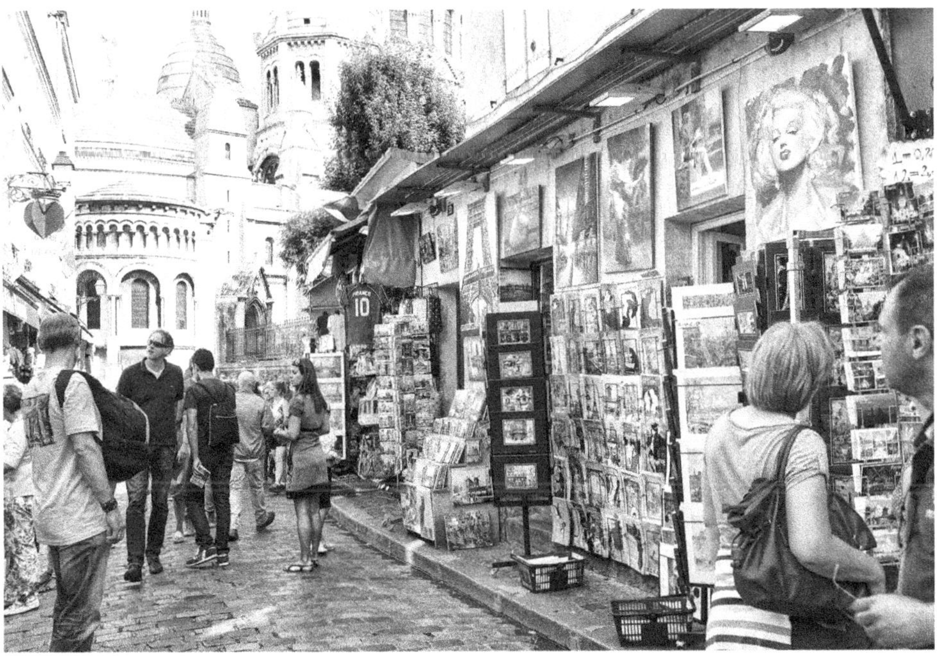

This left my feet and the lower portions of my legs visible to anyone who cared to look. A view of calves and calloused toes was a better option, I speculated, than to have an unknown stranger gaze upon my sleeping face and eyes. Another night might bring a different erotic of seer and unseen. I slept to the murmured hum of a summer night in Paris, air conditioners rumbling in an unseen distance.

July 28. This morning it took twenty minutes to place the contact lenses properly over the watery curves of my corneas. I had to keep taking the instruments out, inserting them again, until the cellophane sheens felt fine and clear over the surfaces without sharp irritation. The body is a reluctant cyborg.

I went to the basilica twice today, this afternoon and again around nine at night. Within the field of intersecting sights and sounds close to the steps, busy with human interests, stood a man with a guitar, singing a bluesy version of the song "Have You Ever Seen the Rain?"

Men coiled the springs of wind-up birds or planes and released them into the air above, the birds clacked about, lofty in their heights, they lost the energy of their whorled motion, grew hesitant in flight, became desultory, inevitably came crashing to the ground, landing on unknowing shoulders or feet or pavement or got entangled within the branches of nearby trees, the path of their flights and the spot of impact seemingly random happenings, there must have been a multitude of factors unseen to an unlensed eye, torsion of motor, wind speed and air temperature, meteorological pressures, warmth of photonic light, the skirting of bodies below, insect trajectories, combined forces of spiraled ascent and descent twisting like images in the world.

Still no trace of the blind man.

I've gotten on friendly terms with the men from India who are selling the water bottles. I've told them I had once lived in Nepal, and can speak Nepali, though our brief exchanges have been in French. I've purchased several waters from them, one euro a bottle, the beginning of amity, and they nod when they notice me by the steps. I've taken to sitting there for an hour or two, while reading a novel (Genet's *The Thief's Journal*, just now), or sketching random notes. The water sellers had become curious as to my reason for returning, day after day. I told them I was a photographer, writing about travels in France.

I sat and watched the unkempt pageantry, taking in the day's sensorials like an anthropologist in a Himalayan teashop—or a spider poised in its web; a spider-ethnographer sensitive to the shimmer of vibrant pulsations. Eight eyes, clear and unclear, two median eyes, the lens of which hold good image brightness; the resolution is poor but good for spotting changes in environmental light intensity; felt vibrations count for the most. This spider sits in the center of its web, patiently attentive. He moves sideways when connective tissues indicate morsels of interest within the reach of his webbing. He seizes words, images, objects, affects, and visions by encasing silk strands around them, preserving them for future digestive use.

One of the water sellers, a man older than the others, caught my eye in holding up one of the bottles. He looked at me and gestured with an index finger. *One euro.* I smiled and shook my head no. He nodded and signaled "one" again. I shook my head no. The third time, yes. I walked down the steps, reached into a pocket and gave him a euro coin. He handed me a water, cool clarity in flexible plastic. I took a sip and pointed to his stash of bottles, set in a bucket of cold water. The silk found its mark; pincers and paralytic juice.

"Why do the police take the waters? I saw them do that before."

"The police? No good! We're doing work here. Why should they bother us?"

"Yes, that's true. And it's good for the tourists to have water available."

"Yes, it's good. No problem."

"Do they arrest you?"

"No, not really. Usually they give us citations, for twenty or twenty-five euros."

He said this while miming the act of writing on a piece of paper.

"Oh, okay. That's not so bad."

"No. Not so bad. Sometimes they bring us down to the police station, and we have to wait there for several hours. It's a hassle. We're not doing anything wrong. There are real thieves in the city."

"Have they come today?"

"No. Not yet. They don't come every day."

The older man noticed that my bag was partially open.

"Keep your possessions close," he warned me. "Do you understand?"

As we spoke, another man stood on the opposite of the gate, a bottle of water for sale in his hand. I believe he was the one who had been accosted by the police officer and dragged around by the collar, when I was here before. We exchanged nods. I could not bring myself to talk to him. We shared an intimacy of which he was unaware, memories unknown to him. The photographs taken that October day had, for me,

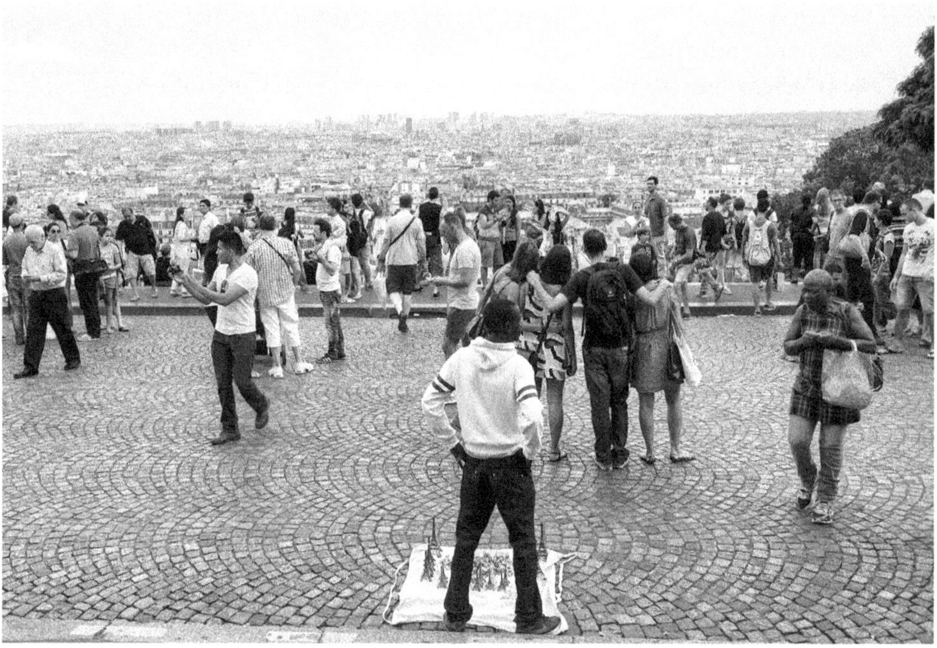

retained an impression of his capture and the distress in his face. He was, to me, remembered, a vivid phantasm.

So went the flow of perceptions, imaginings, memories, and phantasms of an otherwise unremarkable day in Paris, each act of looking splintering into a thousand intensities of sight.

Tomorrow I'll bring the photograph of the blind man with me, with the intent of asking the water sellers if they recognize him at all. Perhaps they've seen him around.

July 28. I photographed a man standing by a supply of miniature Eiffel towers, laid out on a small blanket at the foot of the gate. I glanced at the camera's LCD monitor, chimping at the images just taken. When I looked up again, the man was scooping up the icons with the blanket with a few deft motions. He stood alert, looked about, and ran off. The water sellers and the hawkers of Heineken fled moments later, a flock of sparrows lighting from a telephone line. I could not perceive the threat. I looked around and, seconds later, noticed two police officers, a woman and a man, appearing with bicycles at the crest of the stairs to the east; on the western slope a number of sellers were rushing down a side path into the wooded park below. Apparent now are the complex networks of communication that dart through the clandestine sellers on the butte—rapid looks, calls, whistles, relay points, low-frequency signals. It's as if they, too, weave and inhabit a weblike net of felt vibrations and watchful anticipation of prey and possible attack. The perceptions comprise a nervous system in its own right, flexible, ever-shifting cybernetic assemblages of pain receptors and nerve axons, image sensors, and a nervous, compound eye. There are wolves about, they say with so many looks.

He wasn't there today.

July 28. Early this evening, while sitting at a small table outside a café on rue de Clignancourt, savoring a demi of blonde beer, I watched as a young woman left the interiors of the bar across the way and crossed the street, avoiding passing cars. She walked with slurred steps, weaving from side to side. She came close to the café and glanced at two German girls seated at a table near mine. She walked past them and turned her sights on me. She came to my table and asked if I had some *monnaie*, some spare change. I shook my head sadly no. She stepped to the next table and posed the same question to the two women seated there. One of them answered with words I did not catch. The young woman said in response, "Je n'ai pas les yeuxs fatigués."

I do not have tired eyes.

Her eyes were fatigued from drink, smoke in the bars, late nights, mirror work. She's hooked on the stuff.

July 28. I rely on the contact lenses like a beetle depends on its shiny encasement.

July 29. He was there today, the blind man. He stood by the steps to the basilica, much as he did when I saw him before. This afternoon, my last day in Paris, I approached the hilltop from the northwest, walking up from Place des Abbesses, uneven streets crammed with tourists, their antennas alert to the biochemical scent of wondrous impressions, Manets and Monets. A legion of artists carrying blank white canvasses sought to draw the portraits of charmed tourists, "*pour le souvenir*," a memory, for a fee. Most of the artists began their drawings by first sketching in the eyes. In my backpack lay the black-and-white photograph. Upon arriving at the basilica I expected to encounter much the same scene as the past few days—the carnal pulsations of tourists, the dazzling mechanics of cameras, men selling bottles of water. I turned

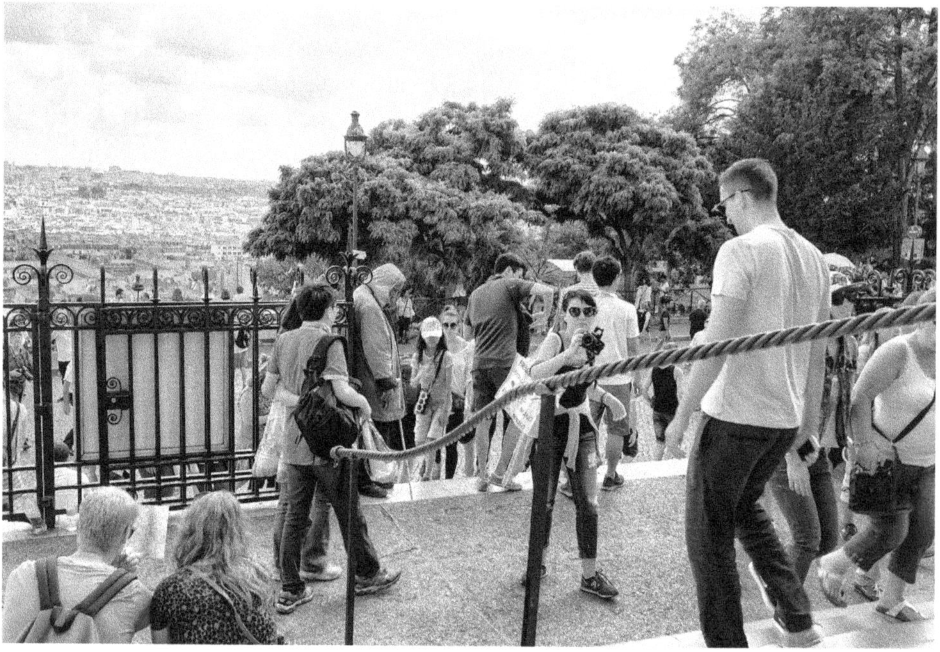

toward the entrance and glanced at a woman seeking alms. That's when I saw him standing by the gate.

He was still there, reasonably well, still on his feet, at the clutch of it. He had assumed much the same pose as in the photographs. His hand was held out, gently. A light metal walking stick lay in the nape of his wrist. He was standing directly in the sun's heat. Sweating, he wiped his brow free of perspiration. He wore a heavy coat, light brown in color, with a large hood, possibly the same coat he had on when photographed two years before. The lower parts of the coat appeared darker in color than those above. The darkening resulted from an accumulation of sweat. I sat on the steps a few feet above and away and felt the same sun as he did. I could not fathom why he would be enveloped in a thick heavy coat on a summer day. The expanses of its coating lent him a sense of protection and kept part of him hidden from the stares and flesh of others. He had to expose himself each day, put himself by the gates and demonstrate his blindness. Did the coat serve as an eyelid, protective and soothing? Clouds passed above, bringing relief for a minute or two, until the searing heat returned. He shook his head at times, as if throwing off a fit of lightheadedness. He retrieved an inhaler from inside his coat and drew breaths from it. Coagulates of people passed. Very few of them gave him any money, one in fifty, at best—women, mostly. Any coins received he measured with his fingers and deposited in his right coat pocket.

"Voleur!" I heard him say at one point. *Thief!* His word caught my eye and I watched as he turned and looked toward the crowd of people below as though sighting or sounding someone who had snatched a few coins from his hand—or to indicate to others the direction to which the thief had taken flight. Perhaps he heard someone running off. Nothing came of his alert. No one responded, as far as I could tell. No one turned or changed directions. His words fell without consequence. He returned to his stance by the gate, hand held out.

He must have been terribly thirsty. I looked into my wallet and saw that I had three twenty-euro bills, nothing smaller than that. A twenty would be too much to give him, I reasoned—he might not discern the amount, or he could lose it later that day. Or someone would see me giving him the money and rob him of it later on. I reached into my backpack, past the photograph, and felt for any change scattered about, ten- or fifty-centime pieces. I came up with a handful of coins. I walked down the steps and approached one of the men selling the water bottles.

"Ça va?"

"Ça va."

"C'est chaud audjourd'hui."

"Comment? Oui. C'est chaud."

The man had two bottles remaining in his bucket. I bought one of them and held it in my left hand. In my right hand was the grab of coins. I opened the bottle and took a sip of the cool water. I walked along the fence, toward the blind man, and stood close to him.

He did not see me standing there.

"Monsieur," I said.

He looked blankly.

"C'est pour vous. C'est un peu de la monnaie."

He turned toward me and held out his hand. I placed the coins in the palm of his hand. My hand touched his.

"Merci," he said.

"Merci," I said.

"Est-çe que vous voulais d'eau?"

Would you like some water?

"D'eau?"

"Oui. Une bouteille d'eau."

"Oui. L'eau."

I doubt he could have recognized me from two years before. How could he be aware, at all, that I had been intensely concerned with his specular image and the condition of his eyes? That I cared for him, and imagined him? Or that I had been hoping to locate him again? He must have been oblivious to the black-and-white photograph that lay in the heated confines of my shoulder bag.

I turned back to where the man selling the water had been. He was gone. I had been counting on that last remaining water still being there. I looked toward the blind man, still by the gate. I gave thought to giving him the opened water bottle, from which I had already drank. If I gave it to him, he would have no way of knowing that I had already taken a few sips. He would hold the bottle to his lips and drink the liquid and the fluids of our saliva would have interwoven in that brief fine stream of comingled time. There would be a consubstantiation of frail, separate bodies now together linked, unknown to him while cognizant to me. It would not be right to give him a water already sipped from, without informing him of this; he could get sick, he would be consuming something tainted, unwanted, beyond himself. He should know the source and nature of things given to him.

I brushed past the gate, past his open hand, and located a man selling water by the concourse below the gate and stairs. I gave him a euro coin and brought the water to the gate.

"C'est de l'eau, Monsieur."

"L'eau?"

"Oui. Un boteille d'eau."

He reached for the bottle, sensed its shape, and took it in his hands.

"Merci."

"Merci."

He looked at me, and said, "Vous êtes gentil."

You are kind.

I am not sure of that.

He looked at me with a gesture of caring regard. He did not have to see me in order to show his regard of me. His voice was rich and grave and tender and sane—and, dare I say, wise and knowing, as if he had seen and heard a lot. In those moments I saw not a blind beggar but a person standing before me, within a moment of mutual regard and respect. His damaged eyes were there, in the pools of his sockets, they did not matter much. His eyes were no longer monstrous. I could have stared at them, and the cataracts looming there, but there was more to his presence. We had spoken, face to face. He was greater than me. He was greater than my impression of him, vaster than the picture I had accrued. His presence before me, and the immediacy of the encounter—it happened so quickly—nearly overwhelmed me.

He took the water, and he turned, I suppose. I walked away, back up the steps. I realized I still had the cap to the bottle I had given him. I held that milky-white plastic, nearly translucent in appearance, in my hand. I thought of returning and letting him know I had the cap, but this would have been too confusing an exchange to force upon him.

I watched as he took a few sips of the water. He drank much less than I thought he would—he looked terribly thirsty, sweat saturated his coat. With care he placed the bottle on the ground, close to the metal bars of the fence, and he felt his way back to the entrance to the gate. The bottle lay there, on the hard ground, the lid crucially open, precarious. Anyone walking past could knock it over with a quick, unknowing swipe of a foot, the water would tear to the ground.

I sat on the steps, in a central prism of vision. He continued to ask for money, I took out a notebook and began to write out notes and observations. I wanted to remember as much as possible, the look of him, his gestures and movements, my thoughts, so much is lost after just a few minutes. He looked my way, toward my body seated on the steps, watching him, writing down words in the space between us. I trusted he could not see me. There was an invisible relation between us. It was as if we were keeping each other company, biding time together, as friends might do. I took a few photographs. There were nine steps between him and me, and a small flat surface, this I counted. We sipped from the waters at the same time, tuned to the same rhythm of thirst.

A woman walked up to him and held a coin out for him. They were facing each other. Apparently he did not see her. There was no glint of recognition of the person or objects held before his eyes. He took out his inhaler and drew a breath. Asthmatic, then. She kept the coin held out; perhaps he would respond. He placed the inhaler inside his coat with no acknowledgment of her presence. I watched her as she reached out and dropped the coin in the front pocket of his coat. Bless her for not walking away, with the coins kept in her hand. He was not aware of her charity. Was this proof that he could not see? The woman moved on. He would never know of her gift to him. Only she herself, and any god of hers, would take in the grace of her charity, along with a lone spider.

I took it that he was completely blind, now. I wondered if he had the ability to see two years back, and then the last of his vision expired.

He reached for the fence behind him and touched it with his hand. Sensing the railing, he moved slowly along the fence, feeling for each metal bar, equidistant from its neighbors. When he came to a larger, more massive bar, bearing a protruding spike, he motioned his body downward, toward the ground. He reached for the lidless bottle of water, touching it with his fingers, and grabbed hold of the plastic without spilling its contents. He brought the bottle close to his mouth and took a few brief sips. He placed it back on the ground. With many walking past I worried the bottle would tip over. I gave thought to walking down the steps and standing close to the water, to protect it from spillage, becoming the protector of the water bottle, but thought my body's interference would cause further turmoil. I stayed put. I saw that another bottle lay close to the one I had given him, the history of which I could not know, perhaps he had been using it earlier in the day, with its water turned warm and musty; the capped container leaned precariously to its side, the weight at its base kept it from tipping over. The man relied on his hands to feel his way back along the fence, back to where he had been standing before, four posts and then the larger post. So this was his topography on the steps, his method of siting where he stood or wished to go. His hands and walking stick worked the fence as a prosthetics of sight, extension of his unseeing eyes, reaching out, anticipating, always hesitant, never more than half certain. I worried how he would fare once apart from the count of steps and posts.

I looked up to see a woman talking to him as he stood by the gate. She was holding a baby in her arms. Several children were close by, below the steps, waiting for her. This woman could have been a nun, caring for orphans. I thought of coming close and listening in on their conversation. I feared my actions would be noticed. I took it that the woman was asking about his welfare, his means of care. He might not be as alone and stranded as I had taken him to be. Envious of their easy rapport, I wanted to talk with him as well. I wished to know his name.

Conversation ended, the man returned to asking for money. Minutes later he felt his way along the fence, back to the larger post and the water on the ground. He sipped from the bottle. He stayed by that portion of the fence. He turned and faced the rush of people leaving the space of the church, moving like logs along a jammed river.

The water bottle remained upright. No water spilled out.

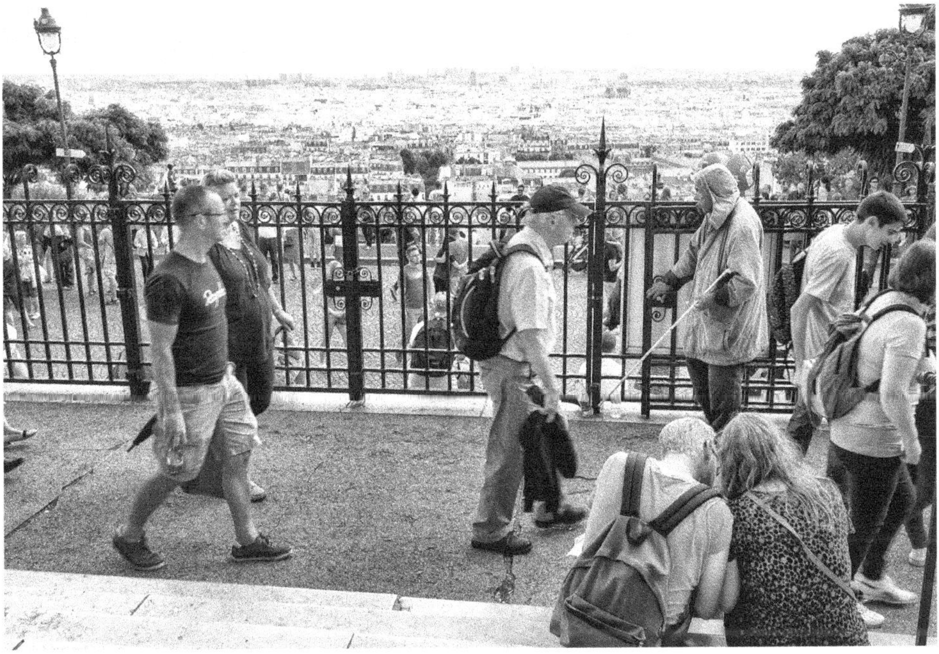

I wanted to stay there, watching continuously. I had to leave the hilltop and walk down to where I was staying, to check in on a scheduled conversation by Skype with a friend. That call never happened.

Back at the apartment I located an assortment of change accumulated during recent travels in Europe, a mishmash of Nordic gold- and copper-covered steel held in a plastic ziplock bag. I placed the collection in my knapsack, left the apartment, and climbed the steps to the basilica. I wanted to give the man this collection of change and talk with him more. I wasn't sure how well I would be able to strike up a conversation with him, introduce myself, ask about his concerns, in French no less, without him having the capacity to see me talking to him, gestures, expressions, the light in my eyes.

I returned to the basilica breathless from a quick jog up stone stairs. He was nowhere to be seen. Another man had taken his place by the gate. The box of hospital documents sat by his side, his hand twitched slightly. Perhaps the alms seekers have arranged shifts, I thought, like buskers at a subway station. Or the subsequent, more able-bodied man had muscled the blind man off.

Could it be that someone, a friend or an aide, came and met him by the gate to the basilica and helped him to climb down into the streets of Montmartre?

In one sense I felt relief he was gone. If he happened to leave while I was there I would have been tempted to trail a few steps behind his uncertain progress. Extending the reach of my web, I would learn how he managed his movements once away from the terrain of the church, where he went to, what he did next, where he lived. I would have held the camera in my hands and photographed him as he crossed a busy avenue and tapped his way around a street corner. I could have arranged to interview him, a digital recorder picking up his words. I could write a life history and give meaning to bare life. I would contribute to the annals of medical anthropology and launch a new theory of suffering, for the betterment of humanity, while bringing attention to his plight and glory to my name.

If I had the opportunity to talk with him again I would ask for his name, only. And leave it at that.

Corneal abrasion

July 29. New York. I wore the contact lenses on the long flight back home today, Paris to Newark. I fell asleep a few hours into the flight and woke up near Greenland, worried that the lenses had congealed onto the corneas. With the contacts coating the surfaces, the eyes do not breathe well, a lack of oxygen can lead to decreased vision from corneal swelling and epithelial cell damage, or so I've learned. I watched the movies just fine, caught a ride over the George Washington Bridge, and was home by early evening. After seventeen hours of relentlessly clear vision my eyes could not take the strain of intensity any longer. Contacts create a kind of caffeinated vision; there's no way to turn down the optics. Once settled in at home I stood before a mirror and peeled each lens from the film covering the eyes. This left me with the feeble use of the broken glasses.

I started up the computer set on the table in the kitchen and opened up Adobe Lightroom. In minutes I was able to locate all of the photographs taken that October day, two years back. They were kept in a single folder, *Paris-6*, distinct images cued to exact times and shutter speeds, more than a hundred pictures viewed on the screen of a liquid crystal display, quadrants of image after image, in color, in RAW format, with lasting metadata, capture time, capture date, dimensions, exposure, focal length; flash, did not fire; lens, 35mm, f/1.8. Clicking through the visuals I flitted from photographic moment to moment, I went back in time, moved through space, sifting through an exquisite, rotating corpus of photographic imagery. I could retrace my photographic steps through that 22nd day, first of a merry-go-round in Montmartre, then the steps of the basilica, a man playing a violin, a woman begging, the policeman, hooded coat, the streets of Montmartre, a glassy Métro line, and rooftop views from the Pompidou Center, ending in dusk, 528 photos in all. I recalled perceptions long forgotten and drank up morsels of time. I could zoom in at will, peer closely, inspect details, and study the digital phantasms, which have come to haunt me. I had control of the surface qualities of these images if not what they signified or portended. I could edit at will these photographic perceptions; reframe them; alter the contrast, add codes and keywords, convert to black-and-white, export files as TIFFs or JPEGs, and soon I'd become a jet-lagged, midnight god of photographic illusion.

The photographs of the blind man are on the hard drive, I was too tired to look closely tonight. I'll consider them all more tomorrow, with fresh eyes.

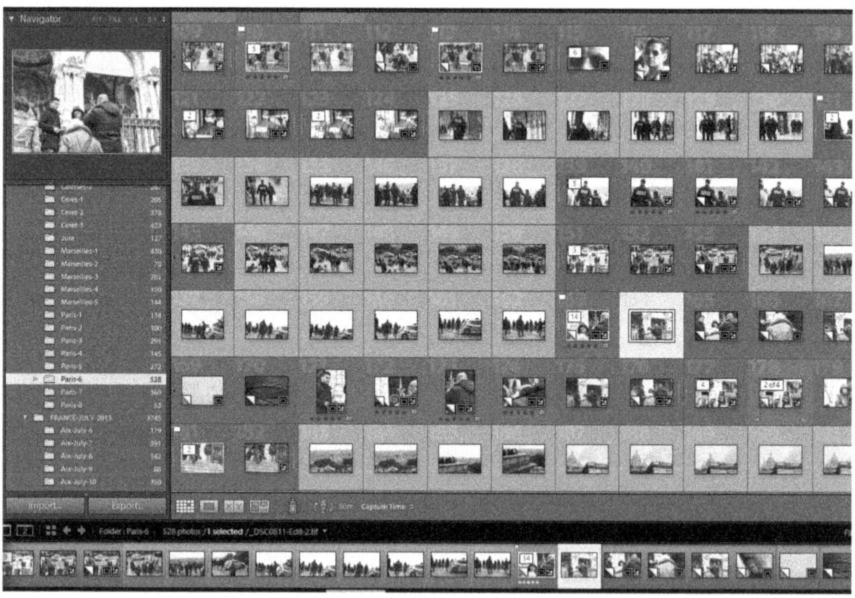

July 30. This past night I dreamed that I was in a suite of rooms, high up in a building, walking about chambers on the top floor of this vast structure, with a number of windows looking out. Nothing could be seen clearly. Everything stood there in a vague and diffuse form, where the very possibility of seeing was an unclear prospect. I woke slowly from dreaming and realized I was walking about my own apartment, past 2:00 A.M., without eyeglasses on. In the dream it was not that I could not see well but, rather, that I was in a place where nothing could be seen well. The physics and metaphysics of the place, the atmosphere throughout, was a world of blurred and feeble vision.

July 30. This afternoon, while at the eye doctor's office in Yonkers, I was able to receive new frames for the lens in the broken eyeglasses. It's good to have the eyeglasses back. It feels like I have my "normal" vision back again—even if this eyeware consists of technologically advanced progressive addition lenses, composed of three distinct optics of eyesight fashioned within a single pair of lenses. The trifocal lenses hold a gradient of increasing lens power, which starts at the top of the lens, for distance viewing; transitions smoothly into an intermediate channel; and then reaches the maximum addition power, for the strength of reading, at the bottom of the lens. Soon after putting them on I was reminded of the triad of lenses involved and the distortions that come with this set-up, with regions of aberration on either side of the optic axis, the associated blur and geometric distortions on the peripheries of eyesight. Not having worn the trifocals for several days has had the effect of denaturalizing the visual distortions I had gotten used to through months of constant, daily use. Pulpy churnings of neural circuits are learning to see anew.

Each act of looking carries a multiplicity of perceptions, a jangled, polychromatic array of optics, haptic touch, uneven memory, assumptions, histories, media technologies, and phantasmal imaginings combined within the gleam of an eye or the wavering sheen of a spectral presence. In what ways are the prosthetics of perception at hand—eyeglasses, contact lenses, camera lens, digital technologies, computer screens, photographic prints—caught up in forms of sensate knowing and fantasy-making? For days and weeks now, and through untimed moments of imaginative fancy, I've been using a gamut of prosthetic devices to process images of a man I've met only fleetingly.

Such visual prosthetics provide the conditions for writing here, for I am writing as if alongside images gathered, in time, through various technological means, lens after lens, frame by digital frame. In turn, the writing itself relies on prosthetic devices. Along with the fabrication of images seen and screened through technological apparatuses, there are the prosthetics of inscription and memory—of marking, grafting, framing, dating, coding, recording, sharpening, revising, copying, transferring—conducted through pen and paper, notebooks, computer screen and keyboard, digital files and folders, laser printers, electronic transfers, cloud storage. The graph of writing, like that of photography, is based on addition and artifice. The perceiver-inscriber of images is, himself, composed of a complex assemblage of technological devices, from the biomechanics of the human eye to algorithms of data processing. Each of these devices, altogether magical in its capacities, is prone to rupture, decay, or breakdown, at any moment.

July 31. I cut myself today. This happened in the late afternoon while I was trying to open a package of books with the narrow blade of a kitchen knife. In the haze of fatigue the knife ran through the plastic wrap of the package straight into the flesh spanning the ligaments of the thumb and index finger of my right hand. The cut was small but deep, a vascular incision. I went to the emergency room at the local hospital to have it checked out. Fortunately no stitches were required, and a gentle doctor cleansed and bandaged the wound. That small nick has thrown off the utility of my hand and my coordination more generally, I can't write or talk or see in the same way. Before it began to heal the cut lay open, a small slice into body. The cut opened farther whenever the fingers flexed or reached for an object. The cut lay there like a small, lidless eye, an alien eye, winking back at me. That eyewound is covered over by a yellow gauze bandage, a secure blindfold. At some point I'll have to release the bandage and scope the wound again.

July 31. Last night I had the same dream as the night before. I was in the suite of rooms, nothing could be seen clearly. It seems that, in the dream, this chamber of rooms lay within the Dome of the basilica, or a structure like it.

When I woke in the morning I could not locate my eyeglasses. They were not where I left them when I went to sleep—on a bookshelf close to the bed. Searching about, I found them under the sheets where I had been sleeping. There's a dim memory of putting them on while half-asleep, half-dreaming, and then falling back to sleep. The eyeware must have fallen from my resting face and come to lie beneath the weight of the

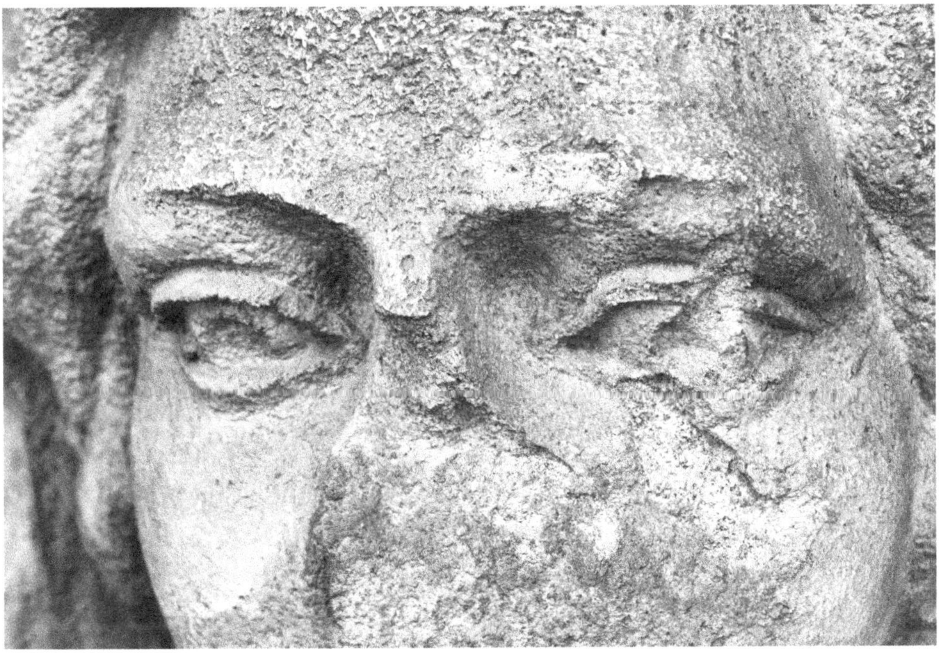

body. By morning, the frames were slightly distorted, but they seem to have returned to their proper shape. Lucky they were not too badly mangled.

July 31. Trouble sleeping tonight. I have been mulling over the strange ruptures to the means of vision. What am I to make of the destructive losses—and by my own hands, no less? Freud said that nothing in behavior lacks a cause—"nothing happens by accident," as they say. The force apparent was striking: my thumbs pressed down too hard on the lens of the eyeglasses; the sunglasses flung from my hands as if with violent intent; a finger dug into my eyelid while I slept; the new eyeglasses lay crushed beneath a body. Two lines of thought come to mind in trying to make sense of this strange and uncommon series of actions. One is that, at some level of my being, I feel guilty or ashamed about photographing and writing about the blind man in such intensive ways; some part of me is bent on hurting myself, punishing my inclinations, in corresponding ways. A lost eye for an eye. King Oedipus gouged out his eyes.

Blind from this hour on. Blind in the darkness-blind.[1]

Another, more intriguing possibility is that, in sympathizing with this man, in trying to grasp the flow of his life, I am coming to acquire certain forms of vision in my own life. All of this is dimly perceived, at best. The psychophysics at work are beyond conscious comprehension, alien to a waking self. There seems a process of phenomenological assimilation at work; I am left to wonder, vaguely, if I am coming to approximate the lifeworld I wish to comprehend. Am I falling into a destructive mimesis of blindness?

If you feel infinitely for someone, can you reach a point where you begin to feel and perceive—and see, or not see—as that person does?

August 1. "Prends garde: à jouer au fantôme, on le deviant."

This warning of a sentence, by Roger Caillois, in his 1935 essay "Mimicry and Legendary Psychasthenia."[2] Take care: in playing a phantom, one becomes a phantom.

August 1. Am I watching myself fall into an image of my own making?

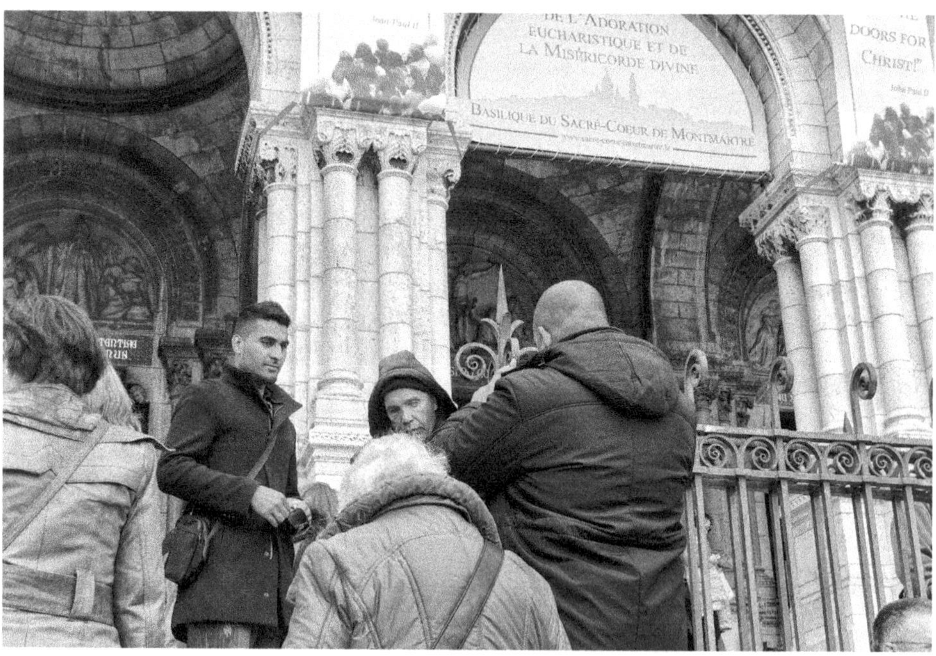

August 1. This afternoon I found the original of the posed photograph on my hard drive. It was taken at 12:21:32, on October 15, 2012. 1/250 sec at *f*/8.0. ISO 200. Lens 35.0mm *f*/1.8.

I had forgotten long ago how different the original was from the one fashioned out of its elements. As with most memories, the edited version had become the perception and reality of that moment. In the initial, uncropped image, more of the basilica can be seen, and there are more human figures within the frame. In concentrating the image close to the three men at hand, I had cut out a lot beyond them. The tight quarters made the image more intense. The tip of the iron fence is fully apparent.

Now that I have observed the blind man's habits around the gate of the basilica, and the ways in which he often stood close to the railing, his hand slightly toward anyone walking up the steps, I've come to recognize that the photograph can be perceived in a different way. Could it be that the man with the sunglasses was not intentionally posing alongside the blind man, as I have been assuming all along? His friend was taking a picture of him alone, with the entrance to the basilica as a backdrop. It's possible that the blind man just happened to be standing nearby, his hands close to the gate, and he was unaware of the actions of the man posing for a photograph, just to his right. He might have sensed someone standing close to him. He heard the shuffle of feet but he could not see the man who was posing or the man taking the photograph, nor my camera below.

Have I gotten wrong the sense of that moment? I remember the transfer of money from the man posing to the blind man, if only faintly, slight as a dream, a few coins placed in a hand and the confirming nod of agreement. Is it possible that I dreamed up a phantasm of that occurrence, which happened not on the steps that day, or any other day, but later on, within the realm of fantasy? And if I have falsely remembered that, in a rush of fanciful interpretation, what else have I spun together within the silk of my imagination?

I doubt that which I see, know, interpret, question.

August 1. While looking at the photograph tonight I faced an unsettling realization: that the young man could be intentionally posing next to the blind man, without the blind man being aware of it. The young man is standing there contentedly, with the fine travertine stones of the church facades behind him and a picturesque beggar to his left. That unseeing man is unaware he is being included within the frame of this photograph.

I find this a horribly unpleasant possibility. I cannot shake this cruel vision from my mind.

August 2. Other forms of perceptual cruelty took form that October day. In my recent excursions into the photographs taken that afternoon I had not noticed two images included there, until this evening, two pictures of the man while he stood close to the railing of the gate. He appears to be looking my way. According to the associated metadata, I took the first of these two photographs at 12:21:39, seven seconds after the one clicked of the young man posing. In the later image, that man's appearance is evident in a space behind the blind man; he is walking toward the church, in conversation with his friend. The woman with the coat, more clearly visible now, has also progressed farther that way. The blind man appears to be looking at me. The look on his face matches the mood I can recall of that moment when I was thinking of photographing him—and he looked my way. I am struck by the resemblance between the mood of my memory and the mood of these images. I had thought I had never taken photographs of this sort. The images suggest otherwise. I had no recent memory of taking them, until now. I wonder now if I had retained the mood of those long slow seconds, of the man's look toward

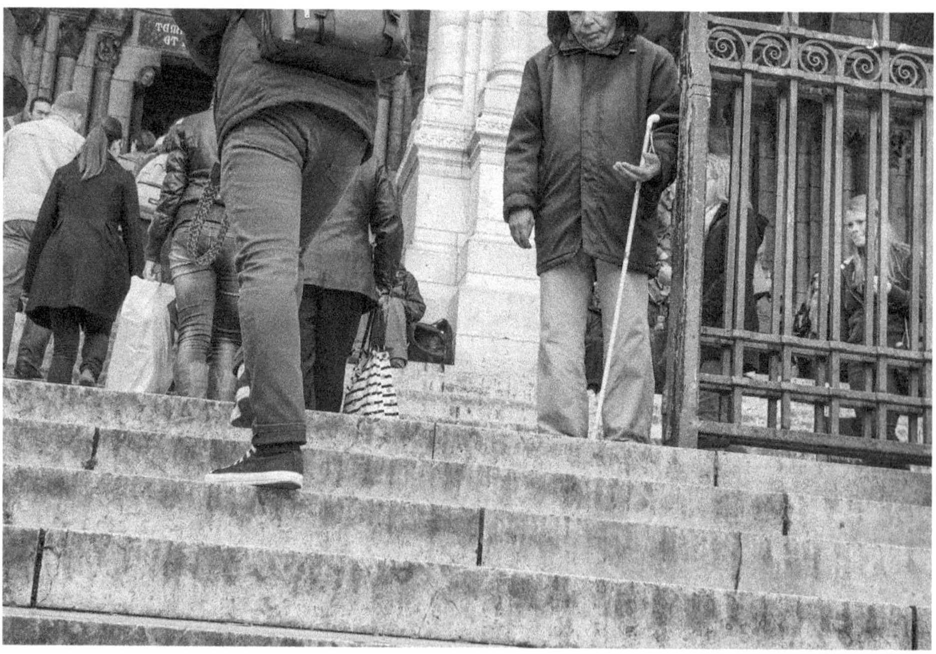

me and my discomfort with that look, while forgetting that I ever took the photographs. Is it possible that some reaches of my psychology had obliterated—"repressed," as they say, rejected, banished—out of discomfort or shame, the cold fact that I took these photographs?

The second image is off-balance. It's a poor photograph, by any means, as though my hold on the camera was faltering, descending into doubt and guilt or hesitation. Or I was shooting from the hip, without looking through the viewfinder, the camera held close to my waist or chest, as I have done while walking down streets or corridors, not wanting others to be aware of the photographic captures; the sly visuals sometimes show something compelling, unexpected.

The man's look has changed here. There is a slight drop of his facial muscles, which I take to be a disapproving regard of my actions. He knew I was photographing him without asking him if I could do so, without compensation. This much he could see. *So this is it*, he seems to be saying. *You are standing there, lifting my image, and there's not much I can do about it, except to look your way in disapproval.* His hand is held out and open, in a show of expected recompense.

Vous n'êtes pas gentil.

You are not kind.

Voleur. Thief.

The second of these images was taken at 12:21:51, a good twelve seconds after the camera triggered the first photo of him alone. What happened in that span of time? I have no memory. Or is the mood of that long, fraught moment the memory I've held onto? It's unsettling to be incapable of remembering a significant action undertaken by one's own hand. Did I stand there hesitantly, with the camera by my chest or waist, mulling over the tainted prospect of photographing him again? Did my interests lead me to sneak one last angled shot of him?

I photographed him like a colonial subject.

August 2. Have I been assuming too much about the sensory means involved? Have I been giving undue priority to sight, while all along hearing might be the primary sense the man relies on when near the basilica? He hears footsteps, bodies brushing past, the gait of their walks, movements and pauses, bodies alone or together. He picks up on murmured voices, hesitation, shared moments, the looks of people. He apprehends the clicking of cameras, the acoustics of which determine for him how far away the cameras are, where their lens are pointed, shutter speeds, rates of capture, all-purpose lenses or telephoto zooms. These many vibratory sounds bounce onto and through him, time and space is mapped acoustically. The finely tuned receiver of his bodymind can tell whether or not he is the intended subject of a given image. The acoustics is a net of aural perceptions and inferences at the center of which lies his hearing.

Looking at the photographs now, I can see how the hood of his coat could serve as a parabolic dish that directs and concentrates sounds toward the inner chambers of his ears. The hood stands as a prosthetic extension and enhancement of his earlobes, much as when a person cups a curved hand to an ear to hear an interlocutor better in conversation. The coat functions as a second skin, as earlobe and eyelid, enhancing oncoming sounds while shielding off oncoming looks. In looking at those photographs taken two years past I see the hood of his coat looming about him, I can picture the upper arch of his coat receiving the vibrations stemming from the clicks of the camera and transmitting them to the appropriate neurons of his brain, which interpret the direction and distance of the camera nearby and rates of photographic exposure. He hears the sounds of photographic looking. He turns his face, eyes, ears, body, and hands toward me in calm, weary disapproval—this now I can see.

August 3. I know I can zoom into the locus of his face and take a good look at his cataract eye. It would be easy to do. A clean click on the computer screen would produce a magnified picture of the appropriate molecules. I'm not sure I want this.

The cataract in the eye appears in a terrifically unsettling way. I cannot look at it for more than a few seconds. It's obscene to dissect and map its contours. This is not the "unsayable" so much as the unseeable, unpresentable; the indescribable. I will not include the magnified image here. The cataract is the misfortunate result of biological processes. The material is of calcified protein, a transparent window turned filmic white. The eye, terribly white, is the patched-up button of a child's doll. The whiteness unfortunate witness to hurricane forces. The cataract is a platelet of the moon viewed from a telescope. It's a continent covering half a globe. The white splotch seen is matter in itself, sheer mass with no meaning to or beyond it, even if we ascribe meaning to it. Unformed. Ill-formed. The unnameable calls for phantasmal imaginings. Notice how an obscure patch of film provokes a glossy sheen of metaphors and resemblances; gauze bandages placed over the gash of a wound.

In the image, it looks like the man can see out of his right eye. I would like to look at his eyes freely and unencumbered. Those eyes keep looking into my own. That twinned look is similar to moments when I've glanced into my own eyes in a mirror: try as I might, those resemblant eyes never leave my own.

I look at the image. The eye looks at me.

August 4. While working on photographs that include his image, it becomes clear to me that I need to treat his appearance with the utmost care. I make sure the seams and folds of his coat look good. I reduce the shadow around his face, beneath the arch of the hood. With Lightroom I use an ingenious device called a "control point" to adjust the contrast, brightness, and structure of his visual form. I want him to look good, and I strive to underline the dignity he deserves. While working on the finishing touches I realize that a better form of care and respect might lie in not representing him at all.

I am the unseen keeper of his image. I can perceive what he cannot. Could it be, now, that I care more for his image than anyone else, except, perhaps, for him? And what, in turn, can he perceive that I cannot? What perspectives on humanity has this life led him to realize?

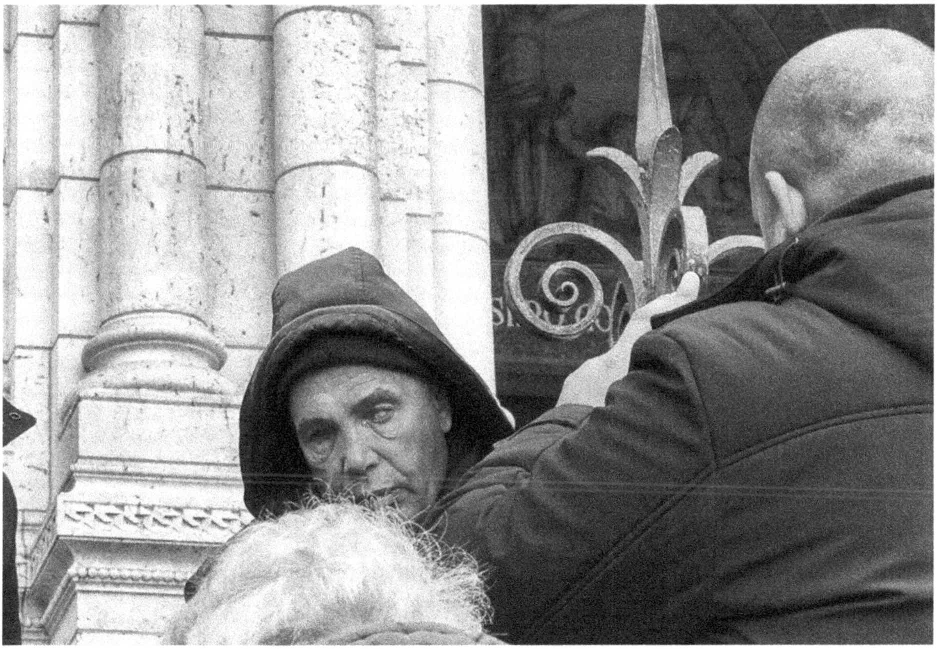

August 4. This morning I took off the bandage wrapped around my hand to take a look at the cut there. It's healing nicely, no redness or infections. The cut is no longer an open wound, the skin has banded together. Where the open wound once stood there lies the bland skin of a pale eyelid, stitched into the place where the alien eye once looked out. The body has taken on any number of optics.

August 4. "The eye exists in its savage state."—André Breton.[3]

August 5. "Do you have his permission to use the photographs you took of him?"

"No, I do not."

This from a conversation with a friend in New York City.

I am having second thoughts about including images of the blind man in anything I might write about him. I'm not sure I have the right to do so. There's a photographer at the college where I teach who tells his students that he feels completely comfortable photographing strangers in the streets of New York City: if someone approaches him and says, "Hey, you just took my picture," he answers, "No, it's not your picture, it's my picture." I'm not so sure. The tension speaks to different conceptions of what a photograph is: (1) a person's image is part of the self, a signature graph of a singular being, and he or she has an inalienable right to protect that image and ward off photographic thefts; (2) an image results from the imprinting of photons on a light-sensitive surface, and the proprietor of that image is the person or agent working the apparatus of photographic recordance.

If need be, I suppose, I could blur out his face in any photos presented so as to obscure the look of his identity. I have tried doing that, experimenting with the software programs I have, but so far I've only managed to use the "clarity" control in Lightroom, bringing the toggle all the way to left side, −100, to soften the details of his face without blurring it much, his eyes are still there, his look toward the camera. Alternatively, I could provide some drawings that show the outlines of people and objects in the scenes involved, making for a scenography penciled with figures without details or distinct singularities. And yet all of this, I believe, would be obfuscations of what is involved. The actual photographs need to be there, the look of him, onto me, my anxious regard of him, if any of this is to speak to the encounters with photography, vision, and perception at work here. Anything less would be a lie, a weak deception to what's involved.

Perhaps any viewers of the images would appreciate how much I care for his image and for his existence and welfare more generally. Perhaps he himself would not mind the transfer of his resemblance. He has to peddle his image each day he's at the steps of the basilica, and he must know intimately the economies of images, how they circulate, get about, are sold and resold.

"It still sounds self-serving," said the friend.

"Yes, I know. But why not be upfront about it? The clarity needs to be there, in a charged and unclear situation."

"Besides," I added, "it's not all that different from what anthropologists do all the time. They observe and write about the lives of others, often in voyeuristic ways. But they tend not to look closely at the ethics and politics of their observations—or the voyeurism implied. Maybe there's a harshness in what I'm doing, a severity. But this might have the effect of showing, in a stark way, what's involved when one person gazes upon the life of another and then goes on to portray that life in words or images."

"Yeah, right."

August 5. On this cool and damp Tuesday afternoon I went for a walk at a wildlife reserve in a remote part of Westchester County. The thickly wooded lands were a sweet change from the industrial forms evident in the cities, in Europe and New York, all the people buzzing about. While walking about this forest of matter I looked out at the trees, leaves, boulders, insects, flowers, mushrooms, and decaying branches all around. I found I could look only, I could not see much in detail or in precise depth. Everything seemed vague and unclear, as if nothing was there in the way I thought it might be. Limiting my visions were tiny particles of mist in the air. Or the hindrance was due to the technology of my eyeglasses, too many lenses clouding any single ray of vision. Too much ultraviolet light. My own photo-graphy is at risk.

August 6. While going to sleep last night I noticed, while soothing my eyes with a soft touch of fingers, that the upper eyelid of the right eye was sore and tender. I do not remember hurting or poking it in any way. I don't have a clue as to what could have caused this. It could have been while I was sleeping. This new event is worrisome. *I do not trust myself.* Such is a strange sentence to write—it's like saying my body is not my body. This body is other to my self, potential betrayer to the flesh of self.

August 6. I would like to understand what has harmed his eyes. In reading online tonight I've learned that some cataracts are caused by blunt trauma to the eye. A severe injury can damage the capsule in which the lens sits. This allows water from other parts of the eye to enter the lens, leading to swelling and whitening, obstructing light from reaching the retina at the back of the eye. The descriptions match what can be discerned, in the photographs, of the white obscurity in the man's left eye. He might have been wounded in one or both eyes at some point in his life. A blow to the head, violent or accidental. Rock, fist, knife. Metal pole. Chemical burn.

August 7. Last night the dream atmosphere reappeared, the suite of rooms where everything appeared unclearly. It seems the sense and look of the dream was not as coherent as before. The atmosphere of that place is fading away, dissipating, a fog dissolving less into clarity of day than dark of night.

August 7. The optic nerve. The iris. Macular degeneration. Opacification of the lens. Lens Opacities Classification System III. Glassblower's cataract. Cataract removal. The aqueous humor. Simple eyes. Compound eyes. Spherical lensed eye. Spherical aberration. Reflector eyes. Refractive cornea. Parabolic superposition. Photoreceptor cells. Scotoma. Binocularity. Sensory fusion system. Visual acuity. Keratitis.

"The basic components of the vertebrate eye are a transparent cornea, an iris with a central (circular or slit-like) pupil, a lens for focusing, and a sensitive retina lining the back of the eye. Light entering the eye is focused by the lens to form an image on the cells of the retina, from which nervous impulses are conveyed to the brain."[4]

"There are ten different eye layouts—indeed every technological method of capturing an optical image commonly used by human beings, with the exceptions of zoom and Fresnel lenses, occur in nature."[5]

August 8. My eyes are not seeing well. They tire easily. I cannot read or write for long. Too much glare. Too many angles of refraction.

August 9. My eyes are fatigued. They tire of looking. At no point am I seeing well. Light hurts them. There's less strain when I keep the pupils closed.

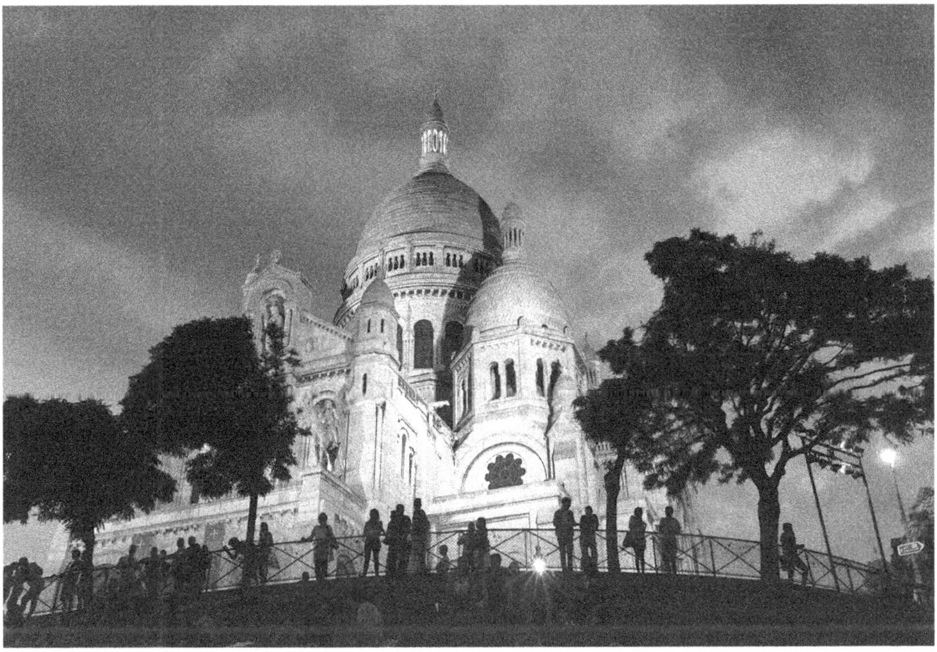

August 10. I should be elsewhere. I should be at Sacré-Coeur. Is there a way for me to get back there soon? I would like to locate the blind man again. I will learn his name, and tell him my own. I could learn his story. I could buy him a lunch or two, at the least, and provide some care for him.

If we were to meet again, what would be the best, most ethical, way to proceed? Friendship? A caring regard for his life and welfare? Silence. Would it be better to not engage with him further? Photographs, or their absence?

Levinas wrote that "ethics is an optics," a foundational way of regarding others.[6] What kind of optics is called for? How might we relate to others in this world?

August 12. Anterior chamber. Zonular spaces. Today I went to the optometrist's office in Yonkers, to get something fixed. While there, I met with the eye doctor and showed him a photocopy image of the photo of the man's face, with the left eye apparent, in vivid colors. I asked him if he could tell me what might have happened to the eye. He held the paper in his hand and looked at the white obscurity.

"It's a cataract, I take it," I said.

"No. It's not a cataract."

"It's not?"

"No."

I had the specifics wrong, all along.

"It was caused by an infection to the cornea. The cornea is supposed to be completely clear."

He pointed to his own eye, while looking into mine.

"An infection can make it glazed over, like that."

"I see. Could it have been caused by a trauma?"

"Yes, it could have been. An injury to the cornea can cause that."

"Right."

"Or, a trauma could have caused an infection in the cornea, and then the eye got like that, all cloudy white."

A blow to the eye. A childhood infection.

"Okay. That's good to know. Is there a specific medical term for this, for this affliction?"

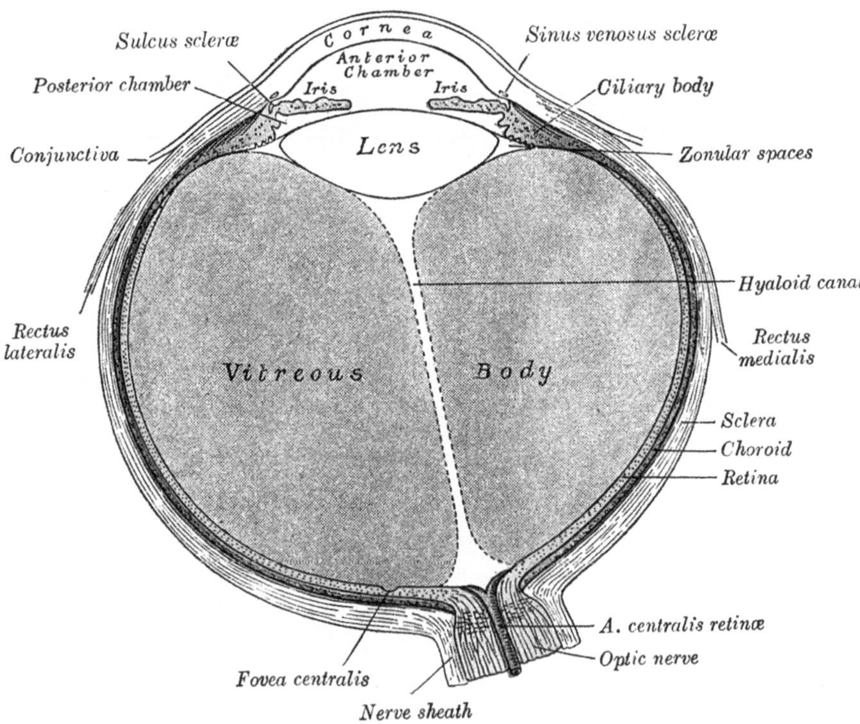

"I'm not sure," he said. "It could be many things. I'd have to take a closer look."

August 13. Cornea. (n). The transparent layer making up the outermost front part of the eye, covering the iris, pupil, and anterior chamber. Late 14c., from Medieval Latin *cornea tela* "horny web or sheath," from Latin *cornu* (genitive *cornus*) "horn." So called for its consistency.[7]

A cornea requires complete transparency. The presence of even the tiniest of blood vessels would interfere with its ability to refract light properly. And so, rather relying on a supply of blood, it gets oxygen directly through the air. Oxygen first dissolves in tear fluids and diffuses throughout the cornea to keep it healthy. Along with aiding in vision, the cornea is protective. In tandem with the eyelid and the sclera, the white of the eye, it serves as a barrier against dirt, germs, and other particles that can harm the eye's delicate components. To see well, all layers of the cornea must be free of any cloudy or opaque areas.

A clear, dome-shaped, watery "watch glass" of sorts, the cornea sits over the sclera and acts as the eye's outermost lens. Wafer-thin, amazingly only about one millimeter thick, the cornea accounts for approximately two-thirds of the eye's total focusing power. Its five intricate layers function like a window that shields the eye from contaminant intrusions and controls and focuses the entry of light into the eye. When light strikes the cornea, it refracts the incoming light onto the lens. The lens further refocuses that light onto the retina. For a person to see clearly, light rays must be focused by the cornea and lens to fall precisely on the retina. The retina converts the light rays into impulses that are sent through the optic nerve to the brain, which interprets them as images. "The refractive process is similar to the way a camera takes a picture. The cornea and lens in the eye act as the camera lens. The retina is similar to the film. If the image is not focused properly, the film (or retina) receives a blurry image."[8]

The cornea is one of the most sensitive tissues of the body. It is rich in unmyelinated nerve endings sensitive to touch, temperature, chemicals. A touch of the cornea causes an involuntary reflex to close the eyelid. Research suggests the density of pain receptors is three hundred to six hundred times greater than skin and twenty to forty times greater than dental pulp, making any injury to the structure extremely painful. If the cornea becomes damaged through disease, infection, or injury, the resulting scars can interfere with vision by blocking or distorting light as it enters the eye. Viral infections of the cornea are very serious and can ultimately lead to scarring and permanent vision loss.

August 14. There's the idea of it, at least. One eye to replace another eye.

"Corneal transplantation, also known as corneal grafting, is a surgical procedure where a damaged or diseased cornea is replaced by donated corneal tissue (the graft) in its entirety or in part. The graft is taken from a recently deceased individual with no known diseases or other factors that may affect the viability of the donated tissue or the health of the recipient."[9]

The absence of blood vessels in the cornea is a valuable feature when it comes to transferring a cornea from one body to another. "Corneal grafting was the first widely successful human transplant operation. The key to its success—particularly when compared with other tissue transplant operations—is the fact that corneas have very few blood vessels; thus, because there's little interaction with the rest of the body, the graft is less likely to be rejected as 'foreign.'"

The cornea grafts are usually taken from the recently dead. It's prohibited to give up a healthy living eye—as can be done with a kidney—apparently two good eyes are necessary for full-fledged, stereoscopic vision. And yet I wonder if anyone has ever considered giving up their own eyes to enable another to see anew or for the first time. I can imagine the gift of it, even if this gift lies solely within the realm of imagination, for the time being. Would this not be a fitting sacrifice, one eye to replace another? Would this be the right thing to do?

August 15. I have learned that, in rare circumstances, a cornea donor may be living. For example, a person who has an ocular tumor in the back of the eye may be able to donate the eye at the time it is removed. Also, if an eye is blind and it is removed, but is healthy in the front, that cornea could be used.

There's the image of it, now. It's a dangerous image, a dangerous perhaps. A good cornea from an eye that can no longer see could be grafted onto the eye of another. I have been looking online at pictures of corneal grafts, with the new cornea shown sutured in place of a removed cornea. Tiny black stitches mark where the glassy prism has been sown into place. In principle, the procedure is comparable to removing a lens from one camera and fixing it onto another. As one medical text puts it, a "button" is surgically removed from the outer layers of an eye, with the fine blade of a scalpel, and another is sewn into its place, a translucent coin moved from one socket to another. If all goes well, and there are no infections or rejections of the new tissue, the person can come to see clearly in several months' time. The minuscule stitches, sown into the eye with the use of a microscope, usually stay in for a year or more.

Are the stitches taken out like the removal of the sutures in a scar wound on the hand; or do they slowly dissolve, erode, fading into the optics of the eye?

Corneal banks. Testimonies. "It is with a grateful heart that I sincerely thank you for the gift of improved sight."[10]

There's the phantasm of it, at least. The idea has come to lie within my body and it has now reached the cortex of conscious thoughts. The image has become clear to me, like an exceedingly complex picture that suddenly comes into focus. Or perhaps I'm faced with the psychosis of a hallucinated wish, the kind where you can't tell what's real or what's imagined.

One good eye should suffice.

I could give him one good eye. That seems fair enough.

August 15. I know that the transfer, the corneal graft, would strike others as a bizarre gift, a sacrifice spun of madness. We're supposed to hold onto our own eyes, aren't we, the very ones with which we come into the world? Those organs belong to us and us alone, and we are not meant to give them away to an unrelated man, poor of vision. And yet tell me, for it's the question that keeps circling back, a perpetually haunting doubt: what sane morality can hold that one should keep what one has while others remain in need?

August 16. Perhaps a calmer, more rational way to proceed would be to sign up to donate my cornea, after death. Then, years from now, the cornea would be recovered from my body—"harvested," "procured"—within hours of its demise and placed in a storage media that preserves the living cells. The cornea would be delivered to an eye bank. In the white-walled, antiseptic laboratories of that high-tech place—I can see the space of this phantasm now—the cornea would be examined visually and underneath a slit-lamp and a specular microscope, their tissues would be rated, on a scale of 0 to 4, for donor suitability. Those old refractions might be a problem. If the glassy cornea passed the evaluation, the lenses would be destined for the eyes of another.

Whoever that unknown recipient of vision might be, he would be a ritual surrogate. He would serve as a stand-in for the blind man. If my lens cannot go to the blind man at Sacré-Coeur, they could go to someone else, in his stead. A sacrificial gift.

This person would be elsewhere. While there is apparently an adequate supply of corneas for transplants in the United States, there is a shortage of corneal tissue internationally. Arrangements could be made to have the eyes sent to a bank in another country, in Africa, say, or Asia. This would be a fitting transfer for an anthropologist who has spent much of his time and thoughts in other places, looking onto the lives of others. It would be a good way to pay back some debts.

The optics here would be an ethics. Eye for an eye. Eye to an eye.

"Don't give up your eyes anytime soon," friends have pleaded.

Yet the image is still there. Several phantasms are at work, obscurely. The drive to sacrifice oneself. The desire to give oneself to others, in the destruction of self. The dilemmas of theft. The urge to give back, and the impossibility of giving back.

August 20. Massachusetts. It's a matter of interpretation, of reading the signs at hand. It's a matter of how certain forms of action and understanding get lodged within a life and body.

While traveling about this weekend, making my way to the ocean shores and marshes along the coast north of Boston, looking for one last breeze of summer, I visited with a friend, an anthropologist, at his home in Lexington. While heading out for an afternoon walk, the same meandering route through suburban woods and grasslands we've undertaken countless times before, I told him about the photographic work I've been involved with in France. I related to him the strange goings-on with my eyesight, the lost and broken eyeglasses, finger jabbing into sleeping eye. I took him through the theories of why all of this could be happening—the prospect of guilt, close identification.

"This is all very interesting," he said. "But couldn't all of this be a random series of events for which you're creating an interpretation? Don't we give explanations to events that aren't really related, except for the fact that we think they are?"

He had a point. It could be that I've been lining up a succession of unrelated happenings, with no causal relation between them, and giving them a psychological force they don't really have. I've been stringing along lines of explanation, telling stories, to myself and now to others. One story is that there is no story. Coincidences only. No synchronicity. The pragmatics of life and existential meaning-making.

Still, I can't shake the sense that certain lines of possibility are taking form, like the emergence of light and dark in a print developed in a darkroom.

That evening, while at dinner, I fell into a conversation with this friend's wife, who has been training to be a psychotherapist. I told her about the curious events with my eyes and took her through the theories.

"Would these explanations make any sense to you?" I asked.

"Yes, definitely," she said. "And guilt and identification are closely related."

"Really? How so?"

"Well, if you feel sorry for someone, then you identify with them. You feel what they are feeling—or, at least, what you take them to be feeling."

"I see. And do you think it's possible for someone to damage his eyes, in unconscious ways even, to the point of becoming blind?"

"Yes, that could happen. And if you identify very strongly with a blind person, it could be possible to go blind without a biological cause. It would be like a conversion disorder—what people used to call hysterical blindness."

And so now, just when I had come to question my interpretive readings of recent events, I am reminded of the strength of obscure forces to inflict psychic blindness on a body.

Conversion disorder. Damage an eye until it can no longer see, until there's no good use left to it but to pass its corneal lens, its means of light, onto another, who might see anew.

August 22. New York. He is here with me now, in the place where I am living. His imaginary presence, certainly imagined, hovers in the air. He stands there when I lie in bed at night, trying to fall asleep. The phantasm of his body rests in the futon bed when I am not sleeping there myself. He is in the room with me when I am reading, or off to the side, when I look at myself in the mirror. He stands behind me, looking over my shoulder, when I sit by the computer, working on the photographs. If he's not doing that, then he's looking out from the photographs as I tend to his image. He is near to my thoughts, even now, as I write these words. It's as if a spectral dimension of his being, a shadow soul of sorts, has left from Paris and jetted to New York and found me in my home, and this spectral presence now keeps company with me as an unexpected guest. Rough on the edges, unshaven, with that heavy coat about him, striving to persevere, his is an unspeaking specter. There are no words about him, or perhaps just a word or two, *merci*, *vous etês gentil*, which recur.

His is not a palpable, touchable body so much as it is an atmosphere, a vague, watchful presence. His difference keeps him near. He's always wearing that burly coat. He remains nameless and unnamed.

I cannot say he is blind. He sees so much.

Remarkable, it is, how you can encounter another person for a few brief instances, or snap a few photographs, and soon that person comes to inhabit vast portions of your life. And slowly, gradually, with the force of a faint breath on a window pane, he comes to shadow your consciousness, or illuminate it.

August 22. Please know that a photograph is a trap that lures the imagination and snares a man's spirit. Once an image grabs hold of a poor soul, chances are that it will never let it go.

An image can be corrosive, destructive of a cohering subject.

August 26. This morning I happened to look for traces of the cut to my right hand. I could not locate any scar tissue distinguishable from the creased lines already there. I keep trying to perceive but see no trace of that once real wound. No eyelid or eyeline, the alien eye has disappeared, just a memory left on the skin of my brain. If I try to bring my eyes closer to that patch of my hand its features become more blurred still. I should have photographed the surface when I had the chance.

August 27. From Borges's poem "The Blind Man":

My every step
Might be a fall

Borges writes, from the perspective of an unsighted man, of the "eye-shaped world."[11]

August 29. The dream of walking about that unclear suite of rooms has gone away. I am too far from it now.

Opticalterities

September 6. Those who can see, she wrote, "were bound to me through an unknown sense which completely enveloped me from a distance, followed me about, penetrated through me, and somehow held me in its power from waking until sleeping."[1]

This remarkable statement from a young blind girl, circa 1840s France, *Souvenirs et impressions d'une jeune aveugle-née*, upon realizing that the people about her have recourse to a perceptual faculty unfamiliar to her: those who can see were bound to her through an unknown sense.

I can imagine a similar sentence being uttered by a sightless person in Paris, circa 2014: those who can see and take photographs are bound to me through an unclear and indeterminate sense which completely envelops me, distantly and close at hand, which follows me about, goes through me, creates images unknown to me, and, from the time I climb the steps of the basilica until I leave hours later, holds me in some way in subjection to it.

He knows the cameras are all about but it must be difficult for him to perceive or foretell the specifics. He hears the clicking of cameras, yet has no way of knowing if he is within the frame of the image, then or

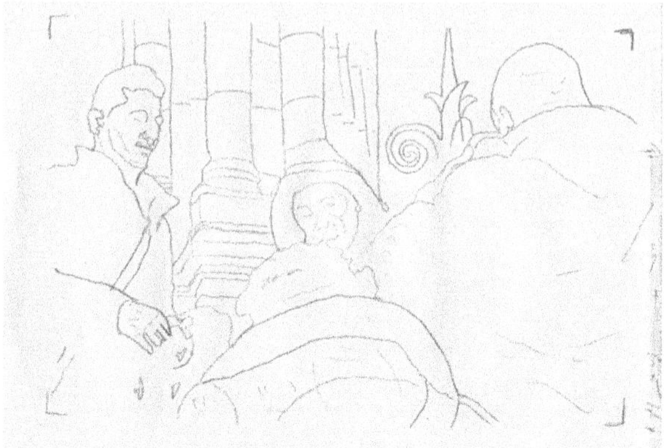

later on. Or he senses a camera pointed his way. He cannot tell if he is an incidental figure within the image or if he is the intended subject. He has no way to know where his image travels to, how his likeness might circulate or recur.

"What a strange power this was," the girl, born blind, named Lucy, continues, "to which I was subjected against my will, without, for my part, being able to exercise it over anyone at all. It made me shy and uneasy to begin with. I felt envious about it. It seemed to raise an impenetrable screen between society and myself. I felt unwillingly compelled to regard myself as an exceptional being that had, as it were, to hide itself in order to live."[2]

The man is subject to the strange powers of vision which others can exercise over and through him. There is an impenetrable screen between him and others. In order to live he feels compelled to hide himself through the veil of an exceptional coat.

September 9. The blind can be deceived.

"The blind man is, first of all, subject to being mistaken, *the subject of mistake*," writes Derrida in his *Memoirs of the Blind*, a book which considers drawings, etchings, and paintings of blind figures, particularly art works drawn from the vast holdings of the Louvre.[3] The blind man is capable of being deceived, either by himself or by others: "The other can take advantage of him." Derrida finds that Jean-Baptiste Greuze's painting *Blind Man Deceived*, 1755, serves as a paradigm: "an old blind man taken advantage of by a young woman."[4] A woman and man are seated close to an older man; they look upon him, secretly, with furtive interest; the "two young lovers" look toward the old husband's eyes to gauge whether or not he detects their efforts; the husband holds his young wife's hand on his knee, resting his hand upon hers. Her lover looks upon the aged man, waiting for an opportunity. The older man appears oblivious to these deceptive actions, this "play of hands." The aged, unseeing husband must not sense the other man's presence close to his person, his wife, his wealth. The beholder of this image observes this scene taking place. He notices the jar held in the lover's hand, the milky contents of which are starting to spill onto the ground. He is a visual witness who sees more than the protagonists do. He takes in the workings of representation.

What I see: the blind man walks about the steps or waits by the metal gate of the basilica. He stands precariously in a field of others, some of whom might not have his best interests in mind. They might try to steal from his pockets or wish him harm. He would stand there, isolated in his awareness, unaware of any lenses trained on his face. He cannot know if any eyes are lit upon him, when or where. He needs someone to watch out for him. I wish to protect him, see for him, to supplement his sentience with limited sight. I stand beyond all of this, higher up on the steps, a visual witness absorbed in myriad angles of sight and sound. I take in the workings of perception. I see this even when I'm not there. I hold the camera in my hands, lift it to my eyes. There are cries of *voleur*. I hear this now.

September 11.

> More naked than others, a blind man virtually becomes his own sex, he becomes indistinguishable from it because he does not see it, and not seeing himself exposed to the other's gaze, it is as if he had lost even his sense of modesty. The blind man has no shame, Luther said in short. Can it not be said that the eye of the blind man, the blind man himself, derives its strange familiarity, its disquieting strangeness, from being more naked? From being exposed naked without knowing it? Indifferent to its nakedness, and thus at once *less naked* and *more naked* than others as a result? More naked because one then sees the eye *itself*, all of a sudden exhibited in its opaque body, an organ of inert flesh, stripped of the signification of the gaze that once came to both animate and veil it. Inversely, the very body of the eye, *insofar as it sees*, disappears in the gaze of the other. When I look at someone who sees, the living signification of their gaze dissimulates for me, in some way and up to a certain point, this body of the eye, which, on the

contrary, I can easily stare at in a blind man, and right up to the point of indecency. (Derrida, *Memoirs of the Blind*)[5]

The disquieting strangeness of a blind person's eyes: we see the eye itself, the organic instrument of seeing, even if that particular organ does not lend itself to vision. We see the protein biology of the eye, faulty or disturbed. It's like viewing a broken bone that has snapped from its proper place and pieced through flesh, the chalky marrow unnaturally exposed. We look upon that broken eye, the sheer matter of it, its bio-organic sinews shown as if obscenely. With an unseeing eye we do not see vision, an interlocking of gazes, so much as the biological capacity to see, even if that capacity is hindered. In seeing blindness we perceive the means of vision itself. We can look indecently upon that eye, over and over, if we dare to; until we look away.

September 14. The other day I asked a student of mine if she would like to make some drawings of the scenes I've been writing about. She agreed to this and has started on several pencil drawings, using a set of photographs as visual aids. The drawings are quite good. They evoke moods and appearances different from those that radiate out of the black-and-white

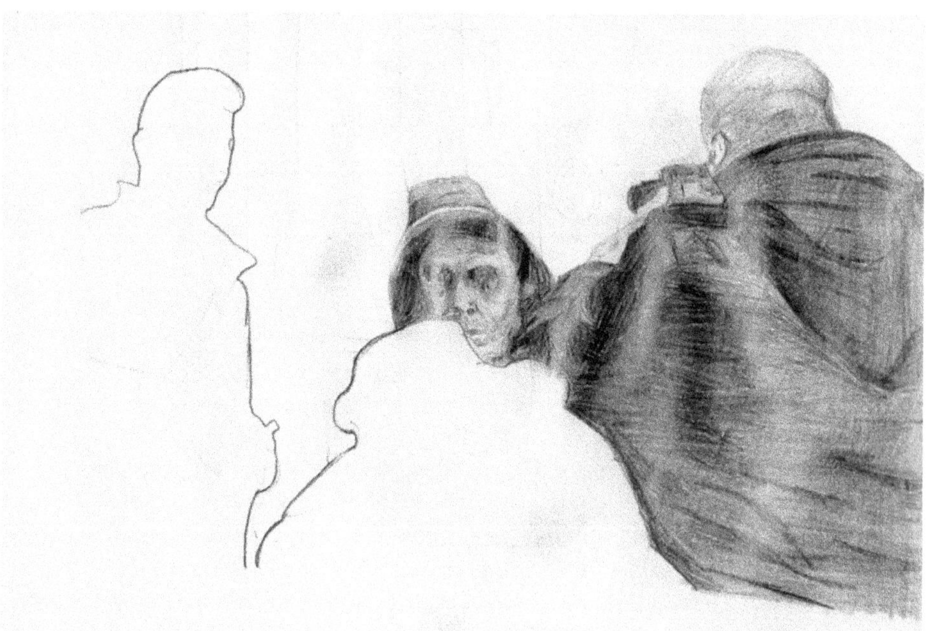

photos. Some of the sketches are incomplete, unfinished, of a subjective hand, much as perception and memory are incomplete, partial.

I may decide, in the end, to use only the drawings of the blind man, and not the photographs. The drawings could have the effect of portraying him and others in ways less direct, less "indexical," than is the case with the photographs. But if the actual photographs are not in the text, would this change the affective force and significance of the writing?

September 18. Yesterday, while I was walking about Manhattan, my thoughts returned to the photograph of the man standing close to the blind man. An insidious possibility crept into mind: that the young man is only simulating a pose for the camera, and the true subject of the photograph is the blind man alone. It could be that the young man and his accomplice had wanted to photograph the blind man in close detail, the pools of his eyes proximal to the lens, and they fabricated a scene where the young man appeared to pose on his own or next to the blind man and at the right moment the photographer trained his camera on the blind man alone. He could have had the camera focused on his friend, shifted it slightly to the right, to portray the man next to him. I have done much the same at times, lining up the focus and aperture on an innocuous scene (a lamppost, a museum painting) and then turning the camera onto the true intended subject of the photograph. Perhaps the two men took a few photographs like this, perhaps they feigned a few photographs of the young man as if posing, and then focused the lens on the unseeing man to his left. That could explain why the young man is not looking toward the camera, for he knows he is not the intended subject of the photograph, and perhaps he's uncomfortable about the sneaky arrangement.

I wanted to look closely at the photo to gauge where the camera was pointing. I only had a visual memory with me and so I had to wait until I got back home last night to look at an actual copy. Once there, I found the photograph in the computer files and was surprised to find that there was no visible trace of the camera itself. The twisting structures of the metal pole are there and the bulky thumb of the man's left hand, but no camera is visible. I could have sworn I had seen the device there before, in the man's hand, his thumb poised above it. The camera's absence is now an aberration, as if the device had disappeared overnight or someone had airbrushed it out of the picture. I guess I had assumed the camera's presence within the secondary photograph, based on the contours of the man's pose and what that schema suggested of the photographic act implied. I suppose I took the curving metal of the pole just there as the arching frame of a camera, and the trigger point near to his thumb—a visual memory came of that impression.

I have been trying to visualize the angle of the camera's lens, presumed to be there, and estimate where the aperture is aimed. No theory of optics known to me can offer any clear understanding of this. Even if I had some geometrical clarity on this, I'd have no way to account for slight shifts of the camera's angle before or after the instance of the secondary photograph. The more I look at the image, the more I sense that the photographer is framing the camera on the blind man alone. His body is hunched straight onto that man, who appears unaware that a camera has him in its sights.

Looking close, I believe I can make out the fine line of the photographer's eyelashes, the delicate lashes of this man's left eye. This might be the mark of a nick in the spiraling metal that forms part of the gate.

September 19. Or, or, or, my head is getting filled with alternate possibilities, neural pathways are lighting up with the transmitters of plausible occurrence. What fecund epistemology, what abundant ways of knowing, would embrace a logic of assorted plausible alternatives? What if many of those alternatives, if not all of them, are imagined or the result of conjecture, a "casting together" of facts, impressions, lines of interpretation, spread out in vertiginous planes of time? Perhaps one that is truer to life, to what most people encounter in their everyday lives, than the smartest lines of reasoning that learning can buy. So much in life, so many improbable conversations and probable scenarios, are imagined, not concretely real, and an anthropology attuned to the imaginary—a fantastical anthropology, an anthropology of the phantasmal—needs to account for the force and tenor of the imagined, the possible, the conjectured, the feared and dreamed of, specters of memory and perception, the dangerous perhaps, within the phantasmal flow of its thought and expression. We need a phantasmography, a writing of the flows and currents of phantasms.

Or, alternatively, we could stick to an anthropology of the empirical, of the facts only, the data right before our eyes, earnest to a fault, and ignore all the phantasms swirling about any situation in life—though that would seem the true madness.

So much of scholarly writing these days is so *earnest*, zealously sincere, calculated, advancing discourses that appear comatose on arrival, the words "peer review" signing a death sentence to any creative singularities;

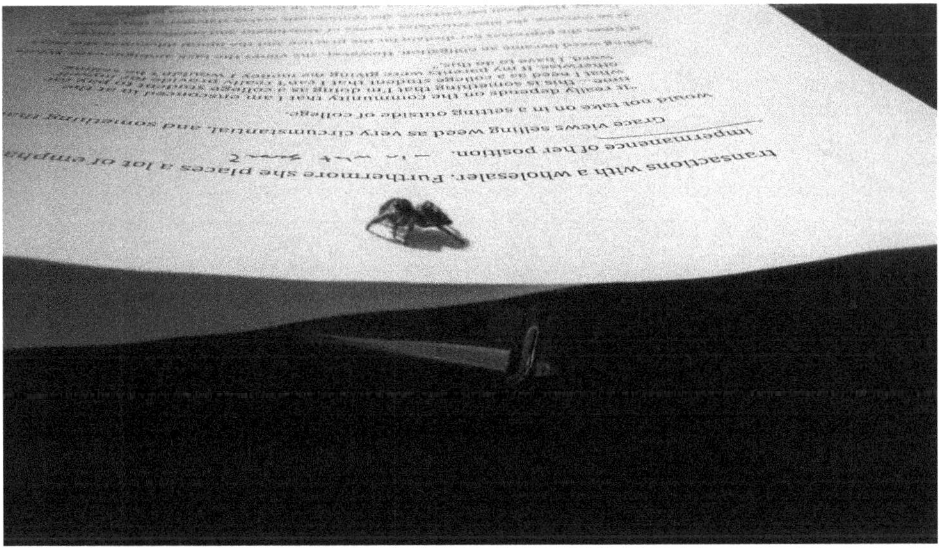

everyone seems afraid of being criticized for not towing the line of political and moral or epistemological propriety. So often there is a clarity of representation, where everything is explained and articulated, to the point of exhaustion. There is no play of life in any of it, except for the barren smiles of wry, ironic commentary. There is little imaginative fancy to most scholarly writing, nothing transgressive, no incalculable desire or longing, nothing strange or unsettling within the reach of its energies. No pathos. No passion. No spiders crawling across the page. No fevered philosopher embracing a flogged horse in Turin.

September 22. No spiders crawling across the page. Strange, strange that a few days after writing this image a spider came crawling across pages of text set before my eyes. This was while I was seated at a metal table at the outside patio of a local Starbucks on a windy afternoon with fast-moving clouds in an autumn sky. Immersed in the work of reading, a double espresso and grains of granulated brown sugar nearby, I felt a slight movement, an itchy presence trailing along the back of my neck.
I reached with my hand and swept whatever it was onto the table before me. A spider landed on the dark graphite surface, this creature soon righted itself, arms and eyes curled into a spool of coordination.
It jumped from the table surface to the black ink white page I had been reading, a student's essay, "a third-person phenomenology" of a young

woman's ambivalence toward her part-time job of selling marijuana to friends and acquaintances in New York City. Surprised by the sudden emanation of fuzzy legs and big goggle eyes I leaned away from the table, fearful of venom. The spider stayed put, hunched over. I grew curious and peered closer, bracing for a good look. The animal was furry, stout bodied, not at all what I expect in a spider, no oval head, no long extended daddy longlegs. I wished to photograph this visitor and drew my cell phone from my coat pocket and stood over the table, torso bent, to picture it precisely. I held the camera to my eyes. The spider came closer, causing me to jump back and lose my footing. *Not so close, dear creature.* I came near to the table and again the spider matched my movement. He stood there, as if waiting for me, matching my regard with his own patient watchful looking. His alien eyes, the two large median orbs on the crest of his cranial head, were looking upon me, watching me, form matching form, parallel mimesis. Whenever I stood squarely toward him and raised the camera to my eyes the bulk of those motions caught his attention, he came toward me, facing my face. The camera came close enough to photograph the creature's eyes. The spider leapt upon the page, skipped over lines of ink, over words like "weed" and "circumstantial," a silk thread lighting in its wake. I bent to photograph and he came close, standing by the edge of the paper, eyes upon mine, fuzzy legs prepared to jump. The closer I approached, the nearer he came. The more I watched, the more he altered forms. This spider was at once frog or toad, crab, ant, and feline insect, furry caterpillar, grasshopper and praying mantis, the morphology of its leaps and the agility of movement affinitive with other apparitions of creatural life. The spider was transmuting its biology before my very eyes, it was multispecies, polymorphic, polyfunctional, ambidextrous, many-limbed and many-eyed. The ghostly apparitions emanating from its body, shifting phasma of an almost hallucinatory nature, spoke to virtually infinite relations with other biofunctions. I lifted up the pages of writing and labored to place the spider in the center of the text; it would not cooperate with my studio arrangements, the spider ran to the side of the page, onto the black graphite of the sturdy table. I say "it" but I took it for a "he" or "she" or "ze," so adventurous was she, bold and undaunted. And he was more a "he" than a "you," even then, given how foreign its sphere of life was to me; third-person phenomenology, indeed. I stood over the table and tried to picture him just right, body eyes and legs distinctive. He kept approaching me, interrupting the ontology of my perceptions. There wasn't time or space enough to take an easy shot. I took it that he was evaluating me, sizing me up; was I something to leap upon, ensnare and gobble up, flee from, or mate with? Who was hunting, and who was prey? How was this arachnid perceiving me, as feline cat or grotesque beast or alter spider, web-weaver, or a shape of death? Dull-eyed creature, pulpy flesh. Obelisk god. Distorted cat. Each brain was taking in measurements, our eyes were engaged in photographic processing, stimuli, likenesses, mimetic play, within the familiar and the novel. In the air lay the shadows of harm, illness, death; the strange otherness of foreign encounters. I noticed the sun lighting up lines of fine translucence across the graphite table and the pulp of the paper. *Why would he be spinning a web just now?* He must have been emitting chords of silk, pissed out in fight or flight, this was not web so much as discrete lines of viscid filament, excreted discharges. I tried to photograph those lucent lines within the streams of sunlight but doubted the camera could pick up the fine grain of filaments. The wind wreaked havoc on our creative designs, pages fluttered about, sugar grains lay scattered on hard graphite, the spider did not stay still. In many of the photographs the cast of the sun, four o'clock in the autumn west, kept him in shadow. I longed for a better camera, the precision of a macro lens catching fine translucent fibers. The arachnid's silk strands, deft leaps from text to table, its stance counter to my own looming presence—I had no theory or *theoria*, no concerted way of viewing, to account for its behaviors; he was acting in ways counter to my imaginary of spiders. An image does not match the real; the map is not the territory; a photograph is not the thing photographed. Any spider is phantastic. Any phenomenon, for that matter. Tired of the nervous commotion, the jerky interruptions, weary of the wind and unwanted contact, spooked by the specter of painful bites, and needing to get back to the mundane task of reading, I scooped up the spider into a set of pages and carried it over to a set of bushes and deposited him, gently, within a patch of green spiny leaves, until I could see it no longer. I did not want to hurt him. *Be safe, dear spider.* I thought by now that others at the outdoor patio would have taken notice of my odd actions. I looked and saw that, within this tidy corporate brick-laid space, no one was looking my way. All eyes were sunk into newspapers or the blue glow of smart phones, oblivious to the insect alterities taking place a few feet away.

September 23. Salticidae. Jumping spiders. The arachnid family Salticidae comprises the largest of all spider groups, with more than five thousand species worldwide. Small and scrappy carnivores, salticids are strongly dependent on their eyesight for prey capture, orientation, and courtship. "Of all the spiders, salticids have the best vision," says one book on arachnids, found at a local library. "Their main eyes detect detailed images, whereas their secondary eyes are primarily movement detectors. They also have binocular vision, which is crucial to establishing distance—a vital attribute for a jumping spider. . . . Their excellent vision gives these little spiders an almost human-like quality; if you approach they will turn around and look at you!"[6]

As often occurs in life, what is at first bewildering and vaguely perplexing comes to be known through certain means of perception and cognition. Apparently it was a jumping spider I encountered yesterday afternoon, an eight-eyed arachnid in search of food, courtship, or alter-curiosities. *Phidippus audax*, possibly: common jumping spider, "bold jumper," audacious. As with many other arachnids, this salticid had a square-front carapace, with four large eyes that faced forward.

> Salticid vision is particularly effective, compared with that of other spider families. The main eyes each have a large lens, a retina with four layers of visual cells and a large vitreous body. Although the visual field is small, muscles at the base partially compensate for this because they can move the retina in different directions. The four-layered retina has 1,000 visual cells, and sensitivities to different spectral wavelengths. The secondary eyes possess relatively large visual fields, and these overlap. As a result, a salticid has binocular vision. Moving prey is usually detected by the binocular vision of the secondary eyes. If the prey is closer than 200 mm (8 in), the spider turns to face it. The main eyes fix the object onto the center of the retinas. If they prey moves, so do the retinas, keeping the image locked. The shape of the object is quickly "scanned" (the main eyes are rotated about the optical axis), and if it is recognized as prey, the spider will stalk it and finally jump on it. Salticid eyes are on a par with the compound eyes of insects, and the resolution is superior.[7]

The phantasmal phenomena of yesterday are coming to make sense within the known zoology of salticids. In its roaming the spider jumped from my head (taken as prey itself, or spiny bush?) onto the metal table—the jumps powered by increased blood pressure in the legs. The silky threads were the "lifelines" it used when making the jumps. When I moved closer to give it a look, within inches of its furry presence, it turned to face me. "Look at a jumping spider, and it will look right back at you with large, forward-facing eyes."[8] The main eyes fixed my appearance onto the center of its retinas with high-resolution vision. When I took the cell phone and switched to camera mode and visualized further, the spider's retinas shifted accordingly and kept my image locked. Its eyes moved to track my movements and the creature's looking matched my own; its eyes rotated about the optical axis to "scan" the shape of its object, segment by segment, like a modern scanner. The jumping spider has specific optical-neural means of perception and evaluation, which came into encounter with the neural-optical procedures of species *Homo sapiens*. The intelligence and sensory acumen in this arachnean mode of being and movement-becoming are remarkable. Yet even though I know and understand more now about yesterday's spider, much of my regard remains phantastical: I try to imagine how an arachnid's eyes and brain might "scan" the world and I try to comprehend the thread and logic of its silk. Unclear still is whether or not the salticid took the image of me as prey or threat or as potential companion in courtship.

Jumping spiders are solitary and curious hunters, like photographers.

September 27. Get out of my brain. These words were tattooed onto the shoulder of a woman's arm, below the pattern of a dark bird, raven or sparrow, the lettering of which I spotted while waiting on an underground subway platform near Times Square this afternoon as she stood by the track which carries an express train to Brooklyn. I believe that's what was written there, in lasting India ink. The dark blue strap of the woman's summer dress obscured a few of the words, only these letters were evident:

Get out o   brain

Seated in a shaky local 1 train barreling beneath Seventh Avenue I was left to wonder what fierce, hauntingly recursive phenomena would call for such an inscription. The image had been seared with liquid ink into skin over the scapula. Perhaps that dark avian creature had come to take flight in her brain, hovering over her left shoulder like a past love or unrelenting demon, complex of guilt; waiting, watchful. This memory-creature was capable (or not) of reading the marks designed for its graphic presence. Or the tattoo was intended as a rite of exorcism, the motions of which left a lasting mark.

I regret not photographing the skin inscription. It would have been easy to flick out the cell phone I carried and feign a phone call—or pretend to snap a picture of the train lines beyond where the woman stood. Others were standing about. I would have felt bad about picturing the woman unaware.

Were the words inscribed on the woman's body intended for those who might look upon that body?

October 12. Yesterday I met with a friend, an anthropologist who works in Latin America. We walked about Brooklyn and eventually made our way to Grand Central Station. He led me to a bar hidden behind a steak restaurant. The place resembled a 1920s speakeasy, with plush chairs and wood paneling and a long dark bar adding to the charm of twenty-dollar cocktails.

We ordered fancy martinis. I told C. of my recent travels in France, of the blind man and my observations of him.

"He probably works with a team," said C.

"You think he works with a team?"

"Yes. This is how it works in Latin America. Several individuals will band together and cover a certain territory, working as a team of beggars. That way they can look out for each other and watch out for the police."

With these words a complete sociological imagination sprang to mind—a network of beggars surrounds the basilica, some of them unsighted, some disabled, most others not, working in coordination with one another. (A mind chisels further.) They communicate by looks and signals, using cell phones. They arrive in Montmartre the same time each day, after a communal breakfast. They work shifts and change locations in a coordinated physics of perception. They pool resources. Some of them stay at the same apartment building, a rundown flophouse that lets out rooms by the week. The men, and a lone woman, compete for resources with other groups of panhandlers. They know the police. They're friendly with some cops, and wary of others. The group has a leader, an unshaven man with piercing eyes. This man carries a knife. He works to keep the others in line. He tries to deter one man from getting drunk each night, unsuccessfully. He looks out for the blind man. He makes sure he gets enough bread and meat at the communal meals. They guide him to his post along the steps. A few of them have been aware of my recurrent presence around the basilica. They picked up on my interest in the blind man and the photographs taken. They watch me with guarded concern, a confederacy of eyes. They've told the blind man about me. When I approach they signal to him with a call, a whistle. That's why he looks my way so intently when I'm near.

I stirred my drink, sipped the blue liquid.

"I had never thought that he would be working with others," I said. "He seems quite on his own."

"I'm fairly certain of it."

I was stunned by the sureness of his knowing, the robust confidence of anthropological theorizing.

What strikes me with this fabulation of a collective of beggars is not how fantastically unreal it might be, or how easily this sober hallucination emerged in the chambers of a mind, but that we humans imagine in comparable ways in many moments in our lives. We meet a person and conjure an entire life. We step into a place and envision what takes place there. We quickly lend it a history, foresee possibilities, stir up phantasms of past and future. This imaginative process happens all the time, though it usually goes unnoticed, for the imaginative schemes are embedded within the fabric of everyday perception. We see imagining all along.

I doubt that the blind man works with a team. Still, you have to wonder.

"What is a beggar to you?" asked C.

I gave thought to the question.

"A beggar is a figure of abjection in a field of perception."

The man before me nodded his head.

October 14. While at the bar the other night I mentioned to C. my thoughts and questions on the ethics of corneal donations. "Have you heard of Zell Kravinsky?" C. asked.

Turns out that Zell Kravinsky is an academic-turned–real estate magnate who had been in the news recently for giving up almost all of his entire $45 million real estate fortune to charity—and then donating one of his kidneys at a hospital in Philadelphia, to benefit a stranger. In reading further today into Kravinsky's desire to give away much of his wealth and possessions, including one of his organs, one statement most caught my eye. "What I aspire to is ethical ecstasy," he told a reporter. "*Ex stasis*: standing out of myself, where I'd lose my punishing ego. It's tremendously burdensome to me." Once this was achieved, "the significant locus would be in the sphere of others."[9]

I can relate to this ethical ecstasis, the extravagant yearning to give up one's body and possession to help others in need of life and vitality. The image here, which glows like the ember of a hallucination, is the rapturous sacrifice of the self, relinquishing parts of the body for the sake of others. The body disbands, radiates outward, reaches toward others.

The delirium of images

December 25

Dear B.

I'm off to Paris tomorrow and I was wondering if you could send me a few pictures of the blind man so I can have a clear image of him. I will let you know if I find him as soon as I get there.

I wish you all the best and I hope you had a wonderful Christmas.

F.

December 27

Dear F.

It's good to hear that you're going to Paris now. I'm sending along an email that contains some of the photographs. The photos should give you a sense of what the man looks like.

If you do make it there, let me know how it goes.

Enjoy your travels, and take care,

B.

January 08

Dear B.

I returned home a few days ago. Paris was wonderful and the weather was pretty nice during our stay. I went to The Sacred Heart and asked different men who were selling key chains and also a woman from the closest news stand about the blind man; they all nodded and said he was no longer there. I asked if they knew any details about his absence but all I got was "one day he stopped showing up."

I wasn't sure what that meant.

I wish you a wonderful and successful new year!

F.

January 11

Dear F.

Happy New Year!

Thank you for your note, and the news about your visit to Paris. And thanks for looking into the status of the blind man. It sounds like he must be elsewhere now, if he hasn't been going there. Perhaps this is a fitting conclusion to our engagements with him.

best,

B.

January 11. New York. I know so little of about this man. Perhaps there is a benefit in not knowing him well. My sense of my engagements with him rests on a few basic aspects of human relations, and these have become apparent in my regard of him. The force of an encounter. The phenomenon of alterity. The nature of perception and photographic images. Phantasmal thought and the play of imagination. Obsession from afar. It's like one of those later texts of Samuel Beckett, in which a few principles of generic humanity take form within the space of a few pages.[1] Movement, rest, the same, the other, imperative of language, the fabulations of a subject, imagination dead imagine; these themes appear, without the distractions of unnecessary details or biography, in an effort of reduction, clarification. Some relations in life entail a phenomenological reduction, in their own right.

It could be that in not talking with the man much, in not knowing him in a direct and familiar way, certain forms of perception and encounter emerge in ways that are usually not so apparent in more ordinary, run-of-the-day modes of interaction. If he and I had gotten to know each other through the relaxed, casual banter of everyday life, with certain commonplaces of relation and amity coming into play, then eventually there would be a strong measure of familiarity, and much, I think, would go unnoticed, unmarked. With this the powerful, disturbing presence of an unknown other in one's life, and the force of phantasy and imagination that sears through encounters with others, would not have come to the fore in my awareness of this man and the many reflections spawned of that.

Most ethnographic research implies a compulsion to talk, to act and converse in the lives of others, to become as if friends with them. The self-spun process here has required a refusal of direct sociality. When it comes to pondering the nature of human relationality, there's a value, at times, in isolation, detachment, and nonsociality. Isn't it because I have

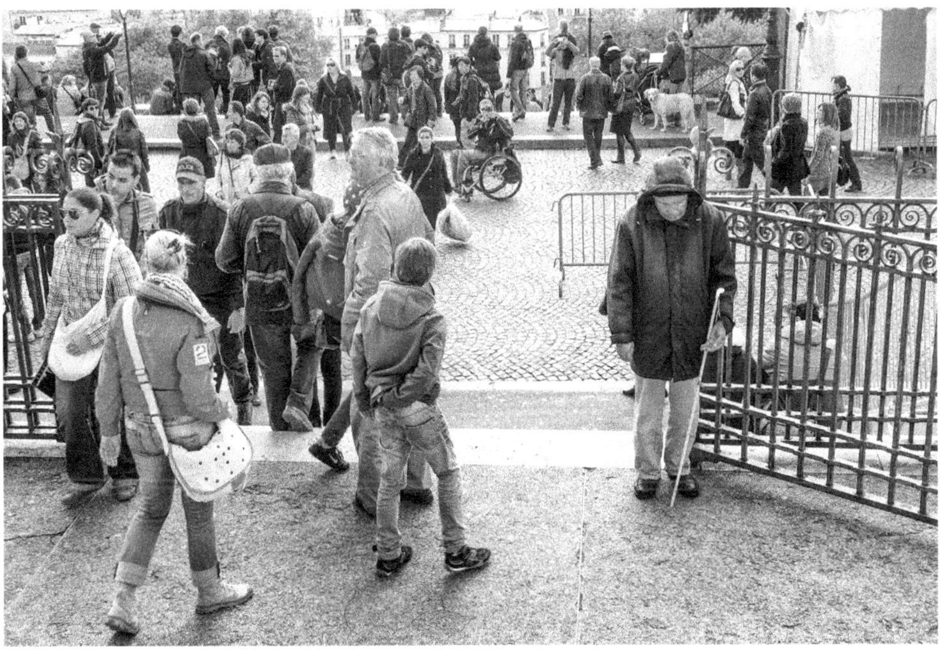

not chatted with the man much, or gotten to know him through the pleasantries of a meal together, that I'm able to sense the intensity of knowing another through a field of images?

January 14. I have another photograph of the man from that October day. He is standing by himself, apart from others, by the gate at the base of the steps. It could have been in that moment that I first became aware of him. I saw how alone he was within that crowd of tourists, how different he appeared in form and demeanor from those passing by his patient body. He was outside the frame of their lives.

I felt a kinship with him, fair or not. In those days I had been traveling a lot on my own. I had wandered through distant provinces in France in order to generate material for a photographic memoir I was working on then, of the year I had spent as a student in France, thirty years earlier. I was revisiting the past, thinking hard on time and memory. After solitary weeks of this I felt much on my own. I spoke a bastard French and seldom conversed with others in any depth, beyond the pleasantries of mundane encounters. Disconnected as a ghost, I was on the margins of other people's lives. I photographed those scenes. I was rarely, if ever, within the frame of an interaction. I was an outsider. I identified most with hobos, vagabonds, migrant workers, hitchhikers, and fellow lone travelers perceived in my travels. I never spoke with them. I was far too shy for that, a loner in my own right. My perceptions were in sympathy with his, despite the differences. We both stood as outsiders in the worlds of others. Like photographs like. We reach for something that matches our feel of the world. "Every photograph taken is a self-portrait," runs one photographic maxim.

I must have walked down the steps some and held the camera steady in my hands. I would have adjusted the aperture and shutter speed and let the autofocus bring the scene into clarity. In the resulting picture the man looks still and abject, motion all around him. He is looking down, toward the ground, shoulders hunched over. His head and face are titled slightly away from those walking past. A white walking stick is resting in the nook of his left arm, close to his hand, held open in a quiet, patient way.

In this hour of looking at the image I am arrested by the many looks and busy lines of interest apparent within. Some folks are moving toward the church above, others are gazing out at the southern environs of Paris. Everyone appears to be within their own moments of awareness and perceptual interest. A man with a dark cap with the word POLICE stamped in bold capped letters is walking up the steps. He is looking ahead, primed for the next encounter. The tip of his tongue is smooth within the bite of his lips as if he's soon to taste imminent action. He is not looking toward the blind man. He appears unaware of his presence and uninterested in the possibility that the man is asking for money from the good souls visiting the basilica. Beyond the cluster of people by the gate, on the stone tile surface level below, occurs a man seated in a wheelchair. His torso is turned toward the church. He is holding a camera toward the line of an opposing camera. That camera is lodged in my own hands, close to my eyes. It looks as if the man is photographing the counteract of photographing, though maybe it just looks this way. I did not see him within the brief time of my own photograph. I suspect he did not see me. I believe he has the church broadly in his sights. Chances are that my presence, along with those of others standing there, will endure as incidental appearances within the canvas of his picture. Our resemblances have ghosted the insides of his camera. We have entered his home. We are on his Tumblr. He has looked at the image carefully in the late hours of the night.

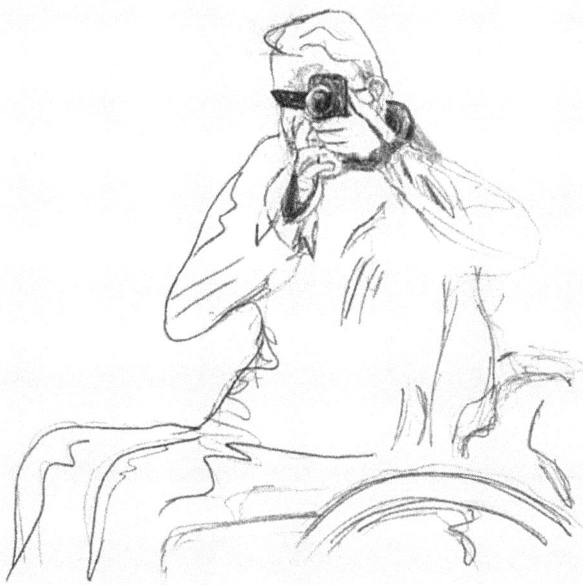

Some distance behind the man's wheelchair stands a dog. The canine, too, is looking our way. His color matches that of the blind man's white pants. I cannot shake the feeling that this white dog is looking at me looking his way, as if with him is a preternatural sense of what such looks imply. Each species has its own prismatic of sentience.

The photograph portrays the blind man as standing apart from those around him. I figured he could not see me doing so. I felt half-bad about taking his image unawares. I wanted to compensate him for lifting his resemblance. I walked down the steps, this I remember. A clamor of people were brushing by, it was difficult to speak or hear well. I came close to him. I went to place a euro coin in his hand, or a fifty-centime piece. He did not see me approaching. He was looking elsewhere, his face turned farther down the steps. I tried to say, *Pardon, Monsieur*, or I said, *Bonjour, Monsieur*. The sounds emerged a raspy mumble. My voice was faint, rough, unpracticed. I suspect he could not hear me well. For us to communicate well I needed him to see me, for him to gauge my eyes and face and gestures of hands and body.

The sudden unexpected contact startled him. He looked down, felt for the coin, took hold of it. I imagine then and now that he tried to feel its size and surface to measure its street value, the touch of his fingers sliding over the ridges of the metal, a fifty-centime piece. I imagine he put the coin into a coat pocket, though I cannot recall this perception. He might have said *merci*. I might have said *merci*. I do not remember looking at him, face to face.

I cannot recall well the flow of time then. There are only a few bit images and the trace memories they bring to mind.

January 27. The delirium of a photographic image lies in the ways in which the mind's eye roams from scene to scene, detail to detail, never following much of a straight line of knowledge but instead "goes off the furrow" (*de lire*, in Latin), off and beyond the grooved tracks dug out by ordinary, straight-laced perception; the eye wanders, dreams up possibilities, skips to other scenes and moments; the mind conjectures events in time, it begins to hallucinate, sees things that aren't there and some that are; the eye picks up on what till then has gone unnoticed and unremarked to the far distant point where there can occur a derangement of perceptions; a mind can get lost within phantasms of ink on paper.

I have been looking at the photographs I had taken of the blind man while he was standing by himself, close to the gate. I had forgotten these

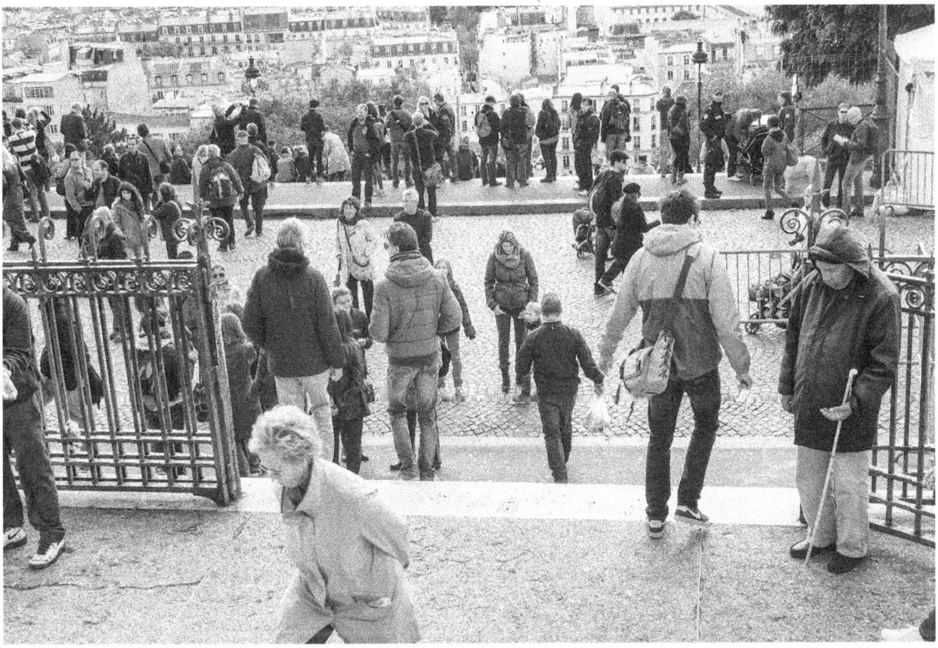

alternate versions of this particular flow of time. Only now, with six original images glowing on the computer screen, times of exposure noted for each, is there the possibility of delving into this particular ricochet of perceptions.

12:14:41. 1/160 sec at f/9.0. Now the man in the wheelchair can be barely seen, hidden behind two hatted folks walking past. We cannot see what he is looking at. The white dog, too, is partially obscured. It looks like the dog belongs to either the women by the baby carriage, or the two men consulting a guidebook. Close to the canine stands the police officer, straight and erect, primed for duty. His right hand is held near his hip, close to a belt that carries the accoutrements of his position. When we zoom into his image and look into this man's eyes it appears he is looking right at us, judging an act of photography. It's possible his gaze is not precisely onto us; he could be looking at an area behind our visual form or just to the left of it. Something or someone seems to have caught his eye, and he's not letting it go. To our left, by the left side of the gate, close to the railings, is the cut-off form of a young man sporting Nike running shoes. A bottle of water, held in his hand, looks chilled and tasty. We can presume this man is selling bottles of water. His back is turned, away from the steps below the gate, and he's looking away from where the police officer stands. We wish to warn the young man, if we could, and tell him about the police officer's proximity and his regard of the area around the basilica, but the photograph remains still and silent, unmoving, we are helpless to alter the unfolding events; any presumed agency involved in looking at a photograph goes only so far. We sense danger. We wish the compound nervous system among the unlicensed peddlers would kick in and sound the alert to the police presence. Perhaps that system was not yet fully developed, the looks and shouts and relay points were not in place in those days, two years back, or they were not intensely in effect that sleepy Monday afternoon. Perhaps the young man was not paying attention, caught up as he was in the moment of selling waters, his face and body turned away from the area from which the police officer is walking. The blind man is standing near the other side of the gate, his hand held out, the cane lies in the nape of his wrist. He looks to us to be alone in the world. We sense there is a good photograph to be had in these circumstances, the man standing alone by the gate, the multitudes of people walking about, zigzagging lines of craved desire. We hold the camera steady and try for another click or two before the arrangements of that time have passed.

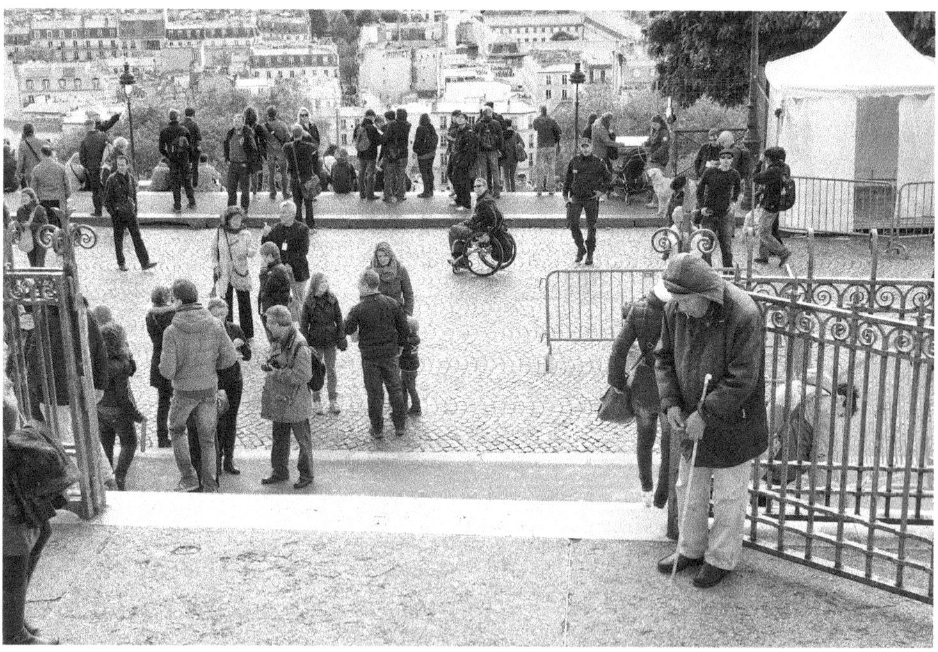

12:14:45. Four seconds later and now the man selling waters is outside our field of vision. Perhaps he has made a sale, or he has changed positions, or he noticed the police officer and he has forgotten about selling waters just now, and he's making strides to leave the premises, fleet on the soles of his Nikes. The police officer is walking toward the gate, his mouth slightly open, intent on moving toward that which has caught his eye. His left hand is held by his waist, by the belt, close to those instruments of power. We're not sure if he is carrying a gun, holstered to his belt, though we're looking for that instrument of violent force, for sure. His open mouth and closed eyelids suggest a look of annoyance, of disgust even, as if saying, *Alright, I've told you before, you can't be selling things illegally, and now you're going to pay for it.* The man in the wheelchair, sporting narrow dark sunglasses, is clearly visible. His hands are on the wheels of the chair. A bulky camera close to his lap hangs from a strap around his neck. Photography has become a hobby of his, a creative endeavor that enables him to extend his perceptual reach beyond the limits of his body: through lens and film he can write with light in the world, his eyes reach where hands cannot. Something caught his sight. The dog is looking toward the energies about the two women tending to the baby carriage. It's becoming clear the dog is with these women and

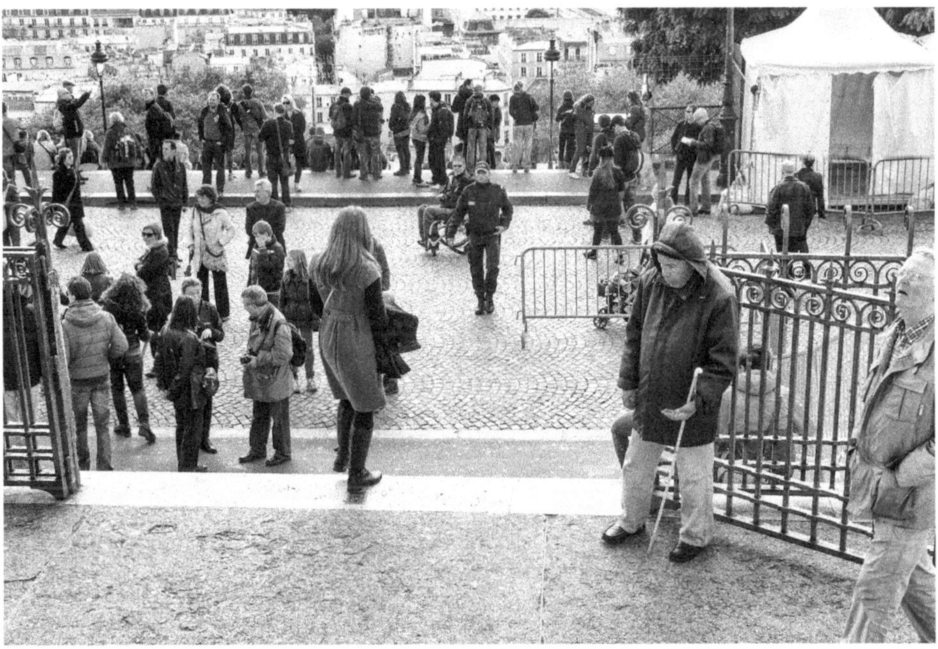

presumed infant. The blind man is by the gate, he is looking down now, fingers and thumbs of his two hands slightly touching one another. The space of the photograph is taking form, there is a certain composition of space and people, but we're not quite there yet. We keep clicking, biding our photographic time. It's unclear if we are aware just then, in the moment of photographing, that the police officer is approaching; he was not at the center of our focal concerns. It's possible we picked up on his looming presence only after looking at the images hours or days later.

12:14:49. Now the police officer is walking intently toward the area by the basilica. His bodily demeanor is clear, authoritative, and confident. He appears well-trained in the arts of policing and command. Near the center of the photographic image, he is looking our way, and he soon might command us to stop photographing. Again it's unclear whether the photographer, or some other subject or object, is the focal point of his gaze. There is an empty, barren space by the area of the gate where the water seller stood eight seconds before. The dog is presently obscured by people passing by. The man in the wheelchair holds the camera in his right hand. His sunglassed face carries a look of discernment, intrigue, or consternation, perhaps. Something interests him, perceptually, affectively. The blind man has returned to holding his left hand out, the

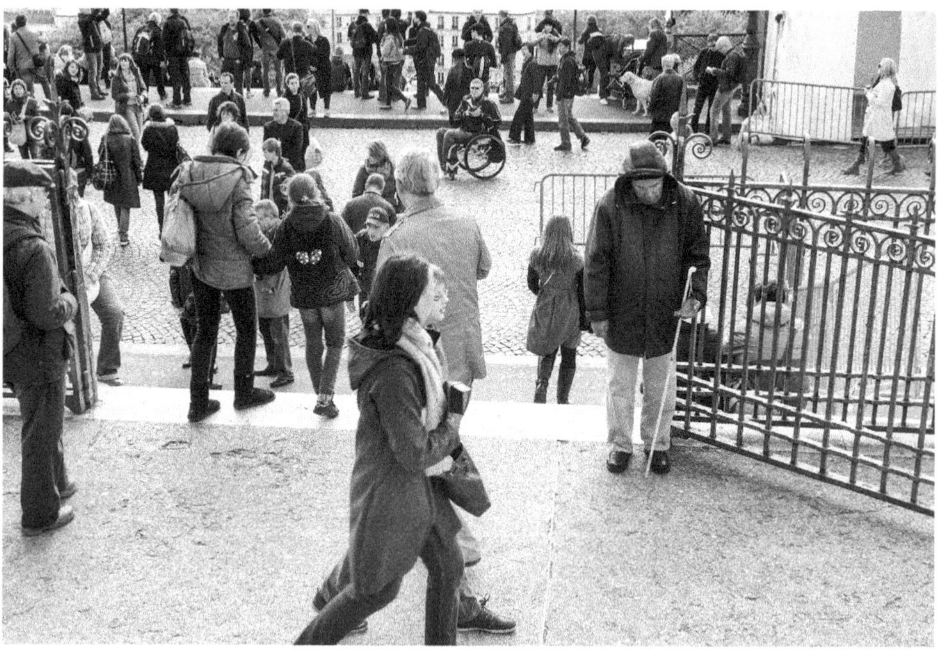

cane lies in the nape of his wrist. At the edge of the image a man sporting clear eyeglasses is walking past, to the blind man's left. His hands are held in his coat pockets in a leisurely, walkabout way. This man is looking up, perhaps toward the upper reliefs of the basilica, the Dome included. He does not appear to be aware of the man standing just to his right.

12:14:53. Now the man in the wheelchair holds the camera in both hands, close to his chest. Two fingers of his right hand, the second and third finger, apparently, are being held around the lens of the camera, in a position unfamiliar to us. He looks as though he is primed to take a photograph. He is waiting, perhaps, for the right moment for the image. The police officer is walking up the steps, effort and intent built into his stride. His eye is trained on someone or something of interest to him, in line with the demands of his profession. Now the investigations of the dog are directed toward other people by the steps. The blind man has changed positions. He is standing as though straight toward the camera. His hand is held out, humbly. The cane lies in the crook of his wrist. Now we have taken four photographs of this scene, but we have yet to hit on the right arrangement of space or an aesthetically compelling formation of people. We're looking for the right mood and affective presence, the sweet spot of life's dynamic.

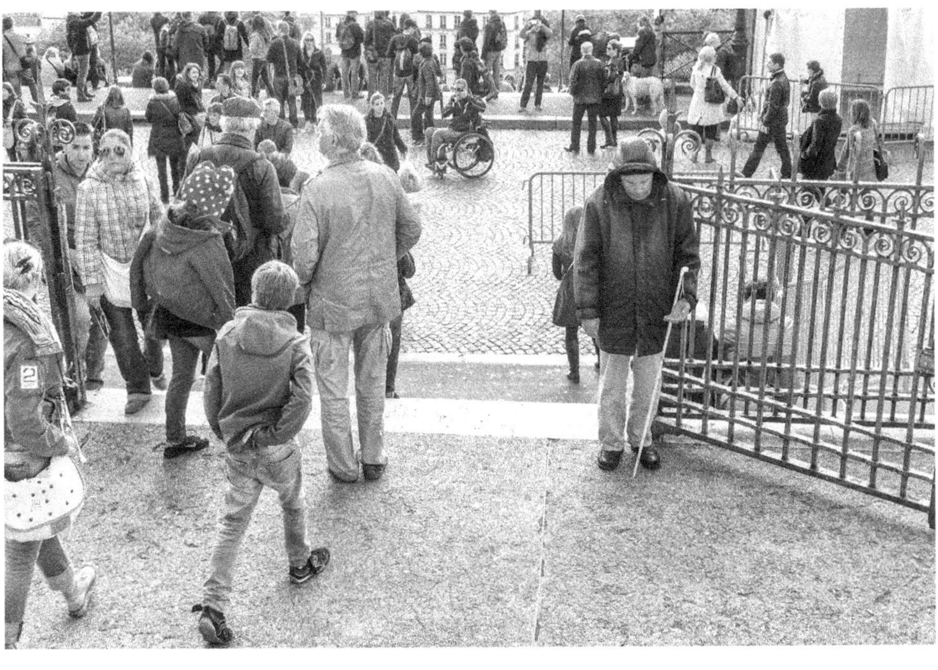

12:14:56. Now the police officer can no longer be seen, three seconds after the previous photograph. In theory, he has either made it up the steps and past the gate, beyond the frame of the photograph, or he is hidden in the crowd of people climbing down the steps. We look for some sign of him, his cap or portions of arms or legs, in the ensemble of bodies in the crowd, nothing is clear. The man in the wheelchair is now holding the camera up to his right eye. The device is being supported by his two hands, held in a vertical position, implying a vertical photograph. The camera is slanted in the direction of the crowd of people climbing down the steps, which is where we presume the police officer to be, or just beyond that. The white dog has turned its attention away from the people by the top step, and is looking to his left, vaguely in the direction of the basilica. There is little change in the blind man's position. If anything, the fingers of his open left hand are lower downward the slightest degree. Why has he turned this way, directly facing the camera? There is no one about him, the tourists tend not to pass by that side of the gate. Is it possible that he has become aware of the photographer and his camera? He could be posing for the expected photograph, perhaps in the faith that he will be compensated for his collaboration. Or he has resigned himself to the inevitable, or he is standing there in an act of passive defiance, *go ahead, take your best shot, if this is what you are reduced to doing, reducing me in the process of your own reduction.* We are struck by the affective force of this man's position, standing close to the gate, away from the others there, oblivious to his forlorn presence. We know there is a photograph in here somewhere, the camera needs to hit on the right combination of forms. Right now there is too much negative space in the foreground, the man should be more centered on the vertical axis, closer to the intersecting lines of the rule of thirds. And so we adjust the frame and camera and lean in for another shot.

12:14:57. Now with this last photograph taken from this perspective, sixteen seconds after the first image, we have hit on the right combination of themes and motives, the man standing by himself, straight onto the camera, hand open, head lowered, the crowds of people passing through the gate, the man in the wheelchair, photographing a camera taking a photograph. Some folks are moving toward the church above, others are gazing out at the southern environs of Paris. Everyone appears to be within their own moment of awareness and perceptual interest. We can see why we chose to hold onto this image. Perhaps it's the best we could do, given the circumstances. The photograph looks different now. The police officer is visually apparent again. He is close to the gate now, his

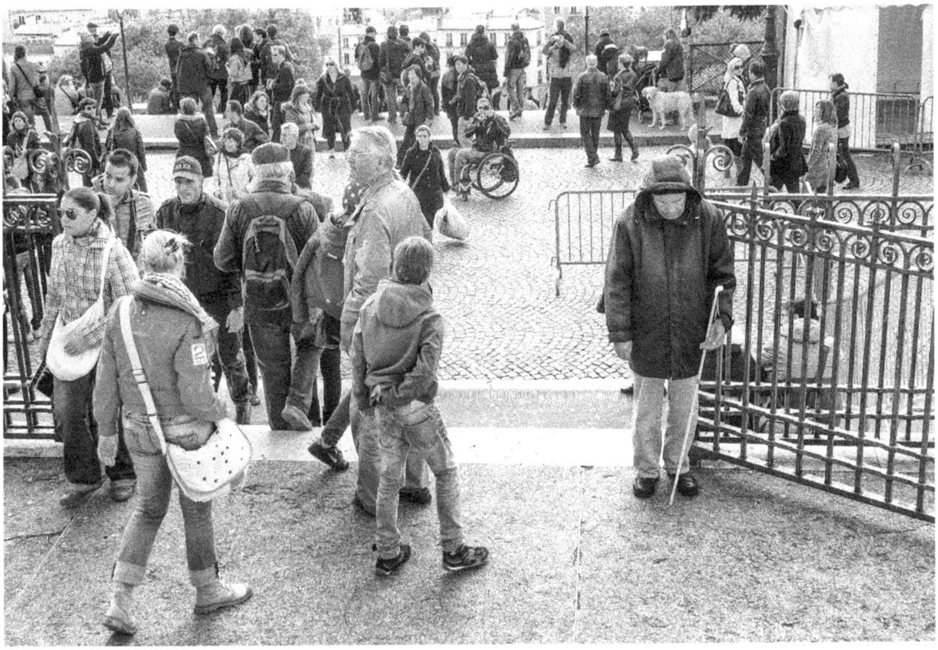

dark boots on the steps, the tip of his tongue smooth within the bite of his lips. He is looking intently forward, toward an area just beyond where our camera lies. The man in the wheelchair appears to be directing his camera in that general direction, as well. It looks as if he is photographing something that lies roughly within the same vicinity to which the police officer's eye is trained. Given the manner in which he is holding the camera, it's likely he is not taking a single still photograph or two, as we had first assumed, but rather he's using the video control to create a digital recording of a segment of time and space. It will remain unclear what moving resemblances have ghosted the inside of his camera. The dog is looking in the direction of the basilica. The dog appears to be less preternatural now, more profane and mundane in his sensory attentions. We are left to wonder what other secret histories yet unnoticed lie within the perceptual zones of the photographs, which hold vast fields of energy. All of this might seem trivial, the many looks, clashing lines of want and interest, but know that many a universe is made of vibratory motion and need.

Thirty-one seconds later and the next image on the spool of that day's photographs, at 12:15:26, shows the police officer by the level

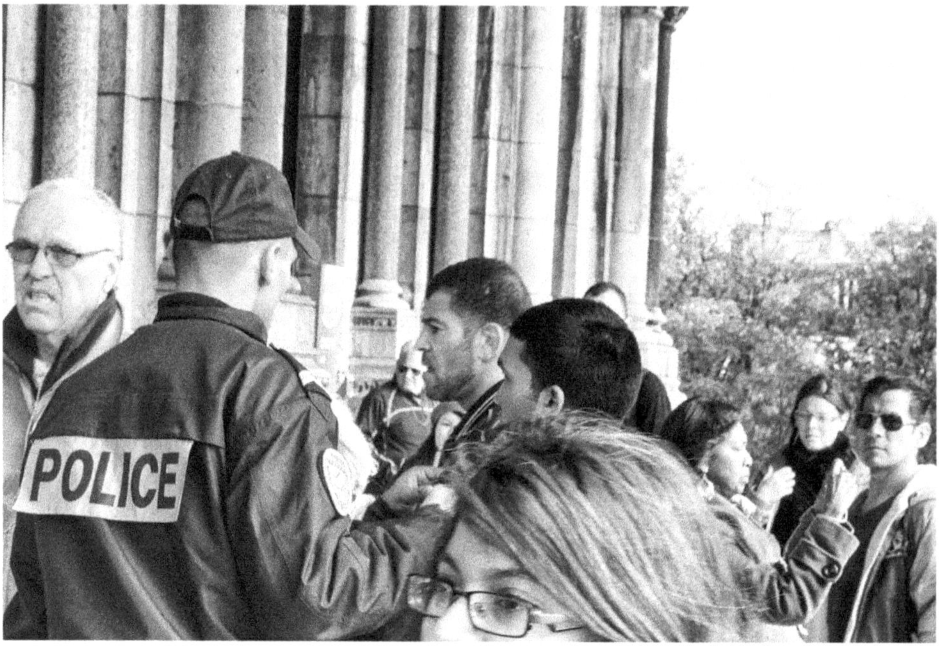

marble ground near the entrance to the basilica, clutching the clothing of the man who was selling waters. So this, apparently, is what caught the police officer's eye, this is the person he was intent on approaching. I cannot recall the clash of their encounter, I must have become aware moments before or after the officer reached his man. Apparent is a handgun nestled into the holster fixed to the policeman's belt. Notice how the young man is looking up toward the police officer, into the latter's eyes, presumably, in a gaze of troubled, unequal communication. The young man's eyes suggest worry and supplication, uncertainty over his fate in the hands of another. Notice how no one else is looking onto this encounter, concerned about the physical force used and implied, they have their sights set on the basilica's attractions—except, perhaps, for a young man to the right of the image, who is just walking onto the scene, his right foot light in the air and wire-rimmed sunglasses shading his eyes. When I zoom in on the details of this man's face eyes pick up on the graphite round of his pupils, they trace a line of sight running from those shaded retinas past the hands of a woman eyeing her camera through a crowd of people onto the officer grabbing the man's coat.

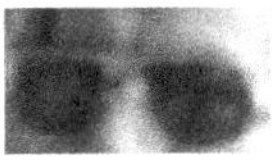

Ensuing from this intersection of physical force and vision was the policeman's tour of the area around the basilica, with the young man caught in the officer's hands, trailed by a stranger intent on photographing. I took twenty-one photographs of their forced coupling, I'm ashamed to say, as the two moved about the area by the basilica, the officer barking commands to the begging woman to move on; I photographed as they walked down the steps, the officer looking about, surveilling the premises as the man surrendered to his clutches, as they made their way to the police car parked below. In the record of these images I catch a person or two looking onto the man being held by the police officer, a quick glance in the pace of their days, looks of curiosity, concern, or apparent sympathy, *tough break, man;* eyes on the officer's strong-arm hold of the young man's jacket. In the next frame they are no longer looking that way, their perceptual concerns turned elsewhere. No one looks for very long.

The last photograph in the police series occurred at 12:19:27. I believe that, after taking this final image of the man being held and questioned by the police, I stood on the steps above where the police car stood, wavering on whether to take more shots of the man's detention. The next image, taken thirty-five seconds later, is of the young man posing next to the blind man. As to what happened within the space of this between I cannot say, I have no visuals to remind myself. It's possible that the man in the wheelchair caught much of that filmic hour within the video loop of his camera—though I see no indication of him in the later photos. In his basement office somewhere, in Rome or Buenos Aires, he has been sifting through the digital strands of film taken that day. Seated at his desk, built of wood planks tailor-designed for him, he watches the flow of video images (*video*, from Latin *videre*, "to see," on the pattern of *audio*) and gets swept into that stream of life. Or he has sliced the thirty-fields-a-second film into a series of still images and through these images he reaches out to a different time and place. With the precision of a surgeon's scalpel, his scopic efforts lead him to pinpoint the actions involved and trace the movements of looks coursing through the images. After a while, he cannot help but come back to the stilled pictures, day after day, late at night, looking for further indications. He is unsure as to what, really, he is seeking to find, and it's not clear to him that the reel of images add up to something greater than the association of their parts. Inevitably, he finds himself lost within a sea of visions. I dream of him, dreaming of us.

Most often, discussions of photography, by photographers, critics, scholars, or others, tend to focus on the aesthetics of a photographic image and/or the semiotic and political import of photographic imagery. But there's so much more going on with photographs, from disruptive shifts in perception to incessant multiplicities of time and perspective to the feverish play of phantasy and imagination to destabilized positions of subject and other to the intense, fractural sociality that underpins many photographic captures. There's a different way of looking at photographs, one more delirious, to which most studies of photography do not admit, or submit.

The delirium of vision lies in the many looks implied in any act of looking, apparent looks and implicit ones, shared looks, direct stares and counterstares, quick glances, a steady stare, sideways looks, delayed looks, a look back, second look and third looks, sneaky looks, looks of longing or desire, care or disapproval, beseeching looks, unseeing eyes, delayed looks, imagined looks, worried looks, forceful looks, potential looks, a rhetoric of looking and an exacting science of looks, haunting looks and relooks; the archaeology of past looks. Such looks veer into different possibilities and impossibilities within folds of appearance and apparition. Vision proceeds through dreamlike associations and lines of force; it gets caught up in intricate geometries of perception; so often a given glance or optical impression sparks imaginative wandering. There is a phantastical sheen to many perceptions. The delirium of looking is in any moment of everyday life. The everyday is far from ordinary; and by no means singular. The everyday is multiple, refractive, and laced with hallucinatory valences.

May 6. In the room, that evening, in Manhattan, far from Paris: his image saw what was going on, though he himself did not see any of this. The photograph of his likeness stood pasted onto the wall; his eyes were watching us, looking onto the proceedings, as those present glanced upon the image.

This was at the Center for the Humanities at Columbia University the other night, during the reception for an academic symposium, titled "Image as Method." The week before we had put up a number of photographs of mine, one series related to the photographic memoir I have been composing of reflections on my life as a student in Besançon, France, thirty years ago. Along with this we had two large, poster-size prints made for the reception area in the center. One of these prints held a photograph I had taken of a man walking on a beach in northern

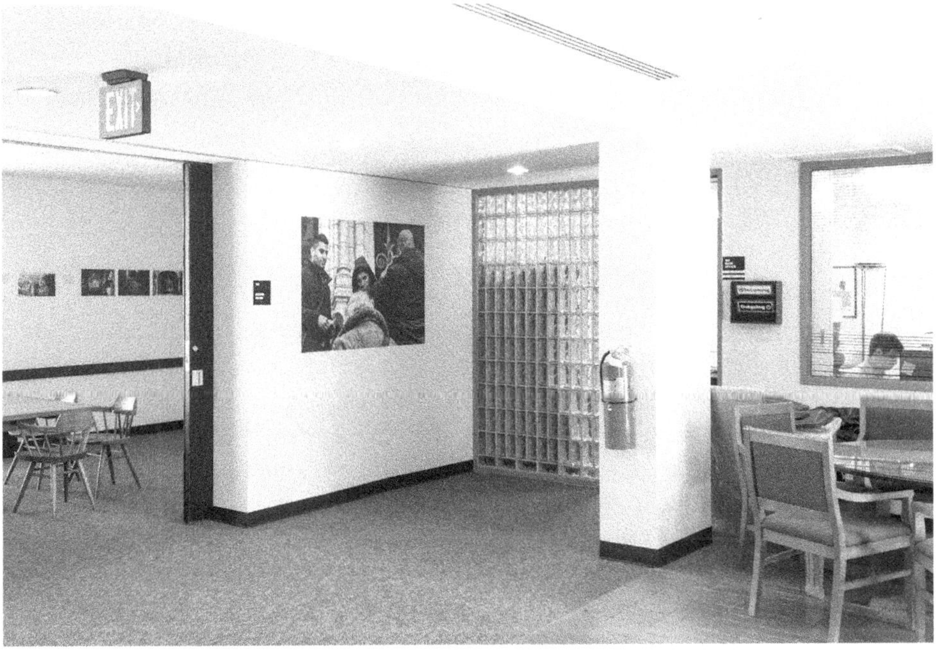

France. The other contained the photograph of the blind man as he stood on the steps of the basilica, close to the two men. We put up this large black-and-white print a few days before the event, on a side wall near a conference room. Working with the sticky adhesive backing, it was difficult to keep the vinyl surface from forming creases or air bubbles as we rolled it onto the plaster wall. Eventually we managed to flatten the fabric in a sufficiently smooth way. The poster stood nearly three by five feet, the people portrayed appeared life-size in stature. You could walk right up to the image of the man and consider the man's face and eyes or regard the younger man, the sunglasses in his hands or the fine shaved line of his stubble beard.

I felt ambivalent about having the image of the man appear in such a sharp and expansive way. I had in fact chosen this image for the wall, in consultation with B., the anthropologist at the center who organized the symposium. It was thrilling to have my photographic work shown as art, in a public exhibit, and yet quietly I had concerns. That unease lingered during the reception, after a round of presentations concluded for the day. A number of participants that night—anthropologists, artists, colleagues, friends, and students, faculty, and staff of the university—mingled and chatted in the reception area, sipping on wine, tasting the sushi served in porcelain plates set on a white tablecloth.

I'm not sure anyone noticed the unstable image as intensely as I did. The photograph was off to the side of the room. The blind man stood there, looking at us, his portraiture forlorn, neglected, without having any say as to if or how his visual likeness should be represented. He had no sense that an image of him had made it to the halls of an esteemed university and people were now gathered, faintly aware of his phantasmal presence.

As I drank red wine from a clear plastic cup and spoke with friends and colleagues I could not shake the complicated gray aura of the physiognomy a few feet away. He stood there as an apparition. He wasn't there at all, just the surface picture of him. We knew who he was and what the gist of his image had become. He did not know us at all. Most likely he was asleep in Paris in those distant hours and he'd go about his next day without any awareness of the force and metastasizing transfer of his captured image. In a way I felt I had betrayed his confidence, even though that confidence was never gained or offered. His image filled the room with a ghostly aura. He watched me as I walked about and chatted theory with fellow anthropologists.

The next day it came my turn to narrate my anthropological approach to images, after several fine talks and films had concluded. For this I presented a paper titled "Photography tears the subject from itself." I stood at the podium on the stage of an auditorium and read through the text while projecting digital images onto a large white screen. The man's image recurred, filling the stage and the possible perceptions of onlookers. I cannot say how these words and images were received or imagined.

I thought that, later on, when two senior anthropologists took the stage to discuss the work presented, they might take me to task for presenting images of this man in such an overt way without the appearance of having his permission to circulate those images. No one asked about this, no one challenged me on the ethics of the research or photography involved, either then or in conversations afterward. The ideas raised related to the thematics of the work, namely anthropological considerations of images in ethnographic fieldwork. "*We need to consider the blind spot in any act of perception. . . .*"

It's possible those in attendance were simply being polite. My sense, though, is that for anthropologists used to gathering "data" in any number of situations, in which they draw from conversations and observations among peoples who have become the subject of their research inquiries, the photographic captures of a man relatively unknown to me—and what I've written about those encounters—are on a par with their own ways of comprehending the world. Apparently, the implied voyeurism did not faze or disturb them.

It was different a few weeks ago, when I presented to the students in an anthropology seminar taught by a colleague at a nearby university. The students had read a draft of the paper I wrote for the symposium and came to the class with a number of questions. Did I have the permission of the man to use his photographic image? Shouldn't I get that permission? Does he know that I am writing about him? Is it fair for me to photograph and write about a sightless man in such cutting ways? I told them I was trying to think through these questions myself, that there were no easy answers. They weren't convinced.

May 22. We dismantled the photographs today. B. and I met at the university and worked with the center's staff to remove the prints from the walls. First we took down the exhibit for the photographic memoir, and then approached the vinyl print of the blind man. We started to peel

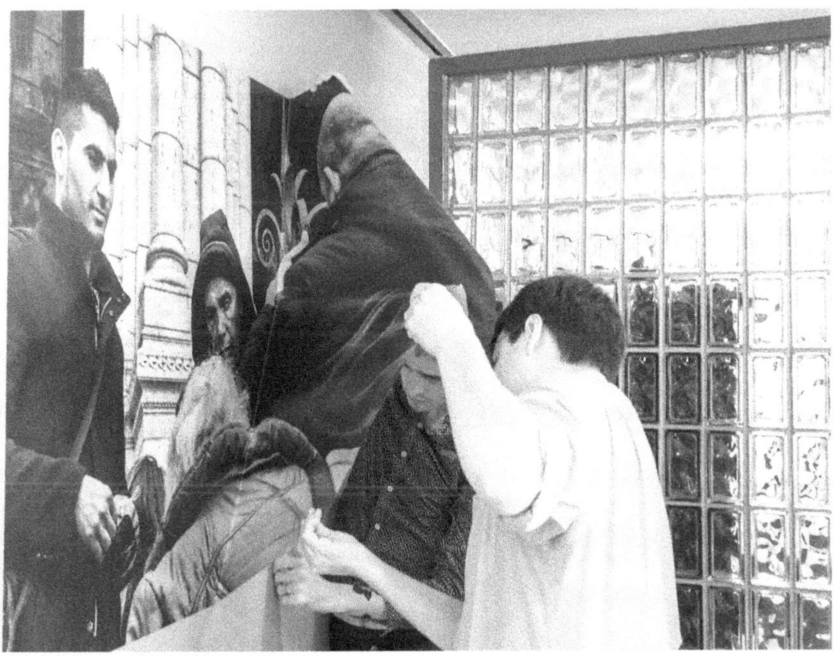

the thick, glossy paper from the wall. Its adhesive backing began to rip off portions of the paint underneath. We tried to drag the vinyl away from the wall, bit by bit, so that it wouldn't tear up the surfaces of the wall. I stepped back and reached for the camera and photographed as two men worked to remove the photo. The print began to crease and turn, twisting into crimpled folds. The persons portrayed grew distorted and took on a jointed intensity. In the photos I took that afternoon the warping body images merge with the bodies laboring to dismantle the photograph until, in slight delirium, it becomes unclear who was in the original print and who was acting to remove it.

Baroque vision

June 1. Paris. The city of mirrors holds reflections and shadows within the savage depths of its history. Each street corner carries a labyrinth of past lives. Churches are sites of toil and death, where tombs and relics lie in crypts below level ground.

On the flight from New York to Paris I read David Harvey's article "Monument and Myth," which tells of the complicated, "tortured history" of the Basilique de Sacré-Coeur, which involves decades of fighting and political contestation, the rise and destruction of the Paris communes, and a leading figure of the church who climbed to the top of the Mont one dull and foggy October morning in 1872: "The Archbishop of Paris climbed those steep slopes only to have the sun miraculously chase both fog and cloud away to reveal the splendid panorama of Paris spread out before him. The Archbishop marvelled for a moment before crying out loud: 'It is here, it is here where the martyrs are, it is here that the Sacred Heart must reign so that it can beckon all to it.'"[1]

For unclear reasons I am being drawn back to this site of multiple, ambiguous, unstable visions and its kaleidoscope of optics. I have become a tracker of visions, a student of the myriad gazes, stares, looks, photos,

blind spots, images, phantasies, and phantasms that constitute many lives these days. A certain baroque vision is required; where there's an eye toward shifting, infinitely multiplying forms, where images are discontinuously in flux and a resplendent play of light and opacity reflects torsions of pleasure and pain, life and death, with no unified way of knowing bringing any singular coherence to it all. I'm not sure where the visions are taking me, or if there's clarity to be found at the far end of the optics. I suspect any truth thereabouts will be multiple, contradictory, recursive, dispersed, a poly-eyed creature contraption of ever-shifting optical refractions. For now, I'm trying to trace certain formations of perception and their implications in time and consciousness for those subject to their ways. With this spectral anthropology, I have become my own ethnographic subject, alongside others perceived.

Yesterday I arrived on an overnight flight from New York and promptly made my way to Montmartre and its blurred world. Soon I was settled into a studio apartment rented from friends, a table, a few chairs, and a futon couch that unfolds into a bed. Amid the jangle of passing cars and motorcycles and the chatter of cafés across the way I fell into a deep stupor in late afternoon and slept through the evening and night.

I dreamed I was photographing a family in a hilly mill town in New York, where steep roads crossed a worn river. I had not used a camera in a while; its bulk felt heavy in my hands. The family included a son who was mentally disabled and his older brother, a possible friend, wary, guarded. The brother said to me, "Don't focus so much on my brother, okay?" Do not represent him, solely. Do not intensify the gaze on him, as he'll be aware of it and our hearts shall bleed. In response I said that I was not focusing on him so much but rather the family as a whole. I showed him the range of photographs the camera was taking. Stark black-and-whites held a range of action and visual dynamics within a coil of effort and energy. I felt sheepish about showing these displays of visual regard and retention. Still, I did not want to destroy any images that spoke of life and the contortions of striving.

I've returned to France in order to revisit the site of encounter. Back at it this morning, I hiked up the stone staircases that led to the basilica. Immediately I saw him there, standing by the pillars, his hand held open to passing bodies. The air was cooler in the shade, the marble cold to the touch, unlike the steps below, where the sun seared its subjects.

It was almost too easy to perceive him right off. This time round, there was no great search to find him. I half-thought he would be away somewhere, panhandling in the South of France or convalescing in a rest home in the margins of Paris. I imagined him at ease by a modest house on the margins of Rabat, sitting in the shade near a stream running through a field of Moroccan wheat, fertile lands seen from the window of a train bound for Marrakech one spring morning. He prefers outdoors to the tedium of a cramped inside.

He looked different now. Slight but perceptible differences marked his appearance, as when one encounters a friend anew after months apart. The cut of his hair was new. The coat looked clean. He wore tan loafers. He appeared worn out the last time I had seen him, expiring under the heat of the sun. Perhaps he had a better situation in life. Was someone looking after him?

The morning suggested an ordinary routine for him. He stood by the exit from the church and he shifted, as people passed, from sunlight to shade, sunlight, then shade again. He must know the rhythms of each day, the flows of people, the most lucrative hours. This time the encounter brought little sense of connection or revelation, no epiphanies of form or recognition between us, imagined or perceived. I walked up to him and held out a few coins and touched his hand with them. He felt the contact and his perceptions seemed to shift. The exchange struck him as a disturbing, off-kilter moment within the busy confluence of his workday. He had no regard for me. Last year's relation was a chimera.

Standing before him, I mouthed a few utterances, "Monsieur," "C'est pour vous." Not more than that, along with a few coins placed in his hand.

"Merci," he said.

"Merci," I said.

I moved away. I walked about, took up watch by the closed doors that led into the narthex. He shifted from sunlight to shade. He kept a bottle of water by the steps at the exit from the basilica, close to where the women like to beg through prayer. A woman was seated by the exit with a bag by her side. He walked over to it, grabbed it, and said, "*Allez, votre sac!*" "Go with your bag!" He handed the bag to her. She took it and rushed off. She returned a few minutes later, once he had returned to his post by the columns.

I noticed a man standing close to the blind man, conversing with him. Who was this? I did not see where this man came from but I suspect he works within the offices of the basilica. He wore dark clothes and carried a gentle, attentive demeanor. He could be a priest. He stood close to his conversant and held the man's arm at one point. He motioned several times to touch the blind man's arm but then held back from doing so. The blind man presumably did not perceive these furtive approaches. The priestly man looked my way and I tried to feign not watching the two of them. I did not want the priest to perceive me as exceptional in any way. The two men spoke while looking in the direction of the woman seated by the exit.

"*Bon, le police arrive*," said the priestly man. A uniformed officer, a young man with a crew-cut scalp, arrived at the basilica and walked up to the woman and asked her to leave. The woman collected her belongings and sauntered off. She returned minutes later and sat again at the doorway. She held her hands together as if in prayer.

The police officer did not ask the blind man to leave. He walked right past him as he stood by the pillars. He showed no concern for him. Apparently he saw this man as a neutral category, not of abject unwanted negative value.

Why was the woman told to move on?

The blind man continued to be perturbed by the woman's presence by the basilica. She was the first person in need that people saw when they were leaving the basilica, her words the first that pilgrims and tourists heard upon returning to the light of day. She was cutting into the flow of possible donations, and so he wished her gone.

I thought I heard him say "Voleur!" at one point. Did I imagine this, or did he say something like "thief"?

June 2. I did not speak with him today. I am altogether attentive when in sight of him, and receptive, but when standing before him I become passive, incapable of speech. Linguistically inept. My mouth contorts into silence and mumbles odd syllables. The left eye causes this, I think. There is an agency to eyes, hands, and sundry body parts, to the flesh and mood of the world, which goes beyond rational calculations.

Could I really ask him for permission to use the photographs I have taken of him? How could I begin to explain what I've been up to?

Recently this sentence from Raymond Radiguet's *Le Diable du corps*: "If we live constantly with the same ideas, if we see only one, passionately desired object, we become unaware of how criminal are our desires."[2]

My ambivalence: I am intrigued by my need to observe and disgusted and plagued by the desire for observation. I am trying to look at looking, while gazing upon acts of voyeurism.

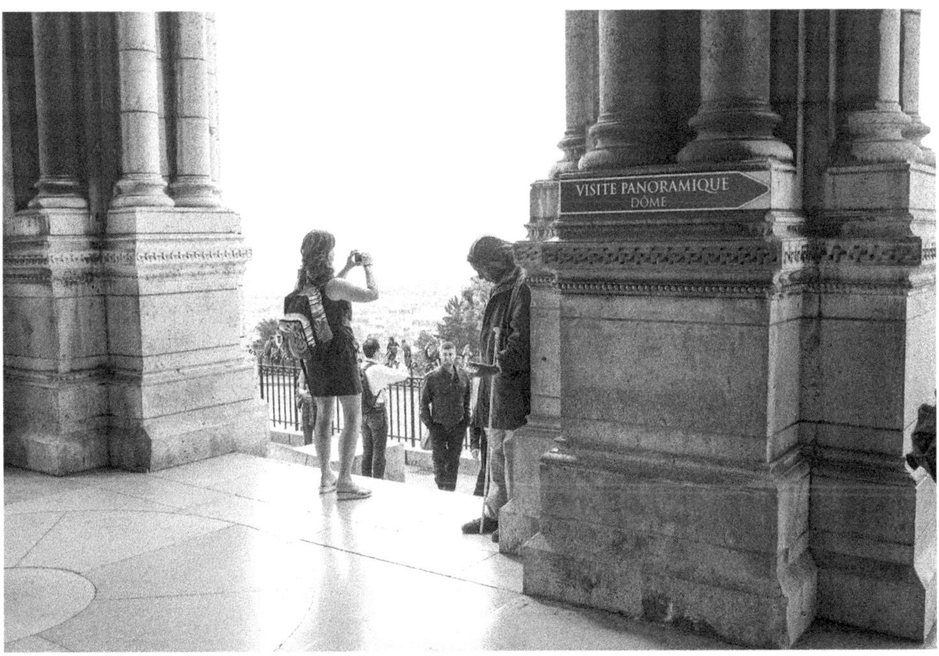

June 3. I hear the clicking of cameras more often. I've become sensitive to that machinery, attuned to the technologies involved. Does he perceive the effects of photography within the range of a similar acoustics? So many cameras are in play in this terrain, so many devices of visual recording; Canon; Nikon; Sony; DSLR; digital; analogue; smart phones; iPhones; tiny cameras the size of spy cameras; video recorders; I spied one camera enclosed within a small leopard-skin case. How many times is a person snared within a photo while moving through a day in Paris? How many photographs am I in within an hour of walking about the basilica? Images recur within the background of Facebook, Instagram; Twitter feeds; adolescent selfies, photo albums, Dropbox; Google Cloud; a family's trip to Europe; reunion of friends; a voyeur's secret rapture. Panoramic scenes. Surveillance video loops, bot technologies. #image. #phantasm.

"*Ojos en los ojos para mirar cómo miran: ojos y más ojos y reojos procurando ser elmirante*," says Argos Panoptes, a monstrous, hundred-eye character in Baltasar Gracián's *El Criticón*, a baroque novel from 1657.[3] The full passage reads in English:

> One has to have eyes on one's shoulders to see what weight one loads; on one's back to see who comes near; on one's knee to see who one adores; on one's legs to see against who one fights; on one's feet to see where one walks; on one's arms to not embrace a lot and squeeze too little; on one's hands to see whose one shakes; on one's tongue to watch what one says; on one's chest to see what one ought to have; on one's heart to see who pulls one in.
>
> Argo says:
>
> "Eyes in the eyes in order to look at how they look; eyes and more eyes on top of eyes trying to be the one who looks."

Just as many optics are required today, though now it's not just singular bodies but corporate systems that require a multitude of looks. One has to have eyes in one's brain, to see what one imagines; on one's skin, to see what pleases; in cities, to see who to watch; in buildings, to see who approaches; in one's phone, to see the spectacle of self; in the Métro, to see how others travel; in airports, to see what they carry; at borders, to see who crosses; on satellites, to see who one fights; on drones, to see who to kill. Vision upon vision in order to see how they look; eyes and more eyes on top of eyes madly trying to be the one who looks.

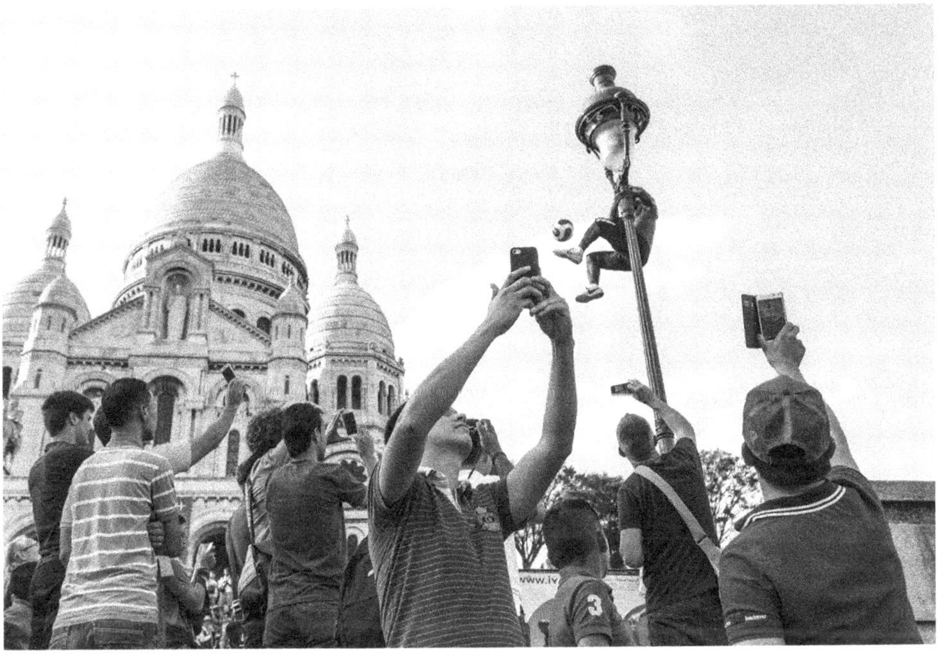

June 5. I had no idea at first what the steel plastic gadgets were. They loomed like ungainly fishing poles raised to the sky by cash-starved sellers wandering the hilltop. Dangling from the top of each contraption was a string, the segue part of a gadget toy that might charm tourists. Only later did I realize the devices were the so-called "selfie sticks" epidemic to Europe this summer. Many travelers carry the devices about with them, the sticks extended above their shoulders like antennas on an army of searcher ants, sensate appendages glistening in the sun. The poles look empty without the cameras in them, as if their holders are carrying around a vacant monstrance used for cult rituals. The frames are full of empty promise, showing nothing. They're all the rage, as are the associated pictures. The environs of Paris have become the backdrop of countless images with smiling selves displayed, the sticks become a prosthetic of the body self, extending the reach of eye or brain. A selfie, they say, is by definition "a photograph that one has taken of oneself, typically one taken with a smart phone or a webcam and shared via social media."[4] I hate the fact of a world where such a definition exists. When people pose for the selfies they twist their bodies until eyes lock straight onto camera and faces demonstrate happiness, delight, satisfaction.

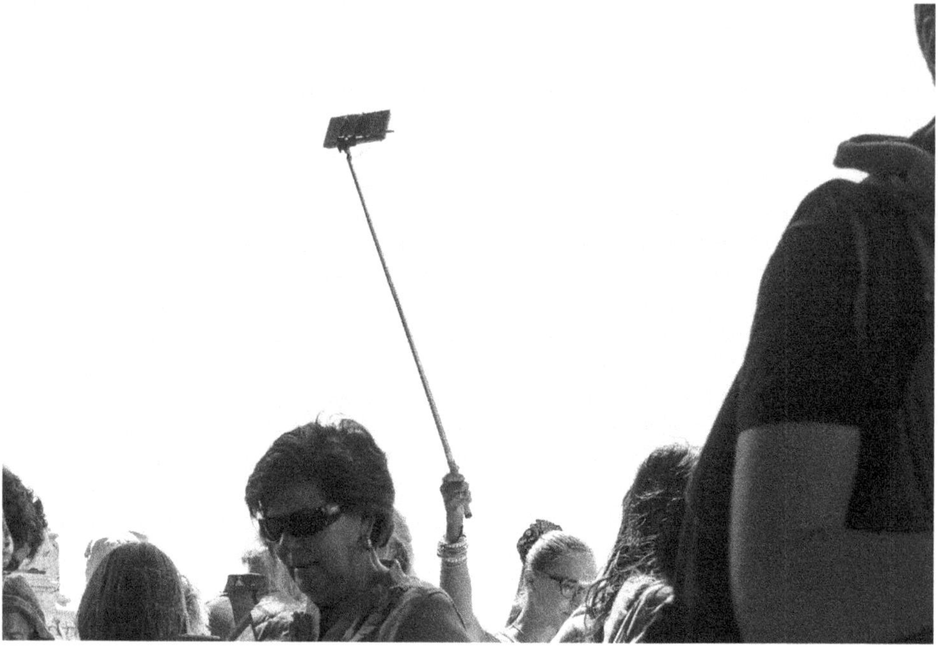

I don't think it's just a show for the selves back home, for the smiles continue long after the camera clicks, the subjects carry a satisfied glow of post-selfie bliss. That was good, say the pleasure centers. Let's do it again. The delight seems real, earnest, authentic, earned—and devoutly narcissistic. "We have discovered happiness," say the last men, and they post on Instagram.

I don't get it. There's something wrong here. Life errs in this rapid circulation of self-posed smiles across time zones for easy display and consumption into iPhones and Instagram within the buzzing of a restive hive. The receiving eyes eat up the visuals with salivary interest and then flick their gazes onto the next images that come along. Look at me, look at me looking, see how I stood by the Eiffel Tower. Know that she exists, know she is happy. iFriends. iLife. Too much focus on the self. Not enough regard of the phantom other, the stranger nearby.

I watched one woman walk down a Parisian street, holding the selfie stick before her. She appeared to be watching herself walk down the street.

I overheard a young couple talking.

"Take my head only, with this backdrop."

"Your head only?"

I do not see like them. Don't want to. The clicks scrape against the skin.

If the cameras are not used for self-portraits, then their users ply them against the world and snap pictures of paintings and gargoyles, trusting with shaky hands that the images come true. The clicks come easily, the photos a spiraling gyre of glimpses. One woman positioned her smart phone on the top of her boyfriend's head to steady the prismatic lens and snapped a level picture of the basilica, the aura of a Parisian sunset imaged by an 8.7 megapixel 16:9 backside-illuminated 1/3-inch sensor, with optical image stabilization. That combination of cranium and technology spoke well to the cyborg-like nature of perception in the new millennium. New arrangements of visuality are shaping our relations in life, what we perceive, or do not; realms of the intimate, strands of connection. The selfies point to a form of life predicated on the hyperintensification of the self and a hypotrophy of an awareness of others. The advent of selfies correlates with the rise of neoliberal subjects, suggest the economics of distribution.

What would Guy Debord, author of 1967's *Society of the Spectacle*, make of the current scene of self spectacularization? "The spectacle," he wrote, "cannot be understood as a mere visual excess produced by mass-media technologies. It is a worldview that has actually been materialized, that has become an objective reality."[5] The reality of the spectacle is now entrenched in everyday life; it recurs through mundane looks and images. The spectacle of the self is embedded in thoughts, anticipated time, modes of visuality, the optics of perception and consciousness. "The spectacle is not a collection of images; it is a social relation between people that is mediated by images."[6] Yet what happens when sociality is focused so much on spectacles of the self?

"Diabolical powers, whatever their message might be, are knocking at the door and already rejoicing in the fact that they will soon arrive," wrote Kafka.[7] The future diabolic can take the form of a look or a way of knowing within the snap of an eye. In the city of glass another swarm of selves are ascending the steps, antennas glistening in the sun. The appendage eyes are multiplying and the tourists took more and more selfies while flaming glances crisscrossed each other ever more wildly and shot their blood-red rays into my chest.

June 6. There is comfort in routine. Safety lies in known syntax. I arrived around ten in the morning and found him there, by the columns.

I returned to the doors leading into the narthex. We lingered in liminal space between inside and outside, sacred and profane, near to the unbaptized and perceived sinful. Each central door is of solid metal, latched together, jointed into stone. When my shoulders leaned against the right-side surface its elements became pliant and shifty. I could not count on anything solid, as I imagined a church to be. My skull rested close to an ornament flower sprinkled with red particles of paint, metallic rose dust. I watched. No tongue: all eyes: silent. One man passed close to the blind man and motioned to donate some money. The man held out his hand, showing a coin or two. He met with no response. He didn't know what to do with the emptiness between them.

He stays close to the structures. The pillars, the hand rails, the steps, marble smooth, the sharp metal poles of the gate; all of this gives him support within the openness of space. The structures help to keep his balance, keep him on track. He needs a quadrant in space. Otherwise his body could be knocked down or get entangled with other bodies. This is the shape of the human, the need for structures. They keep us from falling.

The colors of his clothes, the coat and shoes a light tan, his pants an off-white, blend in with the light-brown facades of the basilica. The coat is a protective device. He belongs there, of the church, within its architecture of devotion and sacrifice. In this figuration he is mythic. His body meshes into the stonework, into the field of perception there, the columns, the steps, the stone surfaces. Each day he becomes an element of its marble physiology.

He moves around a lot. He shifts his body, pillar to pillar, or down the steps, into the sun. He walks back to the locations he had been earlier, within the shade of the basilica. He never stays in the same place for more than a minute or two. Why does he shift positions so much? To try his luck elsewhere? He never appears settled in the space he occupies.

Along the street where I am staying, an uphill lane of shops and cafés east of the sloping mound of Montmartre, someone has set up a life-size, lifelike dummy along the edges of a tall building. At first glance this body looks real, a man holding tight to the precipice of a rooftop. The fall is imminent, any day now. Its catastrophe is apparent. A heavy wind could dislodge its grasp and send it tumbling into the street below. Few people notice its hanging presence.

June 6. At one point this afternoon I walked down to the lower steps of the basilica and tried to photograph the blind man standing among the

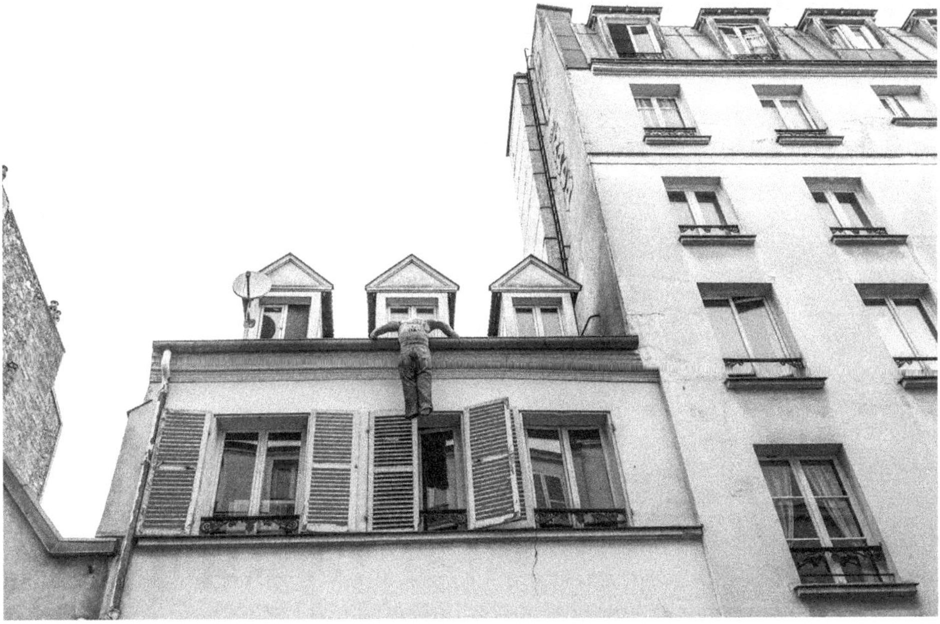

passing crowds. I could not see him that well myself, from that distance. Even so, I sensed he was looking at me, watching me survey the scene. He knew what I was up to. He can't really discern me from that far away, can he? I can barely see him myself, with myopic eyes. When I raise the camera his look turns toward me.

Now that I'm back at the apartment, sorting through the images in the glow on the laptop, the shades drawn in the apartment, conditions right for spectral analysis, it appears that he was not looking at me. In those brief photographed moments he is looking down, to the right or left, attending to the bodies walking past. He adjusts his hood, he holds his hands out and open, the crowd of phantoms lies between us. He and I stand out, unlike the others. We are both watchful, waiting in our separate ways. In no photos is he looking my way. The photographs tell a story contrary to my body's optics. I imagined his eye glance upon me, dank and flinty as a hallucination.

Memory and photography stand as two distinct forms of perception. This suggests how subjective and psychological ordinary perception is. Our eyes see faintly, through optical distortions. We proceed through approximations, guesswork, phantasmal vision.

I cannot trust what I see. I never see true. Last summer, while walking along rue de Clignancourt, I happened upon a sign for an optometrist's office fixed to the stone of an office building. The wording clung to my brain and later on, in offhand moments, I recalled the sign to read, *Docteur des yeux mauvais*, "Doctor of bad eyes." *Mauvais* as in bad, inferior, faulty, wrong. At times, a conscience needs a doctor for bad faulty eyes. A strange sign to establish. I've been curious since. While at home in New York I tried to spot the placard with the aid of Google Street View, cruising the street through virtual means, but had no luck with that. This morning while walking south in Montmartre I happened to pass the sign again. It read, Docteur ———. MALADIES DES YEUX."

Illnesses of the eyes, diseases. Anatomical pathology. Psychosomatic tendencies.

These *mauvais* eyes are bad, doctor. They can't see for real. Dig into them, ophthalmologically, and take a good look.

The doc pried the eyes open and probed for damage.

June 7. It's too much to photograph him straight on. If I try to take any direct photographs of him, he looks at me, discerns me, he makes me out for what I am. He observes and commands. With his eye he regards me. At times he scolds me, silently, much as a grandfather might chastise a child with a devastating look of disappointment.

I need to proceed obliquely, indirectly, and photograph him on the sly, with contorted arms, telescopic sight reaching into curved space. *Photos volées*, snapshots in flight, stolen photos. Otherwise, it's too much, too affecting, altogether too stressful. I've learned to sneak images into the camera, a clinical gaze taken from side angles, while he is distracted, looking elsewhere. Such multiangled devious optics are in line with the baroque photography I've been venturing.

Is it any wonder that the camera stopped working right after I took a number of photographs by the columns to the basilica? The camera display noted an error, fEE. A scary sign "f" as in focal error, "f" as in now you're fucked. Was this a problem with the camera's focusing mechanism? I pressed the shutter button, nothing happened, the camera had become optically impotent. I feared the camera with its image sensors and intricate pentaprism was broken and I would go days without a camera. I tried everything I could think of to fix the problem. I took out the battery and reinserted it and turned the camera on again. I released and reapplied the lens. The error message kept recurring, fEE. I had no choice but to leave the basilica. Without a functioning camera I could not do much work. I could not retain or figure much. I walked down the steps and returned to the apartment in the midday heat. Once there, I opened up the laptop and typed the error code into Google and learned that the aperture ring was not in the right position. My hands must have dislodged it during their photographic fervor. I reset the ring and the camera worked fine.

Magical thinking, the stuff of hexes and witchcraft: I know the content of my photographic work did not cause the malfunction. I think I know this. Yet it's interesting that this is where my thoughts went to when the camera stopped working. A sense of photographic guilt or shame, or a furious ambivalence, led to faulty equipment, went the logic of that magical thought. I had, in effect, unsighted myself.

June 9. The sun writes on a body with its electromagnetic force.

Last night I went to S. and J.'s place in Montmartre for dinner. It was kind of them to invite me into their home. Their apartment is on the top floor of a five-story walk-up. The windows of the living room overlook rue Doudeauville, busy with peoples from Africa. They like where they are living, said the young couple, though they worry about the gentrification, of which they form a part. At night they hear sporadic fights between prostitutes, arguing over customers. They catch bits only of the insults and accusations, as most of the disputes are in English because the sellers involved have come from former colonies of Great Britain. I leaned out past the open glass of a bay window and my eyes followed the long noble line of the street running north. I caught a glimpse of Sacré-Coeur on the sloping hill, the white dome of the basilica shining in the sun's evolving light.

Before dinner we sipped on white wine and snacked on olives and brie. J. asked about my reasons for returning to Paris. I told him about my work around the basilica and showed him a photo taken of the blind man.

"A friend of mine thought he might be Maghreb," I said. "Either from Morocco or Algeria."

J. took the image in his hands and considered it closely.

"When I look at this man's face," he said, "the word Maghreb does not come to mind so much as the word *buriné*."

"I see. Buriné?"

"Yes, buriné. That's a word we might use when describing someone, like a fisherman, who has been out in the sun a lot, and his face has become creased and weathered."

"When I look at this photo," he continued, "I see a man exposed to the sun for many hours. Not necessarily someone from North Africa."

"That makes good sense," I said. "He's been standing outside for many hours, each day."

"Yes, that could be it."

Buriner is to engrave; to chisel, to chip. The verb relates to the noun *burin*, a "cold chisel," a steel cutting tool used to engrave. Metaphorically, memories can be "engraved" in this way, within a book or journal or mind. Writing of a precise nature can be considered an act of buriner engraving. *Buriné* is the past participle of buriner. It means something like "lined, craggy"—as with a face chiseled by the sun, *un visage buriné*.

The man's face had been engraved upon by the heat of the sun's photons. There was no sure cover for his face, no veil or eyelid surface to protect the skin. The face needed to be shown for the sake of encounter, the need for social regard, his face met with constant exposure in daylight hours. There was a writing of ultraviolet light on his body, as with any textured being within reach of the sun's energies. Radiant light hits a body, damages skin cells, the body produces more melanin to protect skin from being further damaged; skin darkens in a slow accretion of line and color. Light sensitive, exposed for hours, the man's body held a photo-graphic trace of the sun's radiance. His face had assumed the composition of a surface imbued with effects of inscription.

"Light which makes life and the visible possible. . . . On whatever it falls light bestows a quality of firstness, rendering it pristine," says John Berger in contemplating what his cataract eyes viewed of light.[8] The innocence of light tires a receptor after pricks and waves of photonic rapture.

Light, and the history of imprinting. For good reason did William Henry Fox Talbot, the author of the first commercially published books of photographs, published in 1844–46, title his collection *The Pencil of Nature*. The twenty-four plates of the work had been obtained "by the mere action of Light upon sensitive paper," he wrote.[9] Talbot said of this new art of "photogenic drawing": "The plates of the present work are impressed by the agency of Light alone, without any aid whatever from the artist's pencil. They are the sun-pictures themselves, and not, as some persons have imagined, engravings in imitation."[10]

The agency of light: "Now light, where it exists, can exert an action, and, in certain circumstances, does exert one sufficient to cause changes in material bodies."[11]

Light affects in unperceived ways. The sun gives life. The sun destroys. The sun writes on skin. The ragged midday heat of the sun on a beach in Algiers blurred and confused a stranger's consciousness, ending in death.

> I walked slowly toward the rocks at the end of the beach and I could feel my forehead swelling up beneath the sun. The intense heat beat down on me, as if trying to force me back. And every time I felt its hot blast against my face, I clenched my teeth, tightened my fists in my pockets, strained with all my being to triumph over the sun and the dizzying fire it unleashed upon me.[12]

Do not stare into the sun or you will blind yourself. The dark solar scribbles in terribly excessive ways upon the surface of a retina and burns it to a crisp. On harsh days sunlight angles from the sidelines into eyes and disturbs their neurons.

> All I could feel was the sun clashing like cymbals against my forehead, and the knife, a burning sword hovering above me. Its red-hot blade tore through my eyelashes to piece my ache eyes. It was then that everything started to sway.[13]

So many forces and materials are at work in a life; cell-phone transmissions, allergenic pollens; the screeching of insects; industrial pathogens; electrochemical charges beyond the human, active agents, somehow inhuman, nearly imperceptible, radioactive half lives; insecticides, drug chemicals held in the vitreous fluid of an eye; the harsh, never-setting light of colonialism. Silent tremors mark the fate of a body.

Light is shimmering force. As vibrant matter, it affects. It works on lives and bodies, on the ways we sense and see.

And so I no longer hold to the theory that the man is Maghreb in identity or perceived origins. A different history of the sun has been toiling in his life.

June 10. His eyes get tired. He was there this morning, at his usual position, his hand held open; the space unfilled. He moved around a lot, shifting from pillar to pillar. He descended the steps. He shifted to the gate and walked back up the stairs, stood near the stone column. A few people gave him change in an awkward way. They did not know how to place the metal in his hands and there ensued a fumbled transfer of coins.

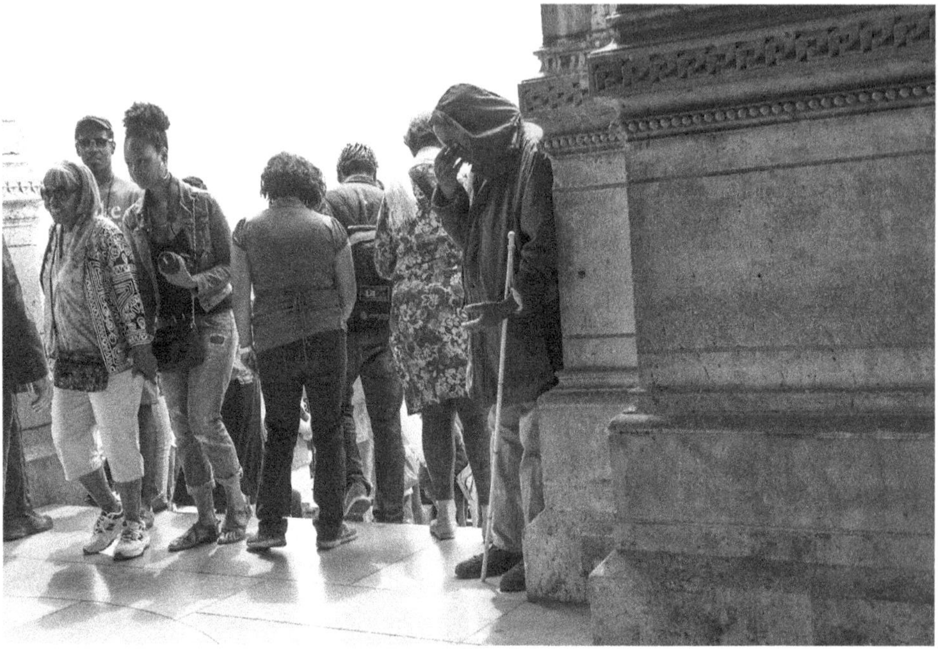

By late morning far too many people were seeking entrance into the basilica on this summer day. Tourists and pilgrims, families on a pleasant Sunday, like a squirming of fish they piled up outside, disturbing the usual flow of bodies. Space became overcrowded and the field of perception collapsed. It became exponentially more difficult for him to be perceived by those passing by. They did not see him well. A few bumped into him while by the stairs to the place. I doubt he received much money. I'm not sure he was aware of how many people were around him. I would have liked to guide him to a better area in which to stand. Eventually he moved down to the gate, where there was less of a crowd.

He is not working in a group. He's on his own.

June 10. Mechant. Cruel.

June 10. He's laughing! He's shouting. When he was down by the gate he was speaking to someone over to his left, where the sellers of trinkets had been yesterday; other salesmen stood there just then. Was anyone listening to him? A few young men were standing there, leaning over some boxes, organizing their wares. They looked toward him when he spoke but they did not engage with him, as far as I could tell. I don't think his words were directed at them.

He smiled in these moments. He stood by the steps and laughed to himself. A private joke, workplace banter.

He laughs in life. He enjoys moments of engagement in the world. There is pleasure, play, joviality, creative expression. His life is not one of pure abjection, contrary to what his image suggests and the phantasms cast upon him.

Any philosophy needs to account for laughter. Or anthropology, for that matter. Laughter trips up staid categories of language and being.

Later on, he smiled again and shook his head in amusement, as if the joke recurred in his thoughts and the world at large.

His laughter has destabilized my regard of him and his figuration in mind. He is continuously changing forms. The image of the blind man, framed by the hood of the coat, is only one design in a larger architecture of personhood. I cannot see this man.

June 11. Fascination with an unsighted man. "Why fascination?" asks Blanchot in his essay "The Essential Solitude."

> Seeing presupposes distance, decisiveness which separates, the power to stay out of contact and in contact avoid confusion. Seeing means that this separation has nevertheless become an encounter. But what happens when what you see, altogether at a distance, seems to touch you with a gripping contact, when the manner of seeing is a kind of touch, when seeing is *contact* at a distance? What happens when what is seen imposes itself upon the gaze, as if the gaze were seized, put in touch with the appearance? What happens is not an active contact, not the initiative and action which there still is in real touching. Rather, the gaze gets taken in, absorbed by an immobile movement and a depthless deep. What is given us by this contact at a distance is the image, and fascination is passion for the image.[14]

This is no ordinary seeing. The man's look touches me with a gripping sensate contact. Seeing him, or being seen by him, is a kind of touch, contact at a distance. Yet this is not an active contact, richly dialogical or assertive. It's not a cognitive, rational relation. My gaze is seized, gets taken in, it's absorbed by immobile movement. I see the image of him, fixed, unmoving, I grasp the image of his eye, his look more generally, and I am passionately fascinated by that image. One encounters the sheer force of matter and is rendered into fascination.

> What fascinates us robs us of our power to give sense. It abandons its "sensory" nature, abandons the world, draws back from the world, and draws us along.

I do not perceive the blind man. I see the image of him, and fascination with that image steals away the power to give sense to the person before me.

> Of whoever is fascinated it can be said that he doesn't perceive any real object, any real figure, for what he sees does not belong to the world of reality, but to the indeterminate milieu of fascination. . . . . This milieu of fascination, where what one sees seizes sight and renders it interminable, where the gaze coagulates into light, where light is the absolute gleam of an eye one doesn't see but which one doesn't cease to see since it is the mirror image of one's own look—this milieu is utterly attractive. Fascinating. It is light which is also the abyss, a light one sinks into, both terrifying and tantalizing.

What I see of him does not belong to actual perceptions but rather to the indeterminate zone of fascination. The gaze of him coagulates into light, a dazzling, semi-blinding light. I risk sinking into this light, tantalizing and terrifying. I risk the dissolution of perception, a collapse of subject and intersubjectivity.

> Whoever is fascinated doesn't see, properly speaking, what he sees. Rather, it touches him in an immediate proximity: it seizes and ceaselessly draws him closer, even though it leaves him absolutely at a distance. Fascination is fundamentally linked to neutral, impersonal presence, to the indeterminate They, the immense, faceless Someone. Fascination is the relation the gaze entertains—a relation which is itself neutral and impersonal—with sightless, shapeless depth, the absence one sees because it is blinding.

I do not see what I see, properly speaking. The look of this man touches me in an immediate proximity, draws me closer, though I'm still at a distance. I regard the image of him in a neutral, impersonal manner; to me he is an immense, faceless Someone, an indeterminate He. I do not know him. I gaze upon him with shapeless depth. The absence I encounter is nearly overwhelming of vision.

"Fascination is solitude's gaze," writes Blanchot. "It is the gaze of the incessant and interminable. In it blindness is vision still, vision which is no longer the possibility of seeing, but the impossibility of not seeing, the impossibility which becomes visible and perseveres—always and always—in a vision that never comes to an end: a dead gaze, a gaze become the ghost of an eternal vision."

I have acquired a dead gaze, the impossibility of seeing.

"To write is to let fascination rule language."

To write is to invoke phantasms through language. To photograph is to create phantasms that rule through images.

June 12. His constant is the coat he wears, despite the summer heat. The hood frames a vision around his face and makes his graphic appearance more singular and distinctive. The look of the hood gives a more pronounced shape to his eyes. The eyes are central to his exposure and commerce. His face looms medieval in appearance, almost biblical. In this way he "gains in forcefulness," to use Nietzsche's language.[15] In donning the hood he becomes a figure of a blind beggar. He creates an image—a phantasm of abjection within a field of perceptions.

How does one shape an image? An effective image needs to be clear and precise and singular. It needs to stand out. What does an image want? An image wants to be noticed and affect perceptions and moods in the world.

His blind eye might be faulty for seeing but it's good at affecting the vision of others. He needs to show himself as blind, uncomfortable as that might be. He provokes affects for the dispensation of coins. In calculating his appearance he has learned to be at once active and passive. He creates his abject, forlorn passivity.

"*Madames, monsieurs,*" he says while people pass nearby. These words are barely heard. Are they meant to be semi-audible? It's as if his body signals that he does not have the force to communicate. A body's passivity. *Pas de force.* The limits of his voice, as heard on the steps, parallel the perceived limits of his ability to perceive and communicate.

June 12. I have to be careful around the Roma women. I've noticed one of them noticing me. I think this woman has picked up on my interest in the activities at the basilica and she might have seen me photographing the blind man. She must have gathered that I'm not the usual kind of tourist, passing through once. My recurrence is noteworthy. After a while I stand out because I do not move on. Her eyes are smart and knowing. When I walked past her post by the doors this morning she caught my look and said, "*S'il vous plaît, monsieur.*" She is a potentially watchful third.

There is always the charged potentiality of being observed by others.

June 12. The Roma women are clearly working as a group. I saw them earlier today, taking a break to the eastern side of the basilica. They were seated on stone slabs, smoking cigarettes, quietly talking among themselves like restaurant employees taking a twenty-minute break. I wonder if they have scared off other potential beggars. They look tough, not to be tangled with.

I take these women to be Roma, though I can't be sure of that. Their appearance fits my imaginary—they wear scarves around their heads, dark hair and eyes. These women keep to themselves, stand apart from other people. French is not their first language. So often we know people through a few select images—the cut of their clothes, the sound of a voice, phantasms of a culture.

I imagine the women and their families taking shelter at night together in cardboard homes leaning against a phone booth in a Paris arrondissement. The children, sleepy-eyed, huddle close to their parents.

The women can be expressive in their emotions. Yesterday, one woman, seated at the entrance to the basilica, was shedding tears. It's unclear if the tears were real or not.

Like the other beggars here, the women are keenly aware of the geopolitics of the place. The flows of bodies have predictable pathways, circuits of movement. Those looking for handouts want to be in the line of movement and sight.

Later on, the blind man began to walk toward the doorway, using his cane to feel the way. He used this prosthesis to sweep an area by the door, to assess if the woman was there, or not. The first time he did so she was there and she got up quietly and moved away, to evade his probes. The second time he approached, his cane swinging left and right, she was not there.

The woman returned a few minutes later. A stream of people came out of the basilica and she spoke to them, "Madames, Monsieurs." He heard her voice, asking for money. He looked that way and said "Les voleurs!" in the direction of his look. *Thieves!*

"Don't give them any money," he said to the passing crowd. I doubt they heard him well.

Upset, he kept looking toward the space the woman occupied.

He approached the woman with his cane, hitting it about, left and right, like the horns of a bull. He approached where she had been sitting. She got up and evaded him. Still, she knows he is not to be taken lightly.

He yelled her way, again. "Je ne travaille pas. Je reste ici."

I cannot work. I need to stay here. You can work, you don't have to be here.

Around eleven thirty the priestly man arrived. I noticed he was carrying a small folder, with a NY Yankees insignia on it. He stood close to the blind man, reaching out, held his hand, and voiced soothing words. They were conversing, relating events, "Oui, elle est gentille." Perhaps the priestly man was giving counsel to him. I sensed an ethos of care in this, the priestly man cares for the blind man and wants to talk with him, to give company, lend a bit of humanity on this hot, crowded, lonely morning heating into afternoon. And yet I sensed something oppressive about this care. It's as though the priest is drawing the blind man into his web of comfort and counsel and supporting him with this pastoral care. This might be his mission in life, to bring people into the grace of his god.

The two of them looked over to the woman, seated at the exit. The blind man was perturbed by her presence.

I can see now why he appeared distracted the other day, when I gave him some money. He was thinking on the problem of the women who asked for alms close to where he wanted to stand.

All of this makes me think back on his cry of "Voleur!" last summer, when he was standing by the gates to the basilica. He could have been upset not because a thief had snatched coins from his hand but because someone else was asking for money in the vicinity of where he was standing, taking money out of deserving hands.

June 12. This morning I heard a high-pitched voice, a rustling of sound which cut like sacred violence into the slanting sunlight and murmur of bodies passing by the entrance to the basilica. This voice, a woman's voice, seemed to carry painful tones of suffering and the promise of a future redemption, as if the speaker was in the heights of an otherworldly prayer, a speaking in tongues, her true audience not the collective of those present but a holy spirit with whom she ecstatically wished to commune. I looked around to locate the source of these sounds. Through a mass of bodies I saw a young woman seated by the entrance. It could have been her. I doubt any of those stepping past would have spoken as such, though it's possible a soul among them was leaning toward transcendence.

The sudden sounds were a cause for tourist rupture. A chosen few must have looked her way and heard her words as a cry for help from forces divine or worldly, and walked on. The sounds shaped a sonic image that seemed to come from another time, a Byzantine church in eastern Europe, archaic rites, lit candles, trembling voice alone in a small chapel calling to a silent savior. The language is unknown. The words elude easy comprehension. Human speech is so singular, distinctive, unmistakable, undeniable, *someone is speaking, just now, hear that she is speaking*; and yet I fail to recall what the woman said, her words are lost to me, specifics of tone and affect remain vague. In speaking so, she altered her surroundings. Was her ecstatic speech sincerely heartfelt or was it a performance—or an intricate combination of the two? There is no pure truth in the human voice. Speech is embodied, partial, performative, affective, glossolaliac, wracked with desire and need. The human tongue is a labyrinthine muscle with multiple possibilities, torsions, visions, truths uttered at disparate times. Voices authentic or persuasive or an intricate combination of real and pretend—it's a blur to anyone listening or speaking. The membranes of the vocal chords are manifold and intertwined, there are true vocal folds and false vocal folds. The larynx vibrates, calls out. Such is one phantasm of a human voice.

June 13. While scrolling through plates of photographs I came upon a picture forgotten the other day. This image includes the appearance of a young woman seated by the entrance to the basilica, a girl around fifteen or sixteen. Within the photo a number of young people are walking past, possibly students on a field trip, around the girl's age. Her face can be seen amid the crowd of bodies, her hair covered in a white cloth that falls around her shoulders. She is looking down, unsmiling. Her eyes appear closed. The downward look suggests she is embarrassed to be there, begging before youths from a world parallel to her own. Perhaps her mother put her up to this. This is her young fate, to show her face and clothing, the history of her people, for the sake of a few coins.

June 13. His eye is like glass to me. His eye has a way of cutting into me, inadvertently, unknowingly.

June 14. I cannot look at his eye for long, or not at all. Nor can I be looked at by it for long. It's a lookless, penetrating, unnerving look.

I cannot sustain a relation with this eye. It's like looking at the sun, or at death. In the moment of looking there is a force field that suggests a span of absence, or physiological removal. In that moment my perceptions are disassembled, displaced. I disappear before that eye.

I am not seen well when he looks at me.

What has no words cannot be put into words. It's not like I can describe this moment of failed vision with any sort of lucidity or clarity

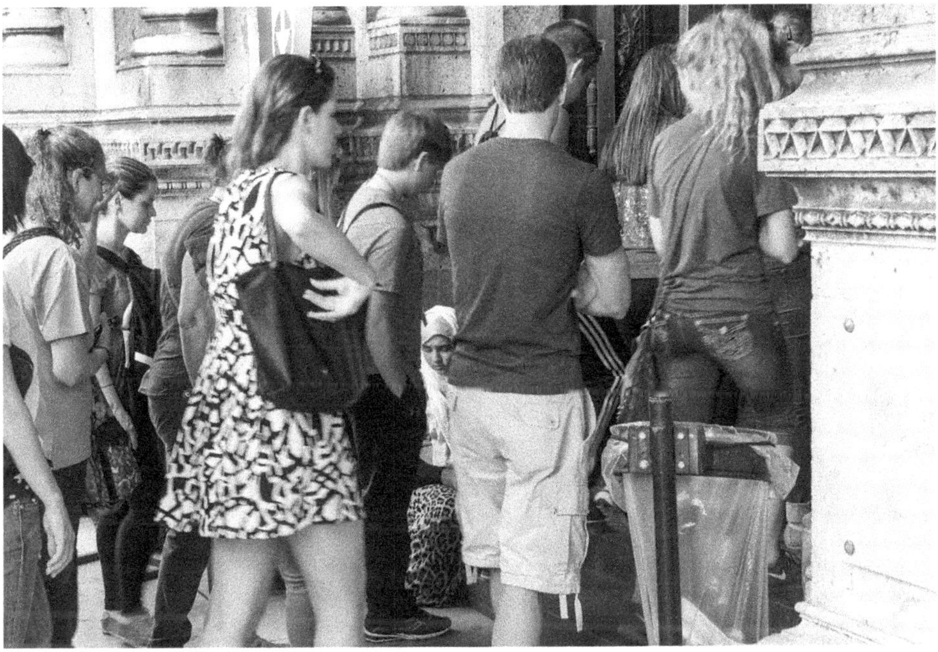

of vision. It's the opposite of defining me, or a state of seeing or nonseeing. It's a blow to my stature, stability, to structures of perception and action that give a self. When I perceive that eye, or am perceived by it, I am bereft of selfhood and agency and a sense of capability and power.

This relates in a heightened way to what I feel when someone, anyone, a stranger or a loved one, looks me in the eyes. I fall into a space of dying and dissolution. There is an intensified collapse of meaning. I cease to appear before that other I. My own eye, my "I," comes into question. There is absence in a locus of knowing. I collapse into a space of dying without any reason or language and clarity of means or nonmad vision.

Usually I soon look away from any gazes counter to my own. The catastrophe of that moment dissipates when the next arrangement of word and meaning arises. The blind man's eye perpetuates the moment of crumbled vision. The man's eye is frozen in that position of skewed intense looking. It never rests, never turns away, and one is left to stare into the blank white heat of the world.

June 14. Late last night, while trying to sleep in the studio apartment, I imagined the blind man standing outside the building where I am staying.

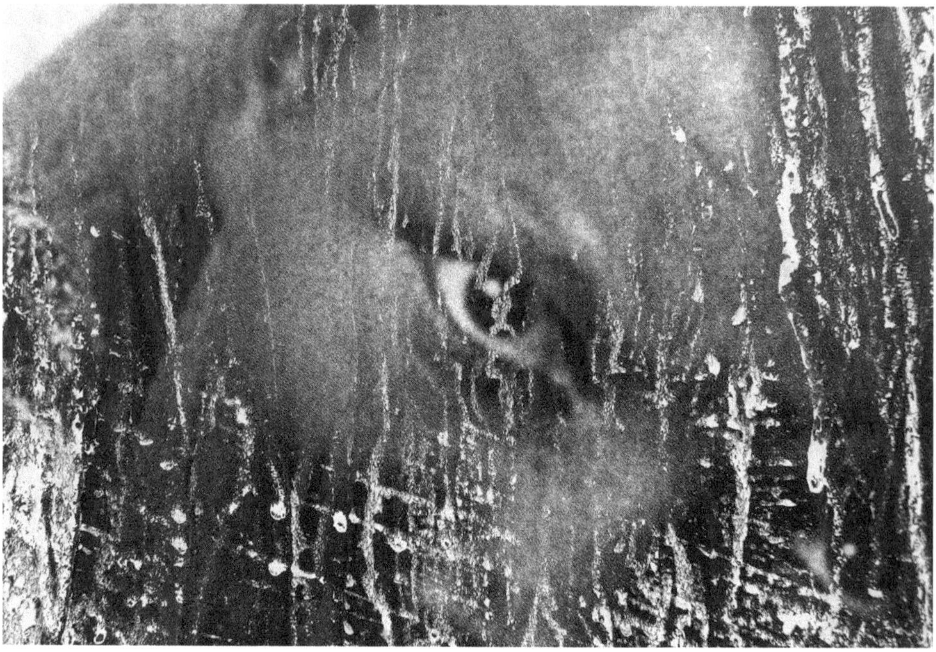

This was long after the neighborhood bars had closed. I got out of bed and walked to the window and looked outside. I saw the fused yellow glow of a street lamp and heard the lone machinery of a street cleaner sweeping an unseen road. I knew the blind man was not there. His phantom form was there, the phantasms of another. The imaginary of him was waiting, watching, looking toward the windows for signs of life within.

June 15. Last night he stood outside the building where I slept. He was standing by the intersection of streets. Throughout the night the sign of the bar across the street glowed in unblinking yellow-red neon.

June 15. His eye is in my eye. It has sliced its way into my vision. It's there, in my look, in how I see the world. His eye perceives my own.

June 16. The eye inscribes itself on me. His eye has written itself into my thoughts and the flesh of my body like the incision of a pen or the sun.

June 16. Fictions are what I see now. That eye, that man, those steps, memories of a city, this body, holding a pen, nothing stable, nothing still and true. Everything is spectral appearance changing forms and likenesses. We inhabit cathedrals of fiction built from the grounds of our lives.

June 17. Imagine always. Arachnid reverie. The spider approaches the butte one summer night from the hilly eastern slope. He decides to forgo the stairway for fear of getting his long legs entangled in the iron railings. He climbs up toward a small park and makes his way along a paved pathway, past benches and stone and overhanging trees. Ascending, he studies the movements of others. He takes his time. His spindly limbs, unused to urban details, gets ensnared in a thicket of branches. He extracts himself and looks around. He reaches the summit and pauses, licks a spiny wound. He finds a plane of space within which to spin a web. Spinnerets lash sticky silk to a corner of the nave. In the net he waits, steel pincers at the ready, eight eyes, cephalothorax alert, book lungs breathing molecules of air. In the moonlit dark he collects bits of nourishment, coating them in paralytic fluid and digestive solvent. Congealed morsels are kept for mastication and consumption. He delights on images sucked from the lives of others, crisp, keen images, ingested at his leisure.

Phanomenology

June 21. It's a vibrant Sunday evening in Montmartre and the man has assumed his post by the gated entrance to the basilica. I had seen him on Friday night as well, while we were both standing by the steps. I could have taken him for a worldly traveler or gentleman scholar carrying maps and documents of historical sites. Bearded, bespectacled, he had a professorial look to him. In another context I could have taken him for an instructor at the Sorbonne, fallen from grace. Studying the scene before the basilica, he looked exasperated, frustrated: far too many people were climbing about the mount for him to receive a fair shake at donations. There was too much Friday-night celebrating going on, the carefree crowds wanted a good time, Heinekens bought for two euros apiece and bottles of wine passed among friends, it was not in their minds to think of giving money to an abbey man seated on the steps. People weren't seeing him at all. Nervous gestures would fail to reach a perceiver's eyes and soul. He soon left.

Looking back, it occurs to me that this man and I were both scholars of such situations, reading the texts of social interactions and finding useful indications in them. He was as much an ethnographer as

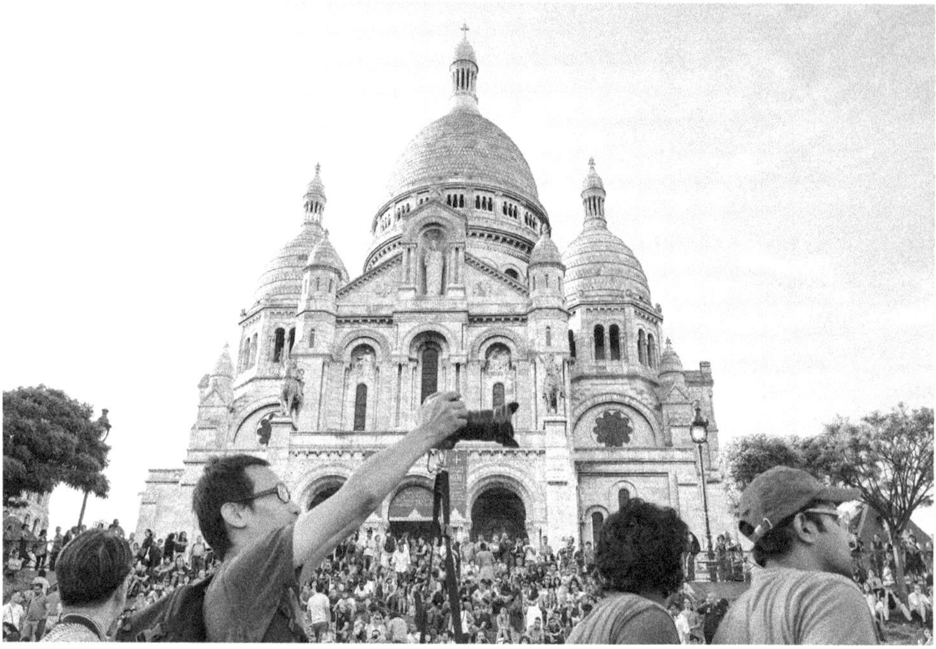

I was; eyes on the crowd, he was participating in flows of tourism while observant of it all, parsing the semiotics of passing bodies for possible gain; the culture and economics of charity, the anthropology of suffering, were his main areas of expertise. He must have sensed parallels in my own vagrant looking. "We deplore the beggars of the south," wrote Walter Benjamin in *One Way Street*, published in 1928, "forgetting that their persistence in front of our noses is as justified as a scholar's before a difficult text. No shadow of hesitation, no slightest wish or deliberation in our faces escapes their notice."[1] Poised in our respective webs, the scholar-beggar and a beggar-anthropologist were scrutinizing the city's vibrations.

Now we are back at it, on this Sunday evening of shimmering light. He is seated by the entrance of the basilica, wielding the living media of his body. With the archway above him, he sits on a cushion of soft downy support, prepared for the night's labors. He keeps quiet, consistent with the code of silence in the church. He nods his head when people pass, a token of acknowledgment of their shared human predicament in this sorry lot of a blessed world. He sports a beard, the barb salt and pepper much like my own though the perception is that his croppings

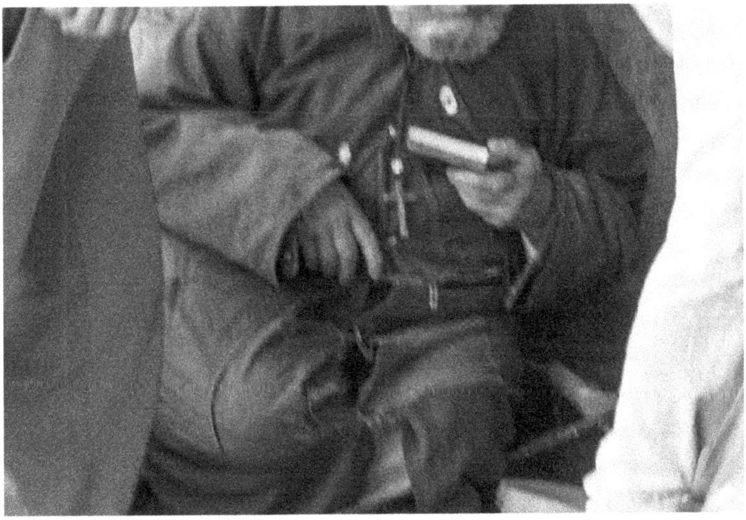

are thicker and fuller, as worn by a monk. He wears a dark-brown coat reminiscent of the clothing of abbots. Draped upon the front of the coat, suspended from a chain looped around his neck, is a small cross, made of wood or metal. Set before him on the ground is an upturned hat. The cap could hold monies tossed within but looks casual enough to pass for something left on the ground if the police question his presence and motives by the glossy marble of the church; *mais non, monsieur*, the old man is not panhandling but merely catching his breath after the long pilgrimage up the hilltop.

He wears eyeglasses with white patches lining the rims. The bandage keeps the delicate structure of the eye ware intact, at least for now. The patch-up job carries a temporality of rupture, repair, decline. A black patch of tape covers the middle bridge of the eyeglasses; perhaps they hold the frames of the two lenses together. The wrapping shows their wounded utility. He fixes the glasses while at home at night in the quiet urban thought of his preparations. He lives alone, give him that. He listens to the radio. He appreciates sitting in a room filled with sparse movements. A thousand dreams gently burn about him.

The eyeglasses appear to be weakened or broken at much the same place of the bridge that my own eyeglasses had snapped in two while I was in France last summer. From that correspondence in ruptured sight it's a quick leap into the fantastical notion that he, too, had gotten caught up in a catastrophe of vision and empathic knowing and he is now living the hard reality of his dreams. He is, in some dreams, the future embodiment of my own fearful fantasies.

My perceptions have been ascribing images onto him, cloaking his appearance in a sequence of phantasms.

The man's left hand holds a small book; a prayer book, apparently. It could be a slim edition of the New Testament or an icon from the relic of a saint. He holds the book up, making it an object to be seen, if not read, a sign of his devotion; the history of a religion is seeded into that text. He might be down on his luck but he is a good man deserving of the Lord's graces. He is hopeful for better times in this world or the next.

He regards the book attentively when people pass. His eyes are trained not so much on those passing his seated body as on the text he holds devoutly in his hand. His awareness lifts to another realm and he barely notices the mortals walking past. The book is not necessarily to be read; the image of the text radiates sacred energy.

When no one is walking toward the basilica he stops reading. He looks up and considers his surroundings. People pass and he uses his left hand to make a sign of the cross as if to give a blessing to the good souls close to the church or all of those involved under the divine grace of God.

The right arm is held stiffly by the body, close to the chest; crimped, impaired. The arm cannot be fully extended without pain to the joints and muscles of arm and shoulder. The right hand dangles from the reach of the long sleeve of his heavy brown dress. His forearm and hand look limp, ineffective, as if the flesh has not been receiving sufficient circulation of blood or neural support. His arm is a sign of misfortune, a neuromuscular disorder in need of medical care and spiritual rejuvenation. He's been hanging on since quitting the drink two years ago. The pale arm carries the imagery of impotency. He is not a full and complete man, capable of useful employment.

Nor is he a threat to anyone. The feeble utility informs passersby that he could not hurt a tourist, unarmed as he is. His weak arms diminish any imaginaries of potential violence.

The fingers are held apart, they do not come together. There is no clasping of a grip, no firm and clear control of the operations of nerve, bone, and muscle. The hand is in a state of collapse, obsolescence and slow, untimely erosion.

The index finger of his right hand twitches. It's as if this finger is tapping the key of an absent telegraph machine, tap-tap, tap, a graphic trace of nerves awry. The quivering appears involuntary, a misfortunate issue of lasting nerve injury. Or the trembling could relate to muscle spasms or dietary deficiencies or even, say medical websites, electrolyte imbalances. The twitching appears, at once, to be indeterminate, unwilled and untimed, and ordered within a pattern of nerves; an irregular fit.

The twitching draws the looks of many passing the body's vicinity. This small tremorous movement occasions slight, irregular movements within the sphere of their perceptual horizons as they prepare to step into the basilica. A rent in his body provokes a rent in perception. *Eyes pick up on movement*, any feline or infant or praying mantis knows intuitively. The perceptual motility can be enough to spark the thought of a good deed: movement stimulates the retina; an eye reckons the misfortune; a brain processes the visuals of the hardship; an arm reaches into a pocket, pulls out a coin and drops it into the palm of another. Telegraph, *télégraphe* in French, is literally "that which writes at a distance," a manual signaling device, and indeed it's as if his finger is telegraphing messages into their brains, tap-tapping a signal that inscribes the message of deformity onto retinal synapse. He is like a boxer who telegraphs his punches, though in this case he's transmitting the record of his own bruised body, knocked about in life. And here I write, telegraphing his ticks.

Some eyes pick up on the finger's patter. Others do not. The twitches have to be perceived within the right coordinates of space and time if the particles of sensation are to hook into the optics of a passing brain. If someone eyes the tremors when she is about to step into the church, then chances are she is not going have the inclination or time to reach for a coin and leave it behind. And so the best field of perception, from the seated man's vantage, is when there is a crowding by the door and people come to a halt and clumsily foot their way into the church, permitting enough time for his convulsions to reach their eyes and seed into consciousness. I can nearly detect a translucent nerve fiber streaming from his hand into the neural wiring of his patrons' souls.

Many a life form relies on twitches—zigzagging insects, bees zipping for pollination, the calisthenics of fleas, the evasive flutter of moths, darting spiders, cicada tymbal, cricket stridulation, rattlesnake spasm, trembling ecstatic. From the first quivering of carbon molecules in primordial ooze to the electric charge of neurotransmitters to the erratic tails of spermatozoa to orgasmic trembling and the contractions of birth, the throes of death, life itself is founded on twitchings and tremors. Or so sayeth a theology of twitches. Life is convulsive or it is nothing at all. The world requires twitching in order to be a world.

The twitching finger implies something at work in the flux of images. Matter vibrates. Meanings oscillate. Images quiver, in contour shape and significance, within a flux of time. Many images are nervous, twitchy. They tweak into our eyes.

Time itself is nervous. It's jittery, prone to the tensions that come from jumbled tempos and colliding perceptions. Any flow of time is strung out on nervous twitches, especially in this day and age.

Blur analysis: later on, while biding time back at the apartment, a curious observation results when I look at some still shots of the man taken the other night while he was seated at the base of the steps. In those moments it is the left hand that appears crimped, tucked into the tender wound of his body, fingers held apart unable to grasp anything solid, while the right hand holds the book in a firm and flexible manner. This arrangement makes sense, given the way he is seated on the steps and the requirements of his body just then, but it's contrary to the pose adopted on the steps two nights later. Seems true that the nervous tremors shift from the body's left and right depending on the way the body leans into the world. The body is pliant, its

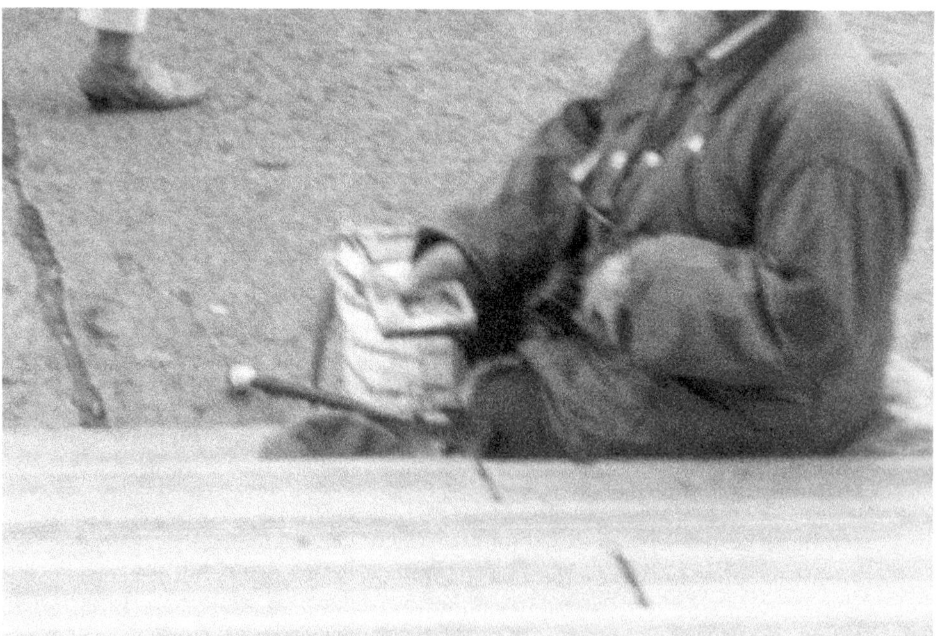

powers ever-shifting; a physiology holds wavering capacities. Nothing is stable or fixed into permanence. In its sensate becoming a body oscillates, twitches, displaces; it alters its powers, the materiality of expression, transformations of ground. The nervous system finds alternate pathways, new possibilities of sensation and perception; ghost vibrations.

At times the man stands upright. Either he is tired of sitting or he wishes to try a different pose and an alternate arrangement of image affects. When the body is upright the index finger of his right hand does not twitch. His hand holds onto a cane which supports his body, in particular the right side, which leans toward the ground. The body cannot sustain itself well without external prosthetic. The prop bears a red handle that provides physical support for his arm when he is using this aid. The cane is wrapped at the base with an off-white masking tape, the bandaged repair of an old walking stick that has seen better days. He could use new equipment, but he lacks the cash to pay for anything, just now. Perhaps if the donations are healthy enough this summer he can cash in at a medical supply shop.

While he is standing the man's head lowers perceptibly when coagulates of people pass. In bowing slightly he acknowledges these fellow beings in a show of respect and humility. Again a slight movement, not twitching this time but a tilting of the head, draws another's gaze into the fulcrum of his bandaged appearance. Imagine a man down on his luck, displaced vertebra, joints ache, diabetic veins, there but for the grace of God. Imagine boozy nights drunk on the street, an open bottle lies on the ground. Imagine a hardscrabble soul saved by the creator's interventions. Imagine all of this. Imagine yourself, imagining. There is nothing beyond the phantasms of vision.

While seated the man keeps the cane by his side, near his legs. Evident is his need for ambulatory support. He closes his eyes and draws his right hand to his chest and touches fingers to his inner heart, this act reveals a state of prayer in commune with vast and otherworldly spiritual powers; the intensity of grace washes over and affects the vibrant tenor of his heart. The body might be in bandaged repair but the soul is rich and in good standing with the Lord.

His eyes, when open, are watchful, tentative, and on edge. He looks to any passing eyes or bodies left or right with a jumpy gaze that shifts with the circumstances. There must be the risk of people, dogs, the police, priests or nuns, photojournalists, selfie sticks, the military, drunks, tramps, sociologists, coke heads, pickpockets, beggar-thieves. Threat intelligence is required. His eyes are nervous, vigilant. In that, they match my own. Each time I look his body's way I sense he looks my way. He responds to my own jerky movements. He picks up on slight turns of my head or the shaking of camera and looks to see if my optics has him in its sights. This I perceive, imagine. We relate eye to eye; twitches and countertwitches. My own wavering image must reflect in the glare of his eyeglasses. I take it that the man is aware of my awareness of his bodily actions and we have fallen into an unsteady correspondence of mutual observation and guarded concern. He might be concerned with the theft of his imagery—that I might rip images from his body. I wish to watch his mastery of the rhetoric of begging but he's not inclined to have his artful ruse detected or exposed and I am not inclined to have him learn that I am keen on him. I am learning a lot from his virtuoso use of text, cross, twitches, crutch, eyes, a telegraph body that affects passing bodies, and I do not wish to cut short this master class on the semiotics of the senses.

His craft is one of phantasmography, a writing and conveyance of phantasms within the world. "An image," W. J. T. Mitchell suggests, "may be thought of as an immaterial entity, a ghostly, phantasmatic appearance that comes to light or comes to life (which may be the same thing) in a material support."[2] The man by the entrance to the basilica inscribes a ghostly phantasm onto the material support of his body and into the world. He creates a figure of abjection within a field of perception. He labors toward an effect of sensation; a "bloc of sensation, that is, a compound of percepts and affects," to draw from Deleuze and Guattari's depiction of a work of art.[3]

How do you shape a body into an image? At the basilica the man's body becomes a font for the rhetoric of suffering. Use the body, he says, to affect the world. Make your body the means of an intersubjective, intercorporeal perception. Seed select phantasms into a body's folds to persuade eyes and minds to give it something of value. Employ fingers, hands, and clothing, a sacred text or cross, weary eyes, to show states of despondency, bliss, hunger, longing, desire; the wince of a hand is damaged history. Conjure up a body to invoke fantasies, reflections, reflex actions. What does an image want? An image wants to be noticed and affect perceptions and moods in the world. An effective image needs to be clear and precise and singular. It needs to stand out, like the twitching of a finger. Here, an assemblage of images is at work: an apparatus of sacred texts and jaunty movements angles toward concerted effects. Display the needy state of a nervous system

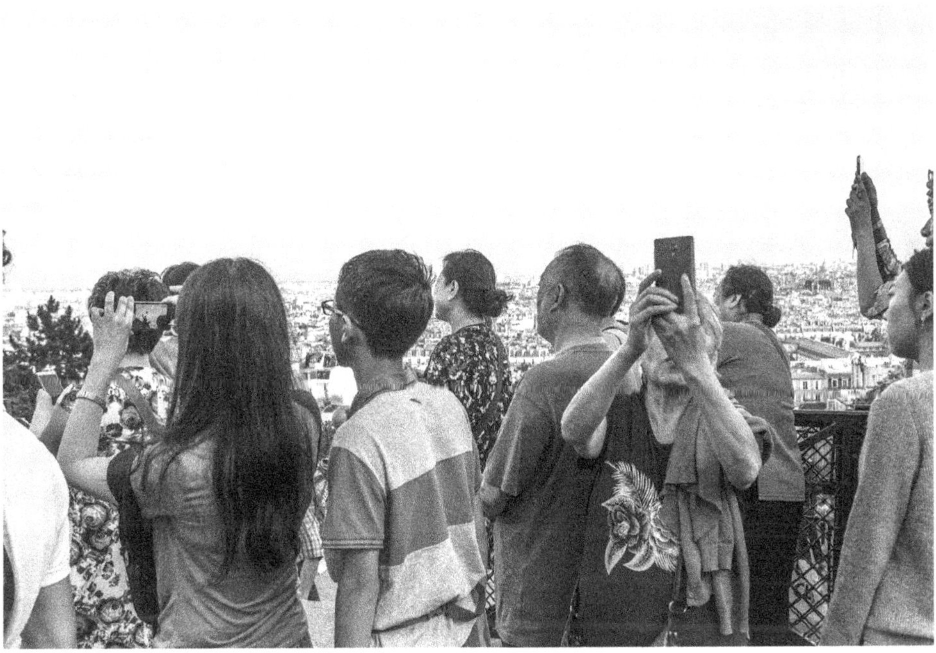

dependent on the charity of others. Contort your limbs until they tell a story. Telegraph your disability. Smile. Nod. Close your eyes. Open them.

From afar I cannot see his eyes directly but instead detect the frame of his glasses and the presumption of watchful eyes and the black patch that holds the frames together. The black patch is a third eye directed toward me, it seems. I take this black middling eye as a dense smudge of unseeing glare or antiglare, a wrapped countereye that wards off the evil eye built into the optics, any optics, of others.

It's a vibratory Sunday evening indeed, just past sunset, with energies binding and disassembling within the flow of bodies, movements, sounds, looks, twitches, tremors, and the light of photons.

Nervous knowledge, I see. My own nervous state of grace, falling upon me during this twilight hour on the mount, is to know that we are all immersed, he, you, I, all those elsewhere eyes, in interconnective tissues of perception white-hot with image and sensation. The trees rustle in the wind and a pale eye looks and a shimmer of perception trembles the body. There's so much to see, far too much for any single mind to take in. The vibrations are everywhere, you just need to look for

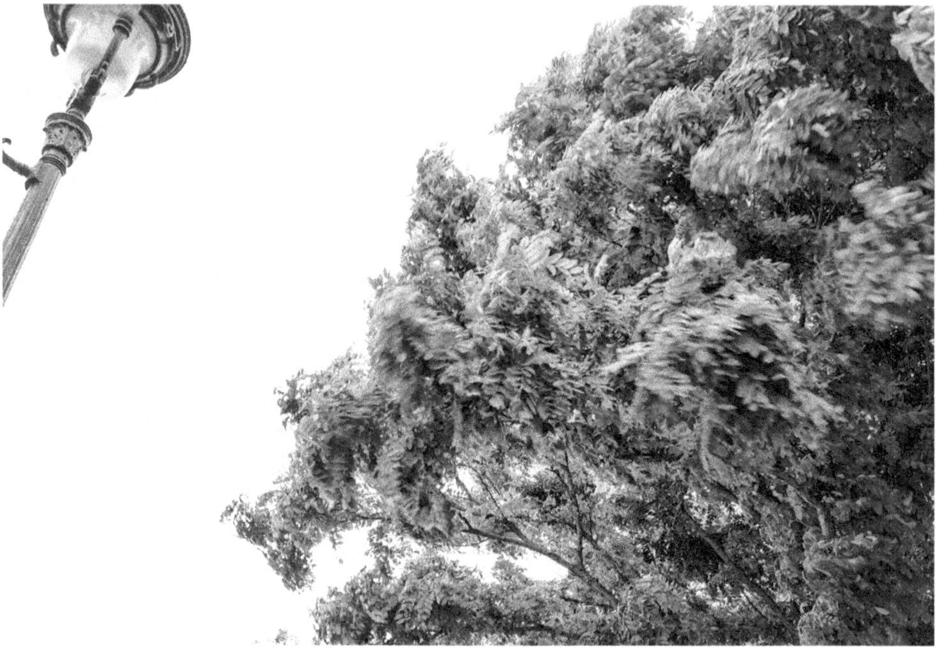

them. Once you start to see all of these particles of light bursting their electric charge through space, fastening into eyes or hearts or bodies, images telegraphed from one eye to another, jumping from insects to buildings into cameras and bodies and infinitely on from there, then it's a matter only of living in a state of nervous knowledge or a clear-eyed madness or something sharply in between.

June 22. For I am a phantom, you see. Or, at least, I now identify as such. I am a walking bundle of spectralities, a ghost haunt haunted by ghosts, rather ghostly myself, a phantom subject among other phantoms, living among phantasmic images, persons, histories. A body of phantasms, I commune with ghosts, appear diaphanous, write phantasmatically. My apparition has *the form, but not the substance, of a real thing*, to draw from an eighteenth-century definition of the word *phantom*. Then again, isn't it the case that any identity assumed or assigned by humans is phantasmic in its composition and designs, stemming, as it does, from an array of suppositions, impressions, imaginings, conjectures, utterances, languages, sensations, performances, hauntings, and virtualities that are no less, or more, than spectral? All identities, all persons and personas, are ghostly, spectral, phantasmatic in form and appearance, and so why not assume the apparitional form of a phantom?

Can a scholar converse with ghosts and phantoms? Jacques Derrida addresses this question in his 1993 book *Specters of Marx* in considering Shakespeare's *Hamlet*, in which, early on in the play, the ghost of Hamlet's father appears to those keeping watch, including Marcellus, who implores Horatio: "Thou art a Scholler, speake to it, Horatio." Derrida observes that "there has never been a scholar who really, and as a scholar, deals with ghosts. A traditional scholar does not believe in ghosts—nor in all that could be called the virtual space of spectrality. There has never been a scholar who, as such, does not believe in the sharp distinction between the real and the unreal, the actual and the unactual, the living and the non-living, being and non-being."[4] Derrida tries to show that,

> though the classical scholar did not believe in phantoms and truly would not know how to speak to them, even forbidding himself to do so, it is quite possible that Marcellus had anticipated the coming of a *scholar of the future*, a scholar who, in the future and so as to conceive of the future, would dare to speak to the phantom. A scholar who would dare to admit that he knows how to speak *to* the phantom, even claiming that this not only neither contradicts nor limits his scholarship but will in truth have conditioned it, at the price of some still-inconceivable complication that may yet prove the other one, that is, the phantom, to be correct.[5]

Derrida likely has Karl Marx most in mind here, a scholar who wrote about ghosts, from the first page of *The Communist Manifesto* on, "A Specter is haunting Europe—the specter of communism." And yet in many ways Derrida himself became a scholar of ghosts, a philosopher who spoke to the phantoms in life, wrote about them, and thought the possibility of the specter. Through his efforts in "hauntology," a logic of haunting "larger and more powerful than an ontology or a thinking of Being,"[6] he broke down sharp distinctions between the real and the unreal, actual and unactual, the living and the ghostly. In learning how to live, and live on (*sur-vivre*), the philosopher scholar took it upon himself to learn how to live with ghosts (*fantômes*, in French). He addressed himself to ghosts in order to question them and, through such engagements, reflect on the "effectivity" and "presence" of a specter, traces upon traces. And yet still through these hauntographic writings one senses a partition, a limit, in which the scholar stands on one side of a threshold and ghosts and phantoms linger on the other. Across a hazy border the scholar looks upon the ghosts, speaks with them, interprets and "reads" any number of spectral figures, other to himself.

Yet can we anticipate, further, a generation of thought and writing later, a scholar who not only speaks to phantoms, but realizes that he is himself a phantom, and that all he utters, perceives, imagines, encounters, knows, worries over, writes upon, is phantasmal, spectral in dimensions and complications? Might we encounter a phantom scholar who proceeds within the uncertain, haunted knowledge that all that he relates to, including his own spectral array in life, is phantasmal, and that all others he encounters are likewise phantoms? Can we anticipate a spectral anthropologist who undertakes fieldwork toward a phantasmography, the writing of phantasms, multispecter ethnography, rather than anything that might appear directly as ethnography?

Through errant walks in Paris I have come to realize that I am, have become, and will be soon a phantom scholar, a scholar of the phantomic, of the spectral, ghostly, a phantomist attending not so much to the phenomenal as the *phanomenal*, to coin a word. *Phanomenology*: a study not so much of phenomena per se, of the purely phenomenal (if such a study could ever be truly achieved), of that which appears, but of *phanomena*, the *phanomenal*, that which apparitions as spectralities of light, as spectral phantom, phantasms, a phanomenologically informed study of phantasmata. "And what is *phenomenology*," asked Derrida, "if not a logic of the *phainesthai* and of the *phantasma*, therefore of the phantom?"[7]

I write the word *phanomenology* intentionally, altering the more customary third letter of a word. This is no typo or orthographic error, though my computer thinks otherwise. When I type "phanomenal" or "phanomenology" at the keyboard, the word processor does not recognize that spelling as a true word, it finds, I think, the writing tainted, semantically incorrect; in a ghostly way its "spellcheck" mode—a ghost technology, if there ever was one—switches *phanomenal* to *phenomenal*, automatically, by linguistic-digital design, often without my noticing the switch at first. The *pha-* as written disappears and *phe-* appears in its place, like a ghostly revenant. I then have to manually revise the spelling, switching the letters back to *phanomenal*, toggling from "e" to "a," an errant mark to set things right. In time, through hours of this, each word, each spelling, carries a spectral trace of the other.

So much depends on a letter or two; in this case, a lengthy, apparitional history of truth and illusion. The words *phenomenon*, *phenomenology*, *phantom*, *phasma*, *phasmatidae*, and *phantasm* all relate etymologically to the Greek stem *phaiein*, "to bring to light, make appear; come to light, be seen; appear," and to the earlier Indo-European base as Sanskrit *bhā-*, "to shine, to be bright, to appear."[8] In these terms, we might say that that which appears or is seen—*phainomenon* in Greek—is apparitional, spectral, a filmy *phantasma*. It appears that, through time, through certain histories, turns of language, and philosophies of thought and appearance, there has arrived a split in appearances and what those appearances connote.

Along one line of thought and language, there occurs the "*phe-*" in phenomena and phenomenal, as relating to "fact, occurrence," as well as perception, evidence, the actual; all the way on to phenomenology, the study of phenomena as they appear to consciousness. One entry in the *Oxford English Dictionary*, dating from 1583, reads, for example: "The second [sign of the Pestilence] is often phaenomena in the ayre, specially in Autumne."

Along another genealogy of thought and language there occurs the "*pha-*" in phantom, phantasm, phantasmagoria, phasma, phantasia, as well as fantasy, fantastic, and fancy, all terms of which invoke schemes of illusion, hallucination, the apparitional, the fantastically unreal, appearances that have the look and feel of something not quite factual, evidential, or actual. From 1483: "The deuylle appered to them in guyse of a maronner in a shippe of fantasme." 1475: "Y tar but fantasms that ye speke." Milton's *Areopagitica*, 1644: "Or else it was a fantasm bred by the feaver which had then seis'd him." Emerson's *Illusions*, 1860: "'Tis all phantasm." Shakespeare's *Henry the IV, Part I*, written around 1597: "Art thou alive? Or is it phantasy that plays upon our eyesight?" And *Hamlet*, written at an uncertain date between 1599 and 1602: "Horatio saies, 'tis but our Fantasie, / And will not beleefe take hold of him." Tis only phantasy, not real phenomena, goes the thought of being in the language—or the phenomenon in question is one of phantasy, apparition, spectral illusion, not quite as real as other phenomena.

Within the histories of these two prefixes, *phe-* and *pha-*, stemming from the same Greek *phaiein*, lies a vast metaphysics of appearance resting on ideas of being and semblance, real and unreal, truth and illusion, perception and hallucination, actual substance and phantom apparition. Is the thing itself, is the *phainesthai* that "shows itself," phenomenon or phantasm? The language employed in perceiving and naming appearances in the world helps to make such distinctions. The shade of sense and image is different for each of these terms.

And yet, what if one was to disturb that asymmetry of appearances and muddy the terrain between the phenomenal and the phantastic? What if one were to insert the "pha-" into the "phe-," rendering the phenomenal the phanomenal, blurring the two together, to emphasize the idea that all so-called phenomena is, in effect, *phanomenal*—phantasmal phanomena. Images shine in a spectral, apparitional light. Any anthropology of images—or of life more vastly—needs to attend to the close imbrication, the haunting entanglement, of the phenomenal and the phantasmal. That which appears to perception, to phenomenality, is the stuff of phantasm. And so there is a need for a bastard, reimagined phenomenology, written as phanomenology.

Martin Heidegger once remarked that phenomenology is best thought of as a "possibility of thinking."[9] The same could be said for phanomenology. In seizing phanomenology as *possibility*, as a potential way of attending to the world, the possibility of phanomenal thought and imagining becomes more important than any concrete theory or philosophical system.

It's a matter of displacing one letter, inserting another in its stead, and making that différance stick. Once phanomena appear on the screen of

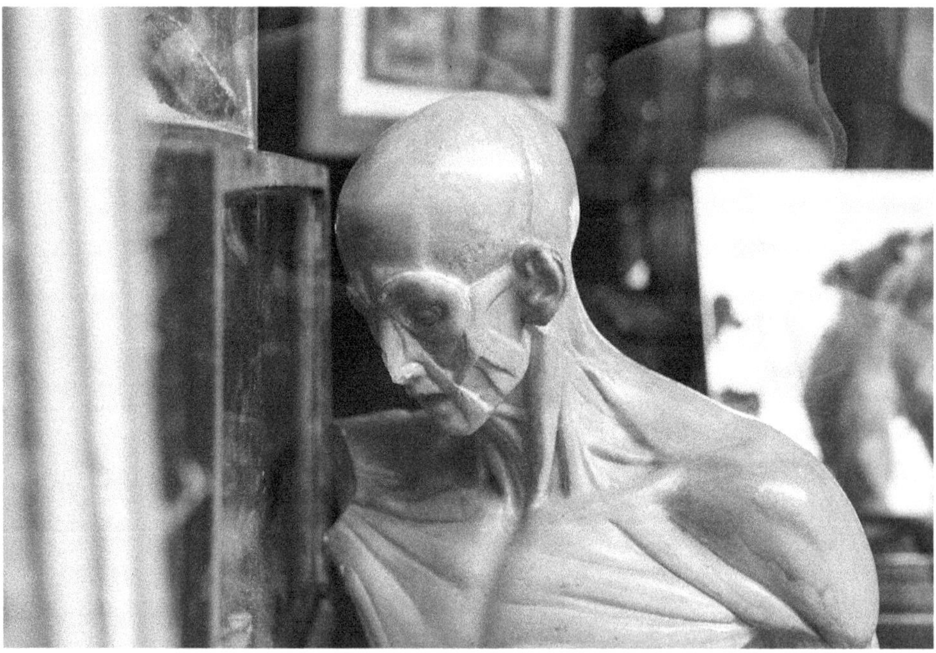

page or mind or in the world at large, once that conjuration is in effect, there is a slight but tremulous shift in the ph/ae/nomenal world. Reverberation, repetition, echo, trace, remnant, revenant, spectrality, and haunting disturb any stable phenomenality. Immediacy gives way to echo and deferral. Ontology reveals itself as hauntology. Life becomes a matter more of apparitions than appearances; more ghostly formations than ancient ideas of presence; more phantasmata than essence; more phantasma than things in themselves; more shifting spectralities than any ground of subjectivity; more force of haunting than intersubjective relations. Writing becomes a medium of spectrality. Phanomena is spectral work. Seen in this light, a phanomenology is called for. And perhaps phanomenology, as phantasmography, as multispecter ethnography, as possibility of thinking, is called for more than ever in these restless, spectral times.

Tis all phantasm.

Nous sommes tous les fantômes.

The collector of eyes

June 26. Athens. Last night I dreamed a biography of otherness. What would be involved if one inscribed and interpreted a life based entirely on scenes of alterity?

June 27. I imagined talking with him today, to consult with him about the possibility of a cornea transplant. At what point would my eye cease to be my own?

June 28. I have become a collector of eyes. These eyes look onto the world, day or night. This work began in Paris, last week. It has continued during my stay in Greece, a country in crisis. While walking about Athens I have taken to photographing eyes found in street art, graffiti, posters, photographs, protest fliers—any eyes that hold interest. Athens is coated with images and sclerotic engravings. It's as if the city is dreaming and the ragged shapes of dream emerge at night on the skin of its structures. *Brain miasma. City of sheet metal.* With no fixed direction I've taken to wandering the neighborhoods of Psiri, Gazi, Exarcheia,

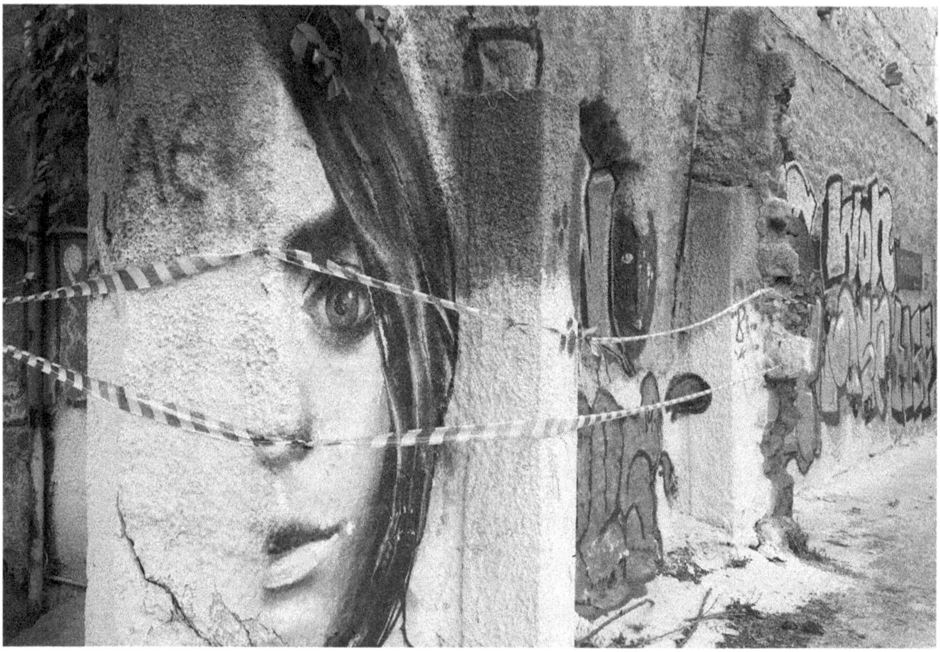

Omonia. I photograph faces, eyes, and lifelike figures, preserving them for a phantom archive.

The eyes appear on iron bridges. Rusting metro cars. Doorways. Electrical boxes. The lux marble of banks. Edge of curbstones. There is a ghostly, mysterious occupation to the faces and figures; they keep silent watch from another night. The photographic images especially, posted onto walls, phone booths, mailboxes, these spectral figures emit a haunting, looming aura, as if these people, the faces and forms conveyed, are looking out onto the world, while stuck in paralytic ether. They hover in a Hades limbo between one realm and another, forgotten by their creators.

The eyes in many images have been violated. Nameless bodies have scratched out eyes or disturbed them with the markings of a pen. Paint covers over some eyes. The materiality of reds and greens drip down a wall. The violence of color blinds and obscures. There are scruffings, blunting, additions, erasures. Some eyes carry pieces of old dried-up gum coated onto them. Other corneas have congealed juices flowing from neglected pupils. It's possible that some people do not like the look of these visions. They do not like looking at the eyes, nor do they want the eyes to see them.

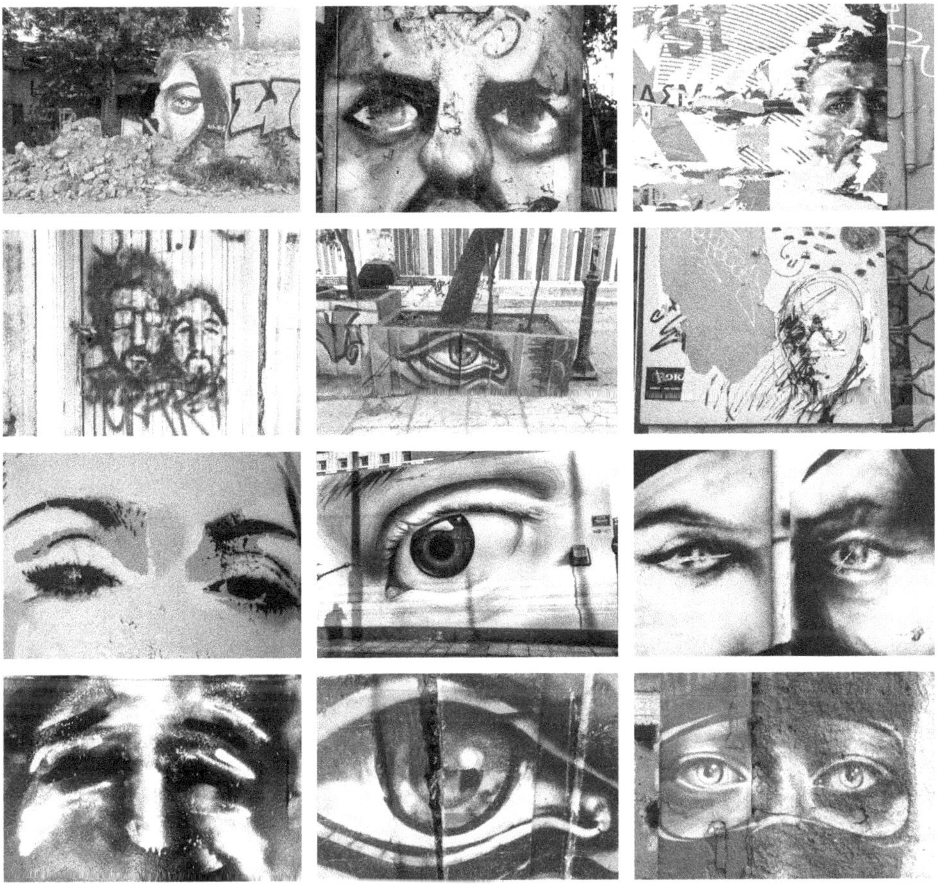

A few lines of a poem read recently:

El ojo que ves no es
ojo porque tú lo veas;
es ojo porque te ve

The eye you see is not
an eye because you see it;
It is eye because it sees you

Antonio Machado[1]

An image of an eye is an eye because it sees you. An image has eyes that look back at you.

In scratching at the eyes, this negating gesture serves as an act of counterlooking; a willful action negates the eye's unwavering vision. It's as if some want to ward off the energies invested in the eyes and neutralize their unending, nocturnal look. A combat of interests provokes a neutralization of the phantasmal force of vision.

(Centuries ago, in Greece, the invading Ottoman forces scratched out the eyes of the icons of saints in Byzantine churches.)

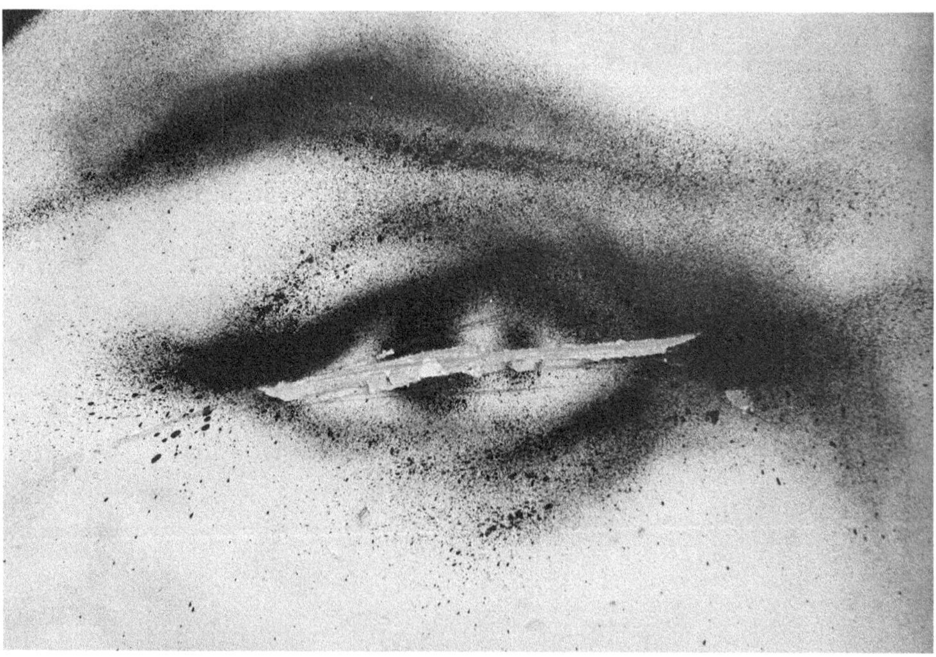

Most often, it is the eyes of women that have been scratched out. Presumably, men do not want those figures watching them with their steady, unwavering looks. And so they violate female eyes, cancel them out. Picture a man standing by a street corner, waiting for friends to arrive. Bored, impatient, nervous from the constant watching, he takes the metal of his house key and scratches into the eye of a Marilynesque figure on a green wall.

I remain fond of the eyes. I try to photograph them in good light, in the hours before sunset, such that the colors come out strong. One afternoon I stood for hours in an abandoned lot waiting for the sunlight to turn just right so that I could photograph the deep aqua tones of a pair of spray-painted eyes. While I sleep at night the eyes are watchful, forlorn, observant. The city dreams these looks.

One inscription, in Greek, on a wall in old Athens:

I saw in your eyes infinity taking shape.

June 24. His eye is a fulcrum of otherness, a white piece of matter. It is inert, neutral.

He reaches me in Greece.

June 29. The camera holds an acid that spills into the eyes of others. This afternoon I walked about the northern streets of Exarcheia, anarchist stronghold. I held the Nikon in my hands and took photographs of paintings and inscriptions written onto the sides of buildings, doorways, windows, images coating the city like the coagulate film of a feverish dream. I entertained the secret nervous knowledge of a photograph. I walked along a sidewalk and stopped to consider photographing a gravel surface splayed in coarse brick stone, dense signs of what I can't recall. I brought the camera to my eyes. Just then a young man turned the corner a few feet away. He was tall and skinny, a gaunt chest, blue jeans, worn running shoes, imagine.

This young man turned and the camera angled right at him. Immediately in seeing the camera he brought his hands to his eyes, shielding them from the monstrosity. Did he have bad memories of the effects and ravages of a camera? I stepped back onto torn ground by the paved road, to let him pass. I lowered the camera to my waist so that there was no chance of any photos of him, no lenses involved or faces seized. I thought we'd move on like passing strangers, pardon, *parakalo.* The two of us never made eye contact but the optics of the moment hurt his eyes with the camera's steely acid, or so it seemed. He stood still and taut, holding his forehead and eyes in his hands. This sudden encounter was not what he wanted or expected. He had just left his mother's place after an afternoon's meal. He can't get a job beyond a few hours at a local bar, this worries him and his family in this summer of crisis, the banks are closed, capital controls, sixty euros a day, lines form at the automated tellers, pensioners worried for their futures, the bright and able speak of a lost generation. Businesses cannot pay the bills or place new orders. There's talk of dropping out of the Eurozone and returning to the drachma. The strain is palpable. Catastrophe seems imminent, the collapse of an entire country, the end of the origins of Europe, a movement toward ruin. He had just visited his ailing father. He can't be like his brother, who is critical of him. He won't see the psychiatrist until next Thursday. It's the last thing he needs right now, this optical collision, a camera bruising light into his retina.

A few blocks away, down east a mile or two, military trucks stand watch by Syntagma Square, holding bands of soldiers on alert for any whiff of protest. Their hard plastic shields lie ready outside the truck. The soldiers can be seen having a quick lunch inside the black vehicle. They carry clubs that can crack a skull. There's the threat of tear gas, stun guns, real guns. Red cameras, video surveillance. We dream of transparent, high-impact polycarbonate.

I was only photographing graphite. It's not the picture itself but the threat and force of the photographic process. The chromatics is a shock to the system, especially when that vital matter points straight and the whirr of the lens locks in. The man sensed that piercing wound of its sharp edge cutting into eyes. He stood stunned by the camera's intentions and afterimages. A camera lingers for hours. There's the risk of optical trauma. I couldn't do much but look or walk away. Cross the street. Lessen the intensity. I turned and saw he was still there, in a posture of grief. His hands had become a bandage or solvent for the wound in his eyes. I would have liked to care for him, soothe his eyes, but there was no possibility for that.

In my notes I wrote that he walked away soon after. He could be there still, for all I know. It's a bad memory, blind light, metallic rupture.

Seeded into the harsh optics of that moment is the violence of negative encounter, circa 2015. Spit on the sidewalk. Fuck you. The flash of metal. Hands to an eye.

June 30. The acid is not just in cameras. It's there in certain looks. A toxicity leaks out of an eye during a cold, lingering stare. It's there in a look of

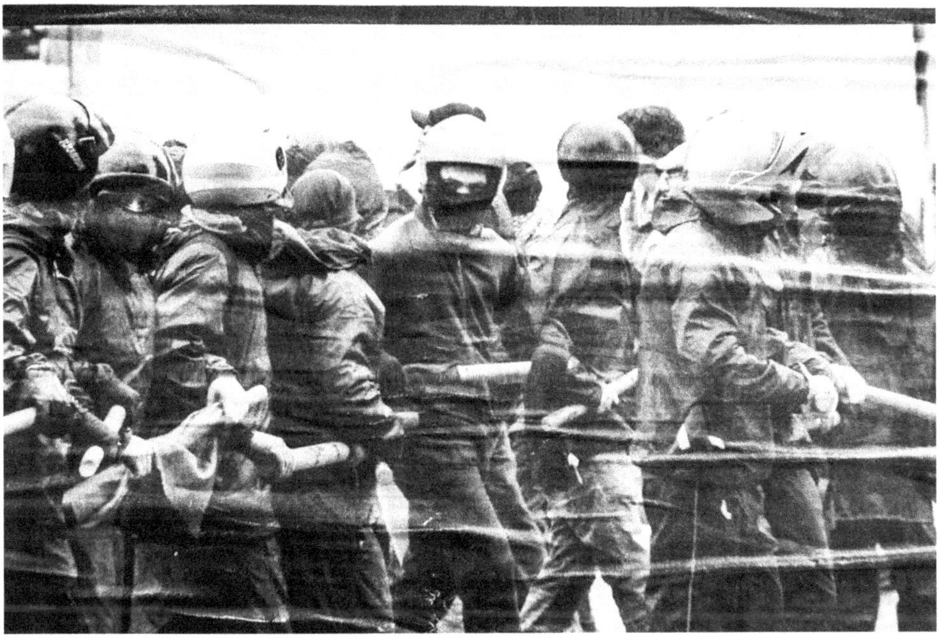

ravenous desire. The eye catches another eye and the pupil slices into the cornea. The women in the city know this. They look straight ahead, aware of the men about them, those many roaming eyes. There are wolf eyes and the eyes of doves, passion eyes. Widowed eyes. Lost eyes. The silent stare of a surveillance camera is noxious. Virulent watchful waiting seeps into thoughts and bodies. There's acid in the harsh words that people write. It drips from computer screens. Noxious acids slip from the mouth, you can taste the stuff in cruel words. They make fun of the old man, imitate his slurred speech. There are acids leaking everywhere. The steely glean of the camera accentuates the points of contact. Turn a lens toward someone and watch the corrosive effects.

Images cut at perceptions, thin as a knife. To see is terrifying, and to stop seeing tears us apart.

July 1. I spent some time at a café today, seated by an open window that looked onto a square. Others were there as well, worried about the economic crisis engulfing the country. A young man approached and stood in front of the window. He held out his hand toward me, assertive and unashamed. I thought this rude of him and ignored his gestures.

The man pushed his hand further through the window closer to us. Only then did I realize that his arm was cut off at the shoulder. He had one good arm. He held the wounded arm out for me to see. I did not like this intrusion, or the man's implied demand that I give him some money. I caught his eye and shook my head no. He looked at me in disgust, disappointed in my lack of charity. I turned my eyes to the book I was reading. He stood there for a few seconds, and then walked on. I imagined him shaking his head, shirking us off.

Late that afternoon, while walking away from the square, I passed by the man. He was seated on the side of the walkway, close to the street, a few coins tossed into a piece of paper. I reached into my pockets and found some coins to give him. He said thank you in Greece. I responded in kind. *Efcharistó. Efcharistó.*

I'm not sure he remembered me from before, nor the futility of our interaction.

He needs to show his arm.

July 3. Yesterday, while leaving the square, I passed by a young man, apparently blind. His eyes looked askew, upward, as if toward the heavens.

I am a monster of eyeful vision.

July 5. In walking about the neighborhoods of Athens I have come to notice shiny metallic compact disks dangling on strings tied to the reach of canopies suspended above balconies nested into the apartment buildings lining the streets. Tied to precarious threads, the diskettes move and shimmy with any slight breeze or gust of wind, they twist and turn, twist again, loop back along the curl of their strings, whorl anew, reflecting sudden bursts of light on the surfaces of walls, windows, metal posts, tables, chairs. The light's brilliance radiates from nowhere, hitting against stable forms within the space of the city. On the sunniest of days a staccato light shifts direction sparking spectral intensities that provoke curving, churning light, slants and prisms tossed about in sporadic, unpredictable motions that match the furious play of the world. Slivers of light enter one's eye; if the angle is right they hit the retina. Yesterday afternoon I sat at a forgotten café and watched as a single disk tied to a string pirouetted above a balcony three stories above an alleyway, shooting manias of light upon Mediterranean surfaces. I reached for the camera and tried to seize this light through the lens; I wanted photons to hurt the digital facade. We seek intensities of bright. Blinding white cancels out other stimuli. Life by light, death by light. I wasn't sure what purpose these plastic metals served, if the hanging disks were decorative or the flashing displays were visually pleasing to those living in the buildings. I've since learned that the disks are used to keep birds away from flowers and vegetables growing in small balcony gardens. What do the birds perceive of frenzied light? Do they sense the threat appearance of a predator creature, with furious optics announcing the descent of furled wings and murderous talons? Or do they know the multiplicity of lights to be the trace of other birds fluttering about? Do the cataracts of light throw off the coordination of sparrows in ascent, disturbing their landing on soft ground? In my own nervous flight of mind I take the compact disks to be watchful, photonic eyes, warding off onslaughts with their physics of shimmering light.

July 6. In many homes in Athens, often by the entrances, there are icons that ward off *matiasma*, the evil eye, a force born of feelings of envy and jealousy. A harmful miasma of the eye can afflict the well-being of others, and so families take measures to deter the visual onslaughts from harming anyone within the household.

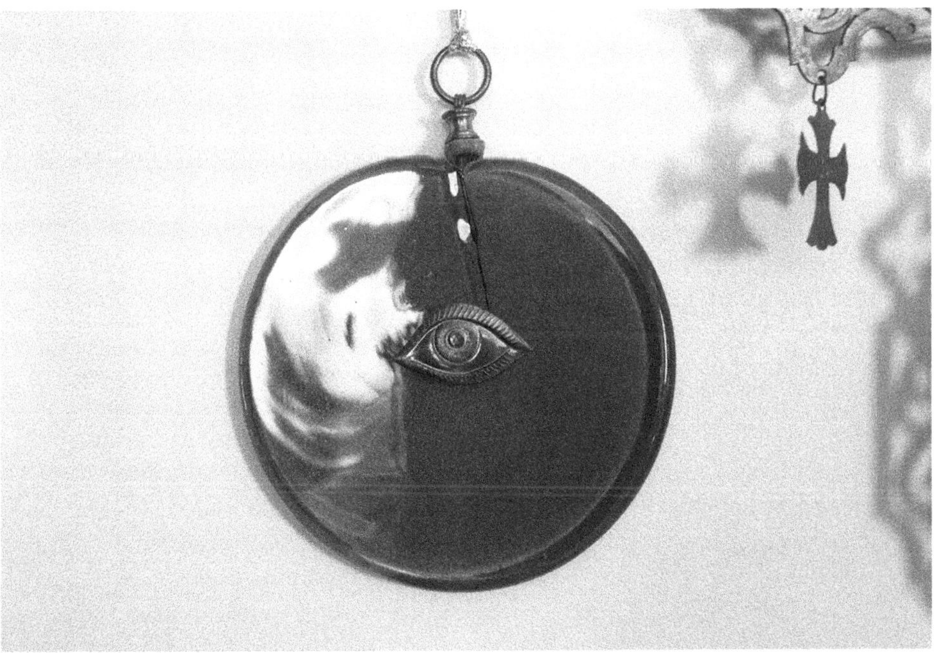

July 19. How long does it take to *process* a photograph? We tend to think it's a matter of a couple of hours in the darkroom or a few minutes on a computer or tablet. Adjust the white balance, sharpen the details, bring out the contrast, and—in this age of Instagram—apply a few nifty filters, and presto, there's a new image to be perceived in a world dense with images. But to truly see and process a photograph can take days, or weeks or months even, years, to know it well and to grasp what is involved in the force of its appearance. Even then, interpretations shift and waver.

I have been thinking hard on the photograph taken at the Basilica of Sacré-Coeur on that October day for a good duration now, months of uncertain looking, tracing the implications. In writing on the margins of the image I've tried to figure out the actors, study the psychology of need and desire, and map lines of perception and refraction. I've contemplated the optics of a self. While I have a keener grasp of the photograph's elements, its backdrop and offstage motives and actors, I am no closer to knowing for sure what is involved in the apparition. That watchful man there, in the center. Those two men nearby, sunglasses and camera. The passing child. The woman ascending the stairs—I can't fathom them.

Still, perhaps there's value in tracing out the history of photographic images within a life or two, or in life more vastly, through the course of days or months, years even. It's worth remarking how images work in or on a mind; how they appear and transfer through different media and technologies of perception; how they take on different formations and apparitions in life; how they claw their way into a body or enter into the transitional space of dreams, fantasy, and imagination; how they can tear a subject from itself, transforming the grounds of perception and consciousness.

Images are not static, timeless icons of abstract meaning to be received cognitively by a rational brain. They work, shift and alter, and disturb, within materiality and imaginary life, through uneven streams of time. A pragmatic, temporal, affective, visceral approach to the phantasm of images is worth the time for it.

July 20. What odd fieldwork I've been involved in, if you can call it that. An anthropologist who conducts ethnographic research usually does so in a particular "field site," such as a village, a city neighborhood, a classroom or hospital, or, these days, a forest or a physics laboratory. With my travels, the field has been dispersed into numerous sites of engagement and perception—the steps of a basilica, a hotel room, a train compartment, a city square, digital imaging, photographic processing, conversations with friends, or strangers, dreams and daydreams, delirious looking, tangents of phantasy and imagination—in which particular crystallizations of thought and image have been the main phanomena considered. The many uneven observations are multisited and multisighted; they're cued to singular intensities; perceptions have shifted in time, along with any understandings involved; they might build, or not, to certain perspectives in life. It's a play of imagining and perceiving where the borders between perception and imagination are altogether blurred and unfixed.

All along, I've been tending to the wound of an encounter.

July 20. And so I might have got it wrong before, when I wrote that a photograph tears the subject from itself. Perhaps it's not in the nature of photographs to do this, to wrench the self from a stable formation of perceiving and knowing, so much as this results from a particular way of engaging with photographs—or with anything else in life: the constant engagement with an image or two; an obsessive reflection on specific moments in time; the incessant digging into motives and potentialities; long stretches of solitary imagining; the delirium of looking and relooking; reflections on meeting a man who is blind, or half-blind. It's not the image, necessarily. It's the encounter that wrenches the subject from itself.

July 21. I'll be heading home tomorrow on a direct flight to New York. I had given thought to stopping in Paris on the way back. One private desire I had was to use the video mode of the Nikon to film the blind man and the other participants of the basilica while they went about their strenuous efforts—the beggar-scholar, the Roma women, the water sellers, the priest, the police, the platoons of military soldiers. I wanted to see if the resulting stream of images would enable a different optics and thus tell a different story of action and perception. I would kneel by the steps and hold the camera discrete and steady and follow the movement of bodies with live view, progressive scan, subject tracking AF. And then, hours later, with the use of computer technology, I could slow matter down to a still pause and look at sixty frames per second. With an editing program I could select single frames from the movie files and save them as discrete files. In no time I'd have a compendium of sequential images; slight movements of a hand, a look or gesture; ethnographic data, tracking subjects.

With me is a perpetual desire for more perceptions; second and third looks. I wish to look again, to have the chance for another, later look; and then look at the first look, to see anew. One needs eyes on the eyes to see how they look. One needs eyes on top of eyes trying to be the one who looks. I wish to see the means and force of vision.

And yet the film images would remain elusive particles. They would escape the scrutiny of any look and knowing. There would always be something unsettling at the edges of the pixels that would tear at perceptions and unsettle the grounds of knowledge.

July 25.

Dear R.

We met during the ethnographic writing course in Amsterdam [. . .].

I am e-mailing to ask how your time in Paris has been, if you have seen the man at Sacré-Coeur? Have you spoken to him, observed him, found out where he lives, if he has a family? Was he wearing the same clothes, did he see you? Interesting how this project on imagination, at a certain point after sharing it and throwing it into the world, is no longer a private/individual endeavor but a social one, as it also triggers and stays in the imaginations of those who have heard you speak about him. Also, why do we have these questions about this particular figure, what does he trigger that others, the man at the bakery or the bus driver do not? Just some thoughts I had, while having to write but finding my thoughts wondering.

I hope you are enjoying the summer, kind regards,

N.

July 31. "Let me look into a human eye; it is better than to gaze into sea or sky; better than to gaze upon God."

Herman Melville, *Moby Dick*

August 6. Massachusetts. Disturbance to a lifeworld, altered optics, the vague vitreous sense of which emerged slowly to sight and awareness yesterday while I was going about a sweltering summer Friday in the western Massachusetts towns where I grew up, where family lives still. In the afternoon I drove to Northampton to meet with S. in a coffee shop, our conversation leading to talk about ethnographic filmmaking and new technologies of virtual reality. Later on, walking along Bridge Street to my car parked along a grassy curb close to the Connecticut

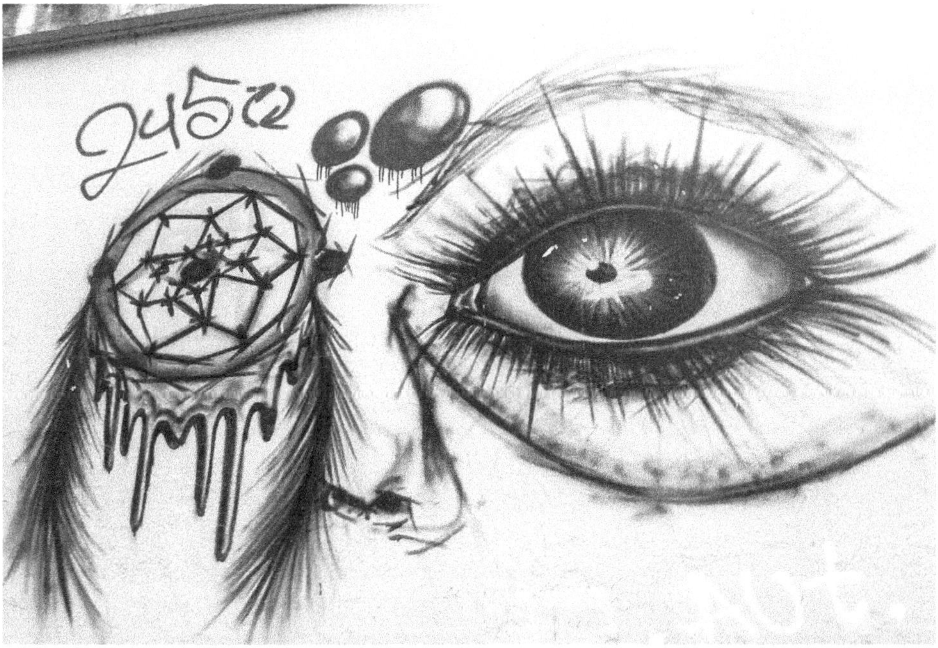

River, I looked into the blue August sky and saw a multitude of tiny dots and circles, as if a constellated force had exploded there, leaving dim, semi-translucent remnants in the ether lens of a dirty sky. The grainy particles shifted with the look of my eye, which meant my own optics appeared disturbed, much as the surface of a camera lens can pick up small marks marring the clarity of its prism or any resulting photographs. I did not give much thought to the distortions just then, figuring the heat and humidity might be causing perceptual aberrations. The marks receded from consciousness as I went about the rest of the day, dinner and cable movies at my mother's place in South Hadley, a body at rest on a sofa sensing only dimly something off with its vision. The screen looked different. That night, while lying in the windowless basement room where I spent my adolescence, I looked up at the white paneled ceiling and saw a number of small "floaters" within the vision of my right eye. They weren't there the night before. They loomed like tiny strands of gunk, insect filaments thrown into the mucus of that eye. Beyond that floated a galaxy of minuscule particles, a big bang explosion of bios matter. Something new and strange to contend with in a changing life.

In the morning I woke to further changes. Overnight some of the floaters had shifted, merged together, as if force and gravity in a prone and sleeping eyeball had brought the strands together into a tangled focal point. To the upper right I saw a blurred dark squashed figure which darted about whenever the pupil shifted its look and focus. Perhaps that knotted constellation would break apart with the movements of day, I thought. It looked obliquely like a squished bug, tangle of knotted hair, or broken spider threads, though I could never see it clearly.

By afternoon I had grown more concerned with the problem, the dark threads especially. Research online suggested that the retina might be at risk of tearing and so I decided to seek medical care. The best and only option on a Saturday afternoon was to go to the emergency room at Holyoke Hospital, a venerable institution (place of birth and my siblings' births, where my mother worked for years as a registered nurse) in the next town over. I drove along familiar roads, crossing the river span of a bridge into Holyoke, city of my grandparents, of my mother's childhood, of my father's work as a chemist at Telegraph Paper, where he devised patents for paper sheets and film coatings, the canal-side factories and paper mills near the river, abandoned long ago. The hospital brought sliding doors, glass windows, insurance card, intake nurses. *I think something might have happened to my right eye. I'm seeing a lot of floaters, and a tangled mass to the side of that eye.* They placed a bracelet on my arm and sent me through the security checkpoint. I found the way to a waiting room where a man with a bruised and swollen foot also waited; he hadn't been sleeping at night. The Red Sox game played on the television bolted into the wall, Big Papi at the plate. They moved me to a small room with curtains and white paper sheets on the examination bed. Seated on another bed, behind a cloth curtain, was an asthmatic boy with his mother, who worried that the boy's crosstown visit with his father had brought on the poor breathing. A nurse came to check my vitals. Pulse, normal. Blood pressure, high. The eye test worked out alright, 20–20 with the eyeglasses on. A doctor rushed for time stepped into the room.

"Is there any part of your vision that is blacked out?" he asked.

"No, not at all."

He peered with an ophthalmoscope into the eye and looked about in bright light. He asked what large floaters I saw. He took a ballpoint pen and drew an amoeba-like shape on the white sheet of the bedding.

"Does it look like this?" he asked.

"No, not really."

He looked into the depths of the eye. He drew a patch of lines.

"Is it something like this? Does it look like a bundle of threads?"

"Yes. It kind of looks like that."

Seeing clearly what I saw only vaguely, he micro-eyed the tangled biology and gave image to the disturbance in the eye.

"Are you seeing any flashing lights?"

"No, nothing like that. Just the floaters, large and small."

"Did you strain yourself in any way lately?"

"No. Not that I can think of."

He looked further, and then turned off the light.

"Ok, you have what's called a posterior vitreous detachment. The vitreous in the eye has detached from the retina."

"Oh. Ok."

"It's usually nothing too serious. It often happens to people over the age of fifty. The retina is in good shape. It's a good sign that you're not seeing any flashing lights, because that could mean that the retina is getting torn or detached."

"I see."

The doctor said there wasn't much that could be done in terms of immediate medical treatment. He advised me to see an ophthalmologist once I returned home in New York. "If you start seeing flashing lights,"

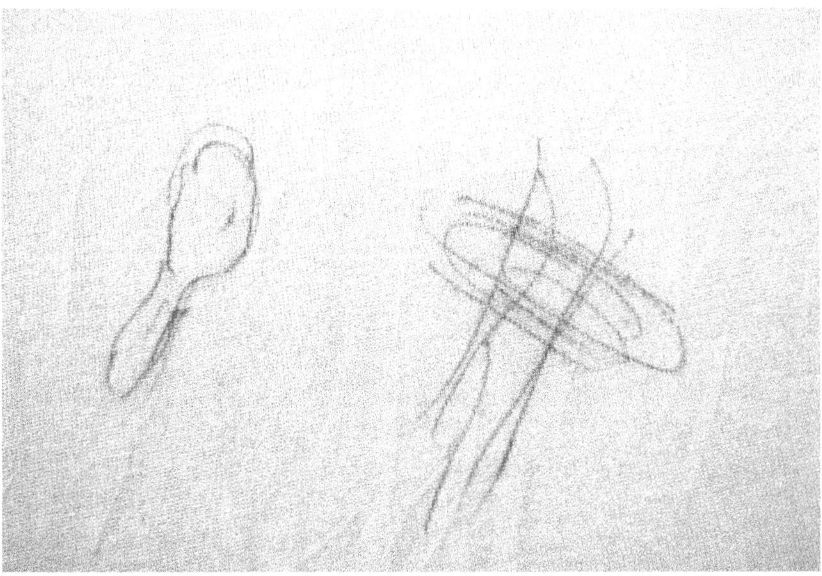

he added, "or you're missing part of your vision, you should immediately seek medical care."

As I write these words the marks coat my eye. I tend not to notice the galaxy of small speckled floaters all that much unless I look into the sky or a bright light. But the squished mar is there like the remnants of a flattened spider. This perceptual inconstant moves about when I'm reading or writing—I notice it just now, going back and forth, hovering about the page and screen like wayward diacritical marks. There's a fly buzzing back and forth within my eyesight, a fly in late summer, energies nearly depleted.

I can never see this sensate knot clearly, it's always to the side of vision, fuzzy and unclear. When I look at written words the tangled mar is to the upper right, around two o'clock. To the far right of vision is the curvature of something congealed, elsewhere. This could be the limits of the vitreous, dislodged and floating. The periphery looms like a tainted, distorting intraocular lens placed over a onetime clarity of vision. A knot, a fold or wrinkle, twisting against the pure optics, someone else's cornea has been layered upon my own.

August 7. There is an animal presence in this. There's the trace of a creature particle within the light and consciousness of natural vision; something other, alter; the squashed, congealed image of another being, distorting vision; a force alter to the biology to which I was born. (As if vision was ever natural; as if eyesight was never always a complex assemblage of biology, neurology, technology, cultural shaping, and the politics of seeing.) A monstrous alterity, and yet I know this spindly arrivant stems from my own changing biology, which now appears monstrous to me.

At any moment particles of the body can break off, become other; disturbances to the self, alien cells. The biological other stems from alterities, mutations, fractures, debris. I am fragmenting in a body that does not belong to me. For all the talk about alterity and otherness, the other is within us.

August 8. Learn the languages of the body, its biology, corpus, genealogies, its phantasma textures. Learn the poetics of its ontology.

Retina. From post-classical Latin retina, from, classical Latin rēte net + -īna; so called on account of its finely fibrillar texture resembling a net. See *rete*, n., a "network or plexus of vessels, nerves, tubules, fibers, or strands of tissue." Some experts take the retina as part of the brain, a neural outpost of sensory uptake. The word is also used figuratively to denote something that retains an image or sentiment; "The image of the future is the last picture which is effaced from the retina of the mind."[2]

Vitreous. From Latin vitreus of glass, glassy, bright, etc., < vitrum glass. Of or belonging to, consisting or composed of, glass; of the nature of glass; glassy. *Vitreous humour* (or body), the transparent gelatinous substance occupying the posterior and larger part of the eyeball. Composed mostly of water and collagen; has a stiff, jelly-like consistency. From R. Boyle, 1663: "We have sometimes . . . speedily frozen Eyes, and thereby have turn'd the Vitreous humor into very numerous and Diaphanous Films."[3]

A posterior vitreous detachment (PVD) is a condition of the eye in which the vitreous membrane separates from the retina. It refers to the separation of the posterior hyaloid membrane from the retina anywhere posterior to the vitreous base (a 3–4 mm wide attachment to the ora serrata).[4] Protein parts of the vitreous detach from the back part of eye and float in the vitreous humor.

Definitions of *floater*, online: "An object in the field of vision that originates in the vitreous body." "A deposit of material in the vitreous humor of the eye, usually consisting of aggregations of cells or proteins that have detached from the retina, perceived as a spot or thread in the visual field." "Any of the protenaceous aggregates in the vitreous humor of the eye, which correspond to degenerative debris." Also, in American slang, a "floater" is "a dead body found floating in water."[5]

The medical term for eye floater is *muscae volitantes*, Latin for "hovering flies." Protenaceous flies that drift in a glassy eye. Dead bodies float in liquid gel.

So much of what we take for our bodies is imagined. This body is a mass of phantasms, fears, longings, imaginings; chimerical spaces and cavities; archives of pleasure and pain; thin tissues of film layered upon another. That body has been troubled by the images it has come upon and anxieties and fantasies emergent from those encounters.

Books have been written on the so-called "ocularcentrism" implicit in many European philosophies, in which light and vision are key modalities and metaphors for knowledge and luminous truth. The way I see it, any pretense to an ocularcentric philosophy of truth and transcendent knowledge falls apart once a body becomes vulnerable to collapse, eyes grow old and distrustful, and vision fragments into a failing organ of limited sight.[6]

August 11. New York. When I met with the optometrist yesterday he confirmed the diagnosis at the emergency room: posterior vitreous detachment. He dilated the right eye and considered the net closely. The retina looks good and healthy, he said, undisturbed by the gel's severance from the back of the eye cavity.

"Are you seeing any flashing lights?" he asked.

"No, not at all."

"Ok, we'll have to keep a close eye on the retina."

He pictured the vitreous up close and showed me the filmed result: a glossy chemical sheet reflected a vast cellular expanse, thin veiny rivers crossing the curving surface of an orange red planet strangely celestial within the orbit of the skull. The inner humor of the eye looked so different from how I saw with that eye. It was like peering onto a distant universe.

"There's a slight twisting fold here," he said in pointing to a crease in the curvature. "It's like a pucker on the surface of the vitreous. I'll let the ophthalmologist know about it."

I couldn't see anything special there. He wrote out a referral note.

"And now you'll be going to a retina specialist to have a detailed examination of your eyes."

With the eye dilated the world took on uncommon luminance; blurred and radiant misty sunlight danced photonically about streets, automobile chrome, shiny windshields, summer sheen in green trees, the dazzling windows of suburban buildings. I wore large sunglasses and withdrew for hours into a darkened room.

August 12. Mydriasis at 2:00 P.M., through the antimuscarinic effects of tropicamide, in combination with p-hydroxyamphetamine: the dilation took place at the office of Dr. M., an ophthalmologist at Retina Consultations in Yonkers, in preparation for the eye exam. He placed a magnifying lens upon the lens of the eye and peered into the fine fibers of vitreous and retina. He found that almost all of the jelly had detached. The retina looked good and intact.

No flashing lights. No dark curtain moving across my vision. No macular hole, no retinal tear or detachment. No threat so far to vision itself. But always the risk of real damage.

Understandably, the eye specialists are less concerned about the floaters in the eye than the health of the retina and its associated optics. The floating flies are epiphenomenal, as it were, but disruptive to my thoughts and vision and a body's perceptions in time. I'm getting more used to the distraction in the visual field. It's still there, especially when I'm reading or writing, a dent in vision. I have come to think of the knotted shadows as a squished spider caught in the gel of eye. A companion species, phantasmally so.

I told the doctor I was planning to go to Paris next week. He said it would be alright to travel.

Usually the proteins break up after a while and fade away, he said.

While preparing for the examination, with pupils chemically expanding, I sat in the waiting room, mostly occupied by elderly patients, eye troubles apparently being the province of the aged; cataracts, glaucoma, macular degeneration. One elderly woman sat in a wheelchair, close to a woman who looked to be her caretaker. The older woman appeared confused and unsure of where she was.

"Why am I here?" the woman asked.

"To have your eyes examined," said her companion. She turned the pages of a magazine.

The woman looked distressed.

"What did I do wrong?!"

"You haven't done anything wrong."

Later, when I came out of the doctor's office and sat at the registration desk, I wore dark sunglasses to shield the photophobic eyes from the dazzling light. From across the room the woman looked at this strange man and the sinister shade of his eyes. Her face took on increasing emotion.

"I don't know why I am here," she cried.

With eyes dilating, the light of the world—the fluorescence of tungsten lamps, the aqua glow of a fish tank, dazzling sunlight—gained greater radiance with each passing moment, as if luminosity was in the molecular structure of life. I thought of the ancient Greeks and their philosophies of immanent light, of the Sanskrit *bha* in *phaiein*, in *pho-* and photon, "to shine, to be bright, to appear." I thought of the suffering of light, sufficient onto itself. I never knew there was so much light in the world. What do other species perceive of solar radiation?

August 13. It's frustrating and despairing to think this optical kink will nag at my vision for the rest of my life. They say you tend not to notice it as much after a while; the brain learns to ignore the difference. I'll have to get used to it. The vitreous becomes a watery wilting balloon deflating in its oracular chamber. Such is a human body through time, the slow demise of vision, downslope of aging. Biography of refractive error.

It's all rather minor, and relatively trivial, and yet the detachment is a harbinger of death and decay. The fragments are a precipitate of future troubles. This body will collapse, one day, and corrode into pieces. The detachment is a minor but telling entry in the ledger of a body.

August 13. What happens when otherness lingers in one's own eyes and vision? The equation "eye = I" no longer applies. Self and other are inextricably entangled.

August 14. A strange foreign body has thrust itself into the sphere of the optical self. With this comes the sense of an intrusion; an intruder has broached the domicile of the eye. "The intruder introduces himself forcefully, by surprise or by ruse. . . . Something of the stranger has to intrude, or else he loses his strangeness," writes philosopher Jean-Luc Nancy in reflecting on the singular intruder that his body encountered—the heart of another human being, inserted into his chest through an organ transplant.[7] Most often, an intruder comes from outside. With the vitreous detachment, parts of the body have broken off and intruded into another realm of the body. And they're here to stay, these intimate strangers. "If, once he is there, he remains a stranger, then for as long as this remains so—and does not simply become 'naturalized'—his coming does not stop: he continues to come, and his coming does not stop intruding in some way: in other words, without right or familiarity, not according to custom, being, on the contrary, a disturbance, a trouble in the midst of intimacy."[8]

A disturbance keeps troubling the interiors of an eye. Parts of the eye break off in a phantasm of imminent sightlessness.

August 14. It's just there, protein filaments stuck in a gel. The materiality of the eye is getting in the way of any transparent optics. An unmovable density presses against clarity of vision. The body contains sheer matter, frayed portions betray its owner. *Il y a, dans les yeux.*

August 15. The eye carries a stain of spilled black ink. (It's as if) something or someone has written on the lens of the eye, leaving a graphic trace.

This semi-legible scrawl adds to other writings on a body self - psychic, genetic, karmic, photonic, environmental, chemical, cicatricial, traumatic, amorous, tattooic—countless graphs inscribed on the corpus of a life.

August 16. With the tear in the vitreous, would this make the cornea less suitable for grafting into the body of another? Are the eyes damaged goods now? I might have to give up on the ecstatic fantasy of giving my biology onto others, especially if the body is in irreversible decline.

August 17. Paris. Tuesday night at the basilica there was the usual crowd of tourists passing through the place. Someone sang "No Woman, No Cry." I walked by the gated entrance and saw the professor-beggar seated by the metal posts of the gate, seeking handouts. He looked well, healthy. I wonder if he has a day job and he comes here at the end of his workday to earn a bit more cash.

A pair of glasses lay suspended on a chain circling his neck. By his right foot, on a lower step, was a dark-blue bag, inscribed with white lettering. I couldn't get close enough to perceive the details of his accoutrements. I couldn't tell if his eyeglasses still carried the bandaged patch in the center. If I tried to get closer, he'd see me seeing. A photograph would have enabled me examine closely, later on, but I didn't have the camera with me, only a cell phone—and I'm wary of taking photos of him.

His hands did not appear to be trembling, neither one. No suffering shown, or to be decoded.

He spotted me right away. He saw me looking his way. Did he recognize me from before?

I walked past him and stood by the wall of an adjoining building, beyond his line of vision. I took out my notebook and wrote out a few notes. He couldn't see me doing this.

With the notebook in my hand I walked back to where I was standing before. I passed near him, again. He held his hand up to his face, as if he didn't want me to see him, or study him, or take his image. Did he think I had a camera in my hands—or a spycam fixed into my eyeglasses?

I saw, or imagined, a hand near his face, to block any direct vision of a gaze upon him.

I kept walking, slowly, and sat on one of the stone curbs, some twenty meters from him. He was looking directly at me, studying me, watching every movement, eyes straight on. He wanted to know if I wanted to know him.

My lingering presence could have provoked a memory for him of my observations back in June. How many others hanging about the basilica would bear a resemblance to me—a tall guy, with dark hair and a slight beard, watchful eyes, not interested in the architectural or spiritual designs of the place so much as the play of people? Does he remember the photographs I took in his presence?

We are like two spiders who spot one another in a shared terrain. We stand still, legs pitched on sensitive ground, and regard the other. Two beggar-ethnographers encounter one another and find they have been studying the same population. They come to observe one another in guarded ways.

By then the man was wearing his eyeglasses close to his eyes. He watched me sit there and look about. I feigned a certain nonchalance. A military patrol walked past—four soldiers, carrying guns. I showed interest in them and performed attentive looking, to show that my intrigue lay elsewhere. The man watched me as I watched the soldiers past. He watched my mode of watching. I stood up and looked around. I walked slowly behind the band of soldiers, trailing in their wake as they crossed the mount. I didn't look back.

August 18. At night the flashing lights came like shooting stars racing across the inner universe of the eye. I first noticed the flares after midnight, when I emerged from the bright lights of the Goncourt Métro station. As I walked in dark streets light sliced through the dark of the eye. I thought at first that electrical sparks might be illuminating the scaffolding of buildings, only then to perceive the light as flaring from a chamber of consciousness or part of a neuronal brain.

The flashes might have been there earlier in the day, but the full glare of the summer sun obscured their effects. Quick paroxysms of light, especially when I look the eye to the right; this is worrisome. It's what the doctors said I should watch out for—the retina might be affected, tearing away. This could be simply a residual effect of last week's detachment; or it could be a neuronal tear requiring immediate medical care. I thought the light might go away if I went home and rested my eyes, but that wasn't the case. When the eyes were closed, there were no flashes. Once opened, the flashes recurred. I lay there in the dark, late at night, in a foreign land, not sure what was going on with my eye or what would come of it. I worried I would have to catch a flight back to New York to submit to urgent medical procedures. I'd have to wear a white gauze patch over the eye and hold my head down to keep the retina intact. I closed my eyes and wished the flashes would go away. When I opened the lids again and looked to the right a camera light flashed in a room of my brain. I fell asleep soon after, so at least I wasn't kept up all night worrying about it.

I fear a potentially catastrophic collapse of sight and vision. I fear the inability to read and to write, or to see light and the rough beauty of the world.

In the morning the flashing lights were still there, though not as noticeable in daylight because of all the luminance around. I decided to try to have the eye examined here in Paris. I located a Foundation Ophtamolique near the Parc des Buttes-Chaumont and gave thought to walking over there, to see if I could talk with someone in person and have the eye looked at. I imagined an awkward encounter, with me trying to explain the situation in French and not having medical insurance in France or knowing the system. I phoned the American embassy and they advised me to contact the American Hospital to the west of Paris. I called there and received an appointment for 17:30.

Waiting through a drizzly day I arrived at the quiet suburban streets near to the hospital before the appointed time. A receptionist at the doctor's office took my name and I sat among the other patients. Black-and-white photographs of the hospital in earlier times hung from the corridor walls. A notice in the hallway stated that surveillance cameras were in place.

A certain Dr. C, ophtalmologiste, welcomed me into his office. He did not speak much English and so we conversed in French. I explained that I had suffered "un détachement du vitreous" the week before and was now seeing the flashing lights. He dilated the pupil of the right eye. Once the mydriasis took effect he dropped a liquid on the surface of the eye and placed a lens flat on the cornea. He peered into the eye's tissues.

"Parfait," he said in taking off his techno-eye. "Pas problème."

The retina was in good shape.

"Bon," I said. But why, I asked, in French, am I seeing these lights, *ces lumières*?

He explained that this can happen when the vitreous is still attached to part of the retina and is "tugging" on it; the brain interprets the stimulation as light. But since the retina is in good shape there's no cause for concern.

I pictured fibers tugging on a retinal net, neurofibrillary tension. I walked with sunglasses in a watery city and entered into subterranean brilliance, eyes downcast, while shielded within the routines of dilation.

August 19. Photo + opia, light-seeing, light-eye. *Photopsia* is the medical term for the "perceived flashing lights" that can often result from a posterior retinal detachment (as well as migraines and other disorders).

As the vitreous detachment proceeds, adherent vitreous membrane might pull on the retina. This traction can stimulate the retina and cause it to discharge electrical impulses. The brain interprets these impulses as flashes of light.

The presence of perceived flashes of light. The word "perceived" here is telling. The light is sensed, but it's not photonic light. The nerve luminance is more neural phasm than solar force, more *pha-* than *pho-*. Epiphanomenal. All of this points to an aporia of sensation: how much of perception is of the world and how much does it relate to the workings of body, eye, and neural mind?

August 20. A *phosphene* is a phenomenon characterized by the experience of seeing light without light actually entering the eye. From the Greek words *phos* and *phainein*. Pressure phosphenes, the rubbing of eyes. Pressure on the eye results in activation of retina ganglion cells. Phosphenes have been detected in situations of meditation; visual deprivation, "Prisoner's Cinema"; psychedelic drugs; visual prosthesis; patterns appear when the eyes are closed. The body emits light like phosphorescent rock inside a cave.

August 21. The history of the eye entails a series of phantasms shifting through time. Pure optics in a clear lens; myopia, astigmatic, presbyopia; broken eye wire; plastic intimacies; vitreous detachment; flying flies; animal other; proteinaceous aggregates; retinal net; tainted gaze; graphic trace; the matter of an eye refracts into different visions with each turn of looking. The detachment and floaters are physiological phenomena (aren't they?), and yet my mind ascribes phantasms upon them. They are phanomenal, like everything else. The recent erring in the eye is an event both biological and phantasmal. Any life is biophantasmal, in that life involves a mix of biological forces and phantasmal imaginaries—an unfathomable jumble of the organic and the imaginary. The force of certain visions has taken hold in the phantasm eye of a phantom self. A range of possible perceptions appear and disappear, change form, take on tonalities, shadings, allusions, these apparitions weave in and out of awareness within the kaleidoscopic workings of an eye.

It's much the same in ordinary life. Phantasmata are part and parcel of the everyday. Each sound heard, each vision, taste and touch, each mode of sensing is phantasmal in dimension. Half-perceived, half-imagined, appears to be a fair ratio.[9]

August 22. The logic of phantasms is not like any ordinary logic or mode of reasoning. Phantasms work through flows of association, analogy, and imaginative force, dream, fantasy, of spectral relations and haunting. Or, to invoke words of Derrida, "The logic of the phantasm . . . is not strictly speaking a logic, it resists the *logos*. . . . There is therefore no logic or *logos* of the phantasm or of the ghost or of the spectral. Unless the *logos* itself be precisely *the* phantasm, the very element, the origin and the resource of the phantasm itself, the form and the formation of the phantasm, or even of the revenant."[10]

The last sentence here touches on something I've begun to wonder about—that the phantasm could be the *logos* of life, the very element of thought and apparition in the world. Is phantasm the form and formation of life, the force of life and image? Is the world itself phantasm?

August 23. What, then, of perception? Any moment of sensing, looking, touching, of "receiving, collecting" (perceptiō), of comprehending, entails phantasmal multiplicities—as well as a phantasm of multiplicity. To perceive in the world, in any flow of time, implies a baroque-like panoply of optics, media, mediations; memories, associations, expectations; displacements and discontinuities; connections, forces, affective tonalities; blind spots and epiphanies; confusions, reversals, ambiguity; certitudes, uncertainties; technologies of projection and reception; frames and screens; neural synapses, liquid crystal displays; images, imaginaries, fantasia; haptics of hand, eye, skin; politics, micro and macro; strange spectral reverberations of violence and beauty. Perception is a jagged story of sensation, force, and phantasm. Vision is riddled with hallucinatory valences. Any field of sensation—an urban expanse, a moment remembered, imagined, a dream, photograph, a lover's touch, a stranger's face, an eye—holds a thousand flickering phantoms.

August 24. See how, in addressing a theory of phantasmal perception, I'm giving clarity to a blur disturbance. With a gauze bandage of abstract words I'm covering over the wound of an encounter.

The phantasm of theory: any theory is a spectral formation that helps with the trouble of looking in life.

See how, with these words, I've added another layer of gauze. It could be torn away.

Writing as gauze. *Gauze*, from French *gaze*, possibly from Arabic قَزّ (qazz, "silk") from Persian کژ (kaz, "silk"), from Middle Persian *kaz* ("silk"), or from غَزَّة (ġazza, "Gaza"), a city associated with silk

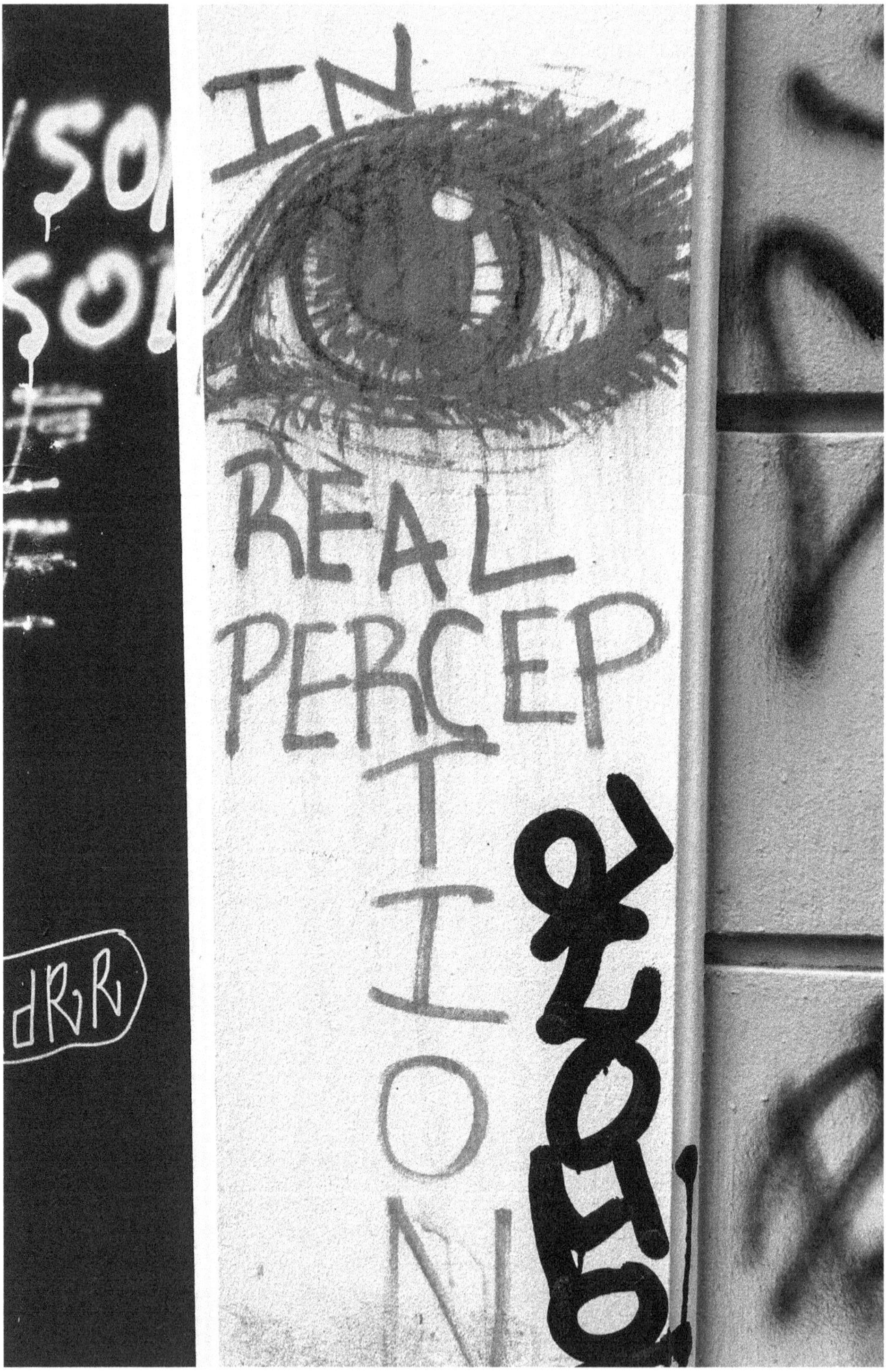
IN
REAL
PERCEP
T
I
O
N

production.[11] A thin, transparent fabric with a loose, open weave. A similar bleached cotton fabric used as a surgical dressing. A thin woven metal or plastic mesh. Mist or haze.

Writing as gauze, fabric, weave, dressing, mist or haze.

August 23. Beyond the optics, I wonder if a plague of phantasmal thought is catching up on me. Is the eye's torsion morphing into blindness? Am I becoming a blind man? In the flesh of the imaginary, the eye marring is a trace effect, a distorting graph of specific acts, simulations, and intrusions. Eye for an eye. Ocular karma. Have I brought this on myself?

I wrote on the eye of another. The specter of that mark now haunts me.

August 29. By the looks of it, we are somewhere off the coast of Scotland. The lands and waters below appear quaintly geographic under the radiance of the sun. Most of the windows in the plane's cabin are hidden behind plastic blinds to allow for better viewing of the digital screens. No one wants any damaging solar glare to cut into the hi-def precision of the pixels. Throughout the airtight vessel rows are lit in darkness by flashes of films and video games. Cocooned within a glow of consoles, we're belted into separate pods, nourished by aluminum-wrapped food, drink, images. Plastic earphones snug within our ears, we have become somnambulant in our plasma dreams, nursing on the tube of images sucking into our eyes through a complex mastication of sight and sound. The man seated to my right has been playing a video game on his smart phone for hours on end. He's pushing brightly colored balls about a tiny screen as the balls tumble and fall into newly fabricated alignments. I cannot deduce the point of the game nor can I fathom the man's thrill of eyeing it for hours on end. *Fancy is his only hope.*

We're in airplane mode, thirty thousand feet above sea level, six hundred miles per hour. The plane is humming across the Atlantic, coastlands of Iceland, Greenland, and on to Newfoundland in that long arc of intercontinental transport. The airplane's moving map system reports on our progress with data sent from satellite to computer to visual display. The flight is ahead of schedule, says our captain, sight unseen. We should arrive at JFK in a few hours, retinal scans waiting for us at customs. My neighbor's head is turned toward the wall of the airplane, the tiny obsession held in the palm of his hand. Apparently he does not want me to watch his electronic adventures. He's coked up on snowy whites and reds, juiced into the feed from the video console fixed to the chair before him. I'm not sure he's listening much to Al Pacino's plight in *Danny Collins*, which is screening on his retina just now. I try to close my eyes but the flashing sheen keeps my eyes pried open. Look at the screen and dream its images. A woman across the way is scrolling through photos she took during her vacation, selfies at the Catacombs. She taps on the images she likes and they zip into a cloud. Each time a flight attendant comes around with drinks my neighbor orders a whiskey and a glass of ice. Apparently he wishes to remove his mind from the press of time and the slow burn of the real, he wants to drown out the anxiety of flight, hazards of crashing. He needs images as much as he does oxygen. We've barely exchanged a word. In the dim light, when I'm not eyeing the screen a few inches from my pupils or scanning those of my neighbors, I'm looking through pictures gathered in Montmartre. Fancy is our only hope. Imagination is our method. Welcome to Air Phantasma, Flight 406.

The one event that keeps circling back to me is of the morning I followed the blind man from the theater of the basilica. This was days ago. He stood by the columns, hand held open. I took a few photographs. He began to walk down the steps, sensing the ground with his walking stick. He came to the longer set of stairs that led downhill, away from the basilica, toward the streets of Montmartre. By then he had taken off the hood of his coat. His hair was grayish and balding at the top. Without the hood covering his head he looked more ordinary, like someone you'd see at a park playing chess with friends, a retired custodian or doorman. He no longer required the mythic image which the medieval coat framed about his face. As he walked away from the basilica, with the hood down, the phantasmagoric force of his appearance diminished in intensity.

I wasn't sure whether to follow him or not. Here was my chance to learn more about him, where he traveled to, how he moved through the world. This curiosity seized me like a ghost. The man made his way along the paved road that led away and west and down the sloping hill from the basilica. He found his way to the glass funicular car that shuttled people up and down the butte of Montmartre, from summit to base and back again. He swiped a card at the turnstile and walked into an open, empty car. I hesitated. *Do I really want to follow him? Should I really do that? Isn't that a shameful thing to do?* I had to think fast. I took one of the Métro tickets I had in my wallet and fed it into the turnstile. I passed the gate and stepped into the car. The machine's facades were built of a thick, clear plastic glass, with metal bars and poles in support.

We were alone there, surrounded by glass and metal. I stood a few feet away from him, all quiet-like. I could have spoken with him, struck up a conversation, laboring through faulty French. He stood facing one of the doors. I could have heard him breathe if I listened for that. The disparity between my yearlong consideration of him and his absolute unknowing of my life made me tremble.

I took out my camera and brought the lens to my right eye. Just when I went to press the shutter a photograph a woman bustled into the space with a young boy—a grandmother with her grandson, most likely. I took the photograph just as the woman was seating herself on a bench at the far end of the cabin. The image shows her face, dimly blurred in an act of motion, looking toward me. She looks startled, searching the Intel of her brain to gauge my intentions. A digital clock above her reads in red, DEPART DANS: *0 min*. In the photo the man stands immobile, as if blankly, forces at rest, waiting for the next effort of motion required.

I sought, this time, to approach him. The machinery kicked into gear and we started down the hillside, four exotics in a glass menagerie. We passed a café seen below, where I saw families seated at scattered tables. We glided past green crops of trees soaking up the morning light. I took another two photographs, using the blind man's body to shield me from the woman's gaze. In the still brief world of that imaged moment the

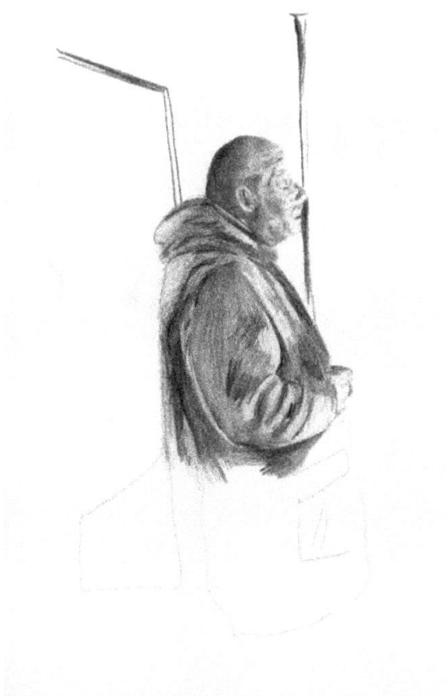

man is facing straight toward the door; the boy, seated on the bench, a round face with curious eyes, has turned his body into light, he's looking toward the streets below; the woman cannot be seen, except for the reflection of her arm and blouse in one of the glass windows. The digital display gives the time to the second, 10:38:46.

We came to a stop at the base of the track and waited for the doors to open. The woman and her grandson stood up and walked toward the door to the left.

"It's this way, probably," she said to the boy.

"It's here," the blind man said.

He meant the door to the right.

The door began to open, smooth glass on metal.

"C'est á la droit," I said, trying to be helpful.

The man turned his head toward me, surprised to hear a voice there. He asked me something quickly, in French, in words I couldn't catch right off—something like, "Accompany me to the Métro, please."

"Pardon?" I asked, hesitantly.

Here, finally, was my opportunity to speak with him. Within a moment's glance I saw a conversation unfolding between us, an exchange of names, a sense of who he was, where he lived, the lineaments of his blindness, within the budding of a friendship. He would have picked up my accent and asked where I was from. I'd come to know him as a person, not just within an arc of images. We might even become friends, buddies in sympathy, bantering in shy and easy smiles. I would visit him when I came to Paris, and I'd meet his daughter, a pensive girl who works in a flower shop. I would learn of his brief marriage, his past life, the days of seeing well. His wife was a small, wiry woman from Nice, of French-Algerian descent, who worked in a factory that produced airplane engines. I needed simply to hear this man well and respond effectively to his words for this friendship to emerge.

"Can you accompany me to the Métro?" he asked.

The woman spoke before I had a chance to respond, undercutting my relation to him.

"I will bring you to the Métro, Monsieur," she said. "We can take you there."

She looked pleased with herself, helping out. She glowed with goodness. The boy, by her side, watched all of this.

The door opened. She took the man's arm in hers and the three of them stepped out of the glass cabin. I stood by the door of the glass chamber, out of the picture, beyond the realm of their sociality. I couldn't think of anything to say.

It's not like I could have guided him well. Still, we could have managed, he and I, through congested streets, until we found the Métro. I imagined him trying to navigate those busy streets alone, avoiding the rush of cars and unwatchful pedestrians as he pushed his walking stick down the pavement.

With little else to do I began to trail behind them, past street lamps and aging merry-go-rounds. The three of them made their way across a busy street, the man's arm held in hers, the boy flitting about. The two elders were laughing, talking it up, sharing perspectives on life in Paris or the vagaries of being a certain age. The boy tagged along, looking here and there, catching glimpses of a window display and a shell game played along the side of the road. He darted toward his grandmother and her companion. I stayed far behind, mixing with the crowd of tourists, street sellers, con men. It's the first time I had "followed" someone for real, like they do in the movies. At times I lost sight of them. I drew closer until I spotted a light-brown coat and could see their slow progress down the congested street. I worried most about the boy noticing me, his eyes active and eager taking in the newness. Future years would bring him other visual pleasures; Asterix comics, video games, the girls at school, films late at night, a trip to India, time served in the military, his true love's raw beauty, the birth of a child, sunsets in Bali, his grandchildren at play. On the street he could have recognized me within the shifting currents of tourists and shop owners and he would alert his grandmother to my shadowy presence and she would turn and stand solidly in the street and chastise me with the sternness of a cruel and damning look. In any films imagined she incarnates a matronly woman, no nonsense, a wry sense of humor, who sniffs out the thief in the apartment complex across the way. As a young girl her prettiness received compliments that made her blush, she married a solid man, nothing fancy, she raised a grateful family, by forty her figure turned stocky, in these later years she foresees possibilities for the future she would rather not have realized; these phantasms of possibility just then, all aglimmer.

The two of them were having a jolly good time, smiling and laughing. She must have been asking how things were going for him. He must have appreciated the conversation. They might have spoken of the ins and outs of panhandling at Sacré-Coeur, the cost of a day's work. I could almost hear them talking, carousing. I wondered if the woman was saintly religious and had visited with her God and she took her assistance that day as a good, charitable deed, a Christian lesson for her grandson in the kindness paid toward blind men or poor crippled strangers in need.

We existed there, in the street, in separate fluxes of time. We came to an avenue, wide and majestic, busy with cars and pedestrian. We began our exactions to cross the street, making for the Métro stop. I crossed the avenue on the far side of an intersection, parallel with the three, their eyes weren't going that way. I followed them to the Métro and walked tentatively down the stairs. They were going slower than I was, I almost ran into them. The bulk of my body had little choice but to pass through the turnstiles within the same timing, a few metal clicks down the row. I thought the woman would spot me right off but she was busy smiling through her escort with the blind man.

There were two stairwells, leading to the two sides of the Métro line. I walked past the three of them and shot down one of the corridors, windowless, with white tiles. There was a 50–50 chance they'd come that way. If they did not, I could retrace my steps and find them along the other stairwell. I waited a few seconds. There was no sign of them, no view of their steps down the stairs, arms clasped together. I hiked up the steps and saw them a few feet away, walking in my direction. I went back down the stairs. I walked down the platform a ways so that when they reached that place they would not see me right off—just like in the movies, where the detective is trailing his suspect in a gritty subway system in 1970s New York.

A train was approaching from the narrow of the tunnel. I stood on the platform and considered whether or not to follow the man into the train. *This will haunt me forever* were the words coating my brain just then. If I followed him on the train, to wherever he was heading next, to his home or to some appointment in the city, a doctor's office or a meeting with a friend, a welfare assistant, then I'd never be able to get that voyeuristic search out of my mind and I'd live always with the stink of that licentious knowledge.

The train came to a stop. The doors opened and people began to step out of the separate cars. I calculated the timing, the slow steady movement of bodies. I turned to see if he would be stepping onto the train. I saw no sign of him, no familiar faces moving onto a metro car. What happened to them?

I walked up the stairs and looked around. I walked down along the walkway that led to the other side of the Métro line, no sight of the man or his companions.

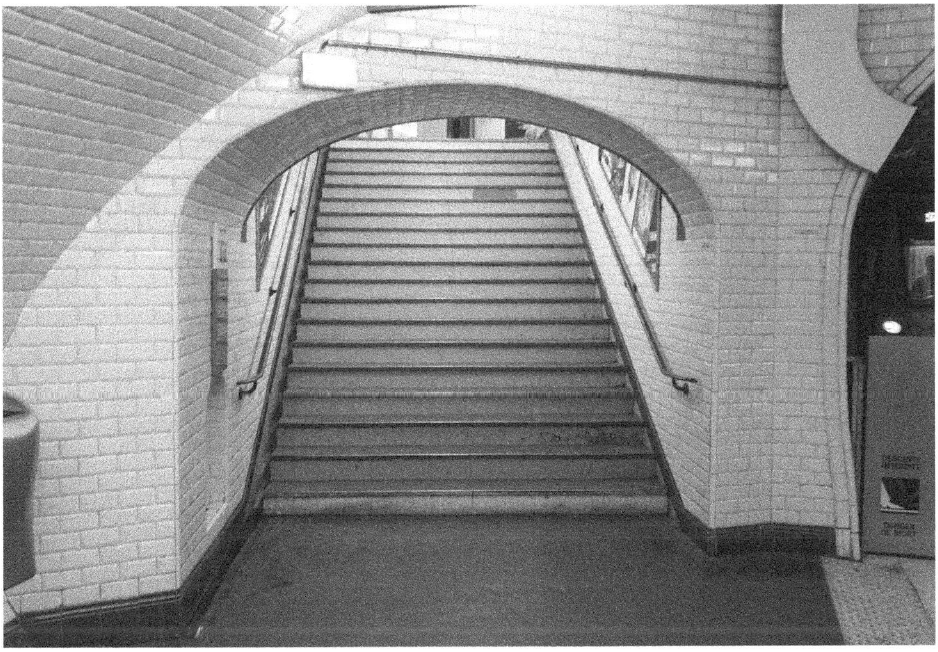

I returned to the platform and tried to comprehend the physics of their movements. I can't say what happened. I faced the vast dark white gulf of not-knowing that lies beyond the easy perceptions.

There is no story to tell. I have no sense of where he lives, outside of what I imagine. I never learned his name. It's better that way. No secret knowledge ghosting up a brain. Still, I am haunted by the optical encasements of the man I took to be blind, or partly blind, I'm not sure.

While in the Métro that day I tried to photograph the descending stairwell, the one I never saw the man descending. People kept walking past as they made their way onto the platform. I tried several times, with trains coming and going and people navigating the stairwell. I gave up on the effort. Too many bodies were getting in the way of the absence I sought to photograph.

Only now, while eyeing one of the photographs, do I notice in the lower left corner of one picture a sign that reads in French:

Descente
interdit
Danger
de mort

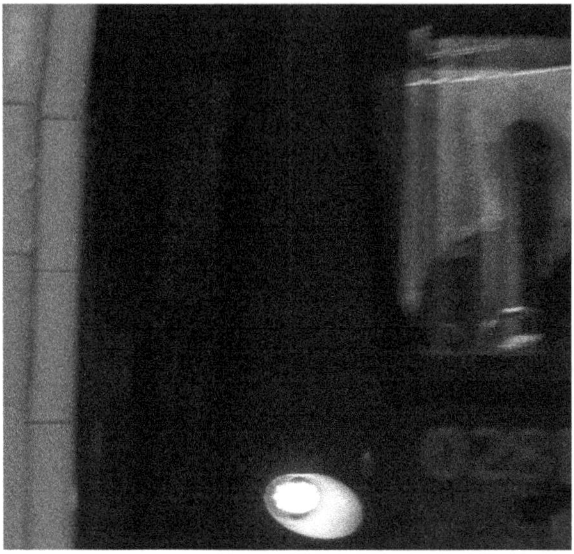

Descent prohibited, danger of death. In the folly of my fancy I take this notice to stand as a cautionary warning of the dangers of looking too closely at the forces of vision, all those eyes and optics and fevered looks stirring within a crowd of phantoms.

August 31. New York. And what of the vague, spectral image above that sign, hovering like a hallucinatory blur along the edges of the photograph? It didn't catch my eye back then. The visuals suggest the shadowy form of a man looking through glass onto the emerging scene.

September 16. My eyes hurt when I write. I can't write for long. There's too much light, too much glare. So much depends on the retina's ability to focus on a hovering screen.

I foresee myself sightless, with impaired vision, facing an obscurity of light.

October 23. Each day something is different. I'm not sure where it's all heading. The dark knot stains my sight. The flashing lights have lessened in the right eye, they are rarely seen. Occasionally, in lower portions of the left eye, grainy glows of white appear and float away, ghostly specters passing through the film of vision.

ALLUSIONS AND ACKNOWLEDGMENTS

In the text are allusions to writings by specific authors, namely William Shakespeare, E. T. A. Hoffmann, Friedrich Nietzsche, Jean Rimbaud, Virginia Woolf, Walter Benjamin, Maurice Blanchot, Samuel Beckett, Pierre Klossowski, Joan Didion, Alain Robbe-Grillet, and perhaps others.

The drawings in the text are by Safiya Husain (except for the anatomical drawing of the human eye, and the sketch made by the doctor in the emergency room). All of the photographs are by the author. The cover image is a photograph taken by the author in July 2015, of street art in Athens, Greece.

The sentence from Maurice Blanchot's *Madness of the Day*, appearing as an epigraph, is reproduced with the permission of Station Hill Press.

The text draws, in part, from two earlier publications by the author: Robert Desjarlais, 2016, "Phantasmography," *American Anthropologist* 118:400–407; and Robert Desjarlais, 2016, "Photography Tears the Subject from Itself," in *Anthropology and Alterity: Responding to the Other*, ed. Bernhard Leistle, 282–307 (New York: Routledge).

The research, writing, photographic work related to the composition of this book was supported, in part, by the Ziesing Fund and the Faculty Research and Development Fund at Sarah Lawrence College. Portions of the text benefited from discussions following presentations given at the University of Amsterdam; the University of California, Davis; at annual meetings of the American Anthropological Association; and at the 2015 symposium "Image as Method" at the Heyman Center for the Humanities at Columbia University.

Thank you to Tanja Ahlin, Nick Bartlett, Manon Capo, Samuele Collu, Vincent Crapanzano, Una Chung, Helen Desjarlais, Aurora Donzelli, Ned Dostaler, Christopher Garces, Angela Garcia, Maria Elena Garcia, Cristiana Giordano, Brian Goldstone, Alexa Hagerty, Caroline Hoepffner, Jean Hoepffner, David Hollander, Jennifer Bianca Hook, Safiya Husain, Michael D. Jackson, Mary Kairidi, Eduardo Kohn, Justine Kurland,

Bernhard Leistle, Eduardo Lago, Natashe Lemos Dekker, Francine Lorimer, Anne Lovell, Dejan Lukić, Stuart McLean, Todd Meyers, Anand Pandian, Albert Piette, Sarah Pinto, Mattijs van der Port, Mariana Rios, Andrés Romero, Mamourou Samassi, Aidan Seale-Feldman, Peter Skafish, Stephanie Spray, Anthony Stavrianakis, Joel Sternfeld, Lisa Stevenson, Laurence Tessier, Jason Throop, Sylvia Tidey, Charles Zerner, Jarrett Zigon, Tyler Zoanni; to Tom Lay and the editorial staff at Fordham University Press; to Clara Han and Bhrigupati Singh, editors of the series Thinking from Elsewhere; to my students and colleagues at Sarah Lawrence College; and to others encountered in life whose names I do not know.

NOTES

PHOTOGRAPHY TEARS THE SUBJECT FROM ITSELF

1. Nietzsche (1878) 2014, 7.

2. Foucault 2000, 241–42. Another translation of this interview in English can be found in Foucault 1991. In this earlier translation, the word "tearing" is used instead of "wrenching."

3. Ibid., 248.

4. Ibid., 240–41.

5. Ibid., 239–40.

6. Beckett 1958, 36.

7. Blanchot 1982, 264.

CORNEAL ABRASION

1. Sophocles 1982, 237, lines 1408–9.

2. Caillois (1935) 1984, 16. The statement, which goes without citation in Caillois's essay, apparently relates to a sentiment voiced by Socrates in Book 3 of Plato's *Republic*, on the dangers of imitation: "And if they do imitate, they must imitate what's appropriate to them from childhood: men who are courageous, moderate, holy, free, and everything of the sort; and what is slavish, or anything else shameful, they must neither do nor be clever at imitating, so that they won't get a taste for the being from its imitation" (Plato 1968, 74).

3. Breton (1928) 2002, 1.

4. Oxford English Dictionary Online, s.v. "eye, n.1," January 2014 (Oxford University Press), http://www.oed.com/view/Entry/67296?rskey=SGnGq6&result=1 (accessed August 7, 2014).

5. *Wikipedia*, s.v. "Eye," https://en.wikipedia.org/wiki/Eye (accessed August 7, 2014).

6. Levinas 1969, 29.

7. Online Etymological Dictionary, s.v. "Cornea," https://www.etymonline.com/word/cornea (accessed August 13, 2014). The anatomical drawing of the human eye is from Henry Gray's *Anatomy of the Human Body*, 20th ed., 1918.

8. "More about the Cornea," Washington University School of Medicine in St. Louis, Ophthalmology & Visual Sciences, http://lasik.wustl.edu/HowtheEyeWorks/MoreAbouttheCornea.aspx.
Information in this and the following paragraph are drawn from several Internet pages, including Wikipedia, s.v. "Cornea," https://en.wikipedia.org/wiki/Cornea (accessed August 13, 2014).

9. Wikipedia, s.v. "Corneal Transplantation," https://en.wikipedia.org/wiki/Corneal_transplantation (accessed August 14, 2014)

10. Lions Eye Bank, Testimonials, http://www.eyebankmanitoba.com/lions-eye-bank/testimonials/ (accessed August 15, 2014).

11. Borges 1999, 311.

OPTICALTERITIES

1. Dufau 1876. For an English translation of this passage, see Senden 1960, 61–62. The current translation of the original French is my own.

2. Senden, 1960, 62.

3. Derrida 1993, 94.

4. Ibid.

5. Ibid., 106.

6. Beccaloni 2009, 41. Other texts drawn from in this passage are: "Jumping spiders," https://ednieuw.home.xs4all.nl/Spiders/Salticidae/Salticidae.htm; and "Jumping spiders, Family Salticidea," https://www.thoughtco.com/jumping-spiders-family-salticidae-1968562.

7. Beccaloni 2009, 42.

8. "Jumping spiders, Family Salticidea," https://www.thoughtco.com/jumping-spiders-family-salticidae-1968562.

9. Parker 2004.

THE DELIRIUM OF IMAGES

1. On this, see Badiou 2003, 44.

BAROQUE VISION

1. Harvey 1979.

2. Radiguet (1923) 2011, 31.

3. Gracián (1657) 1960, 670.

4. Oxford English Living Dictionaries, https://en.oxforddictionaries.com/definition/selfie.

5. Debord (1967) 2014, 12.

6. Ibid., 2.

7. Kafka to Brod, in Wagenbach 1967, 256.

8. Berger 2012, 14.

9. Talbot (1844–46) 1969.

10. Ibid.
11. Ibid.
12. Camus (1942) 2012, 52.
13. Ibid., 53–54.
14. This, and the following, passages of Maurice Blanchot are from his essay "The Essential Solitude," in *The Space of Literature* (1982, 32–33).
15. Nietzsche (1878) 2010, 44.

PHANOMENOLOGY

1. Benjamin 1986, 92.
2. Mitchell 2015, 17.
3. Deleuze and Guattari 1994,164.
4. Derrida 1994, 12.
5. Ibid., 39.
6. Ibid., 10.
7. Ibid., 153.
8. The Sanskrit bhā-, "to shine, to be bright, to appear," is also the Sanskrit *bhati* "shines, glitters" and Old Irish *ban* "white, light, ray of light". The "pho-" in words like photon, phosphorous, and photography, from the ancient Greek *phōs*, "light, brightness," also relate to this semantics and genealogy of light.
9. Heidegger (1962) 1972, 82. Or, as Heidegger puts it in *Being and Time*, phenomenology's "essential character does not consist solely in its *actuality* as a philosophical 'movement.' Higher than actuality stands *possibility*. We can understand phenomenology solely by seizing it as possibility" ([1927] 2010, 36).

THE COLLECTOR OF EYES

1. Machado (1917–24) 1988.
2. David Brewster, *More Worlds Than One: The Creed of the Philosopher and the Hope of the Christian* (London: John Murray, 1854), cited in Oxford English Dictionary Online, s.v. "retina, n.1," January 2015, Oxford University Press, http://www.oed.com/view/Entry/164293?rskey=fAR59e&result=1 (accessed August 8, 2015).
3. Robert Boyle, Robert. *Some Considerations Touching the Vsefvlnesse of Experimental Naturall Philosophy: Propos'd in Familiar Discourses to a Friend, by Way of Invitation to the Study of It* (Oxford: Printed by Hen: Hall Printer to the University, 1663), cited in Oxford English Dictionary Online, s.v. "vitreous, adj.," January 2015, Oxford University Press, http://www.oed.com/view/Entry/224084?redirectedFrom=vitreous (accessed August 8, 2015).
4. Wikipedia, s.v. "Posterior Vitreous Detachment," https://en.wikipedia.org/wiki/Posterior_vitreous_detachment (accessed August 8, 2015).

5. http://www.medilexicon.com/dictionary/34034; https://www.ahdictionary.com/word/search.html?q=floater.

6. See Jay 1993, for instance.

7. Nancy 2008, 161.

8. Ibid.

9. To draw from William Wordsworth's poem "Lines Written a Few Miles above Tintern Abbey" (2000, 134):

> Therefore am I still
> A lover of the meadows and the woods,
> And mountains; and of all that we behold
> From this green earth; of all the mighty world
> Of eye, and ear,—both what they half create,
> And what perceive; [. . .]

10. Derrida 2011, 184–85.

11. Wiktionary, s.v. "Gauze," https://en.wiktionary.org/wiki/gauze (accessed August 24, 2015).

SELECTED BIBLIOGRAPHY

Each sentence written occurs in conversation with other sentences, and every image proceeds in relation to other images. This book is no exception. A number of works of art and scholarly writings have informed, in ways both direct and indirect, the words and images found in the main text, from literature, films, and photographic art to writings on the politics and phenomenology of photography, baroque aesthetics, vision and sensory perception, and ideas of phantoms, specters, phantasm and fabulation. Along with writings cited directly in the text, a selected bibliography follows.

WORKS CITED

Badiou, Alain. 2003. *On Beckett.* Manchester, U.K.: Clinamen.

Beccaloni, Jan. 2009. *Arachnids.* Berkeley: University of California Press.

Beckett, Samuel. 1958. *Endgame and Act without Words.* New York: Grove.

Benjamin, Walter. 1986. *Reflections: Essays, Aphorisms, Autobiographical Writings.* New York: Schocken.

Berger, John. 2012. *Cataract: Some Notes after Having a Cataract Removed.* Berkeley: Counterpoint.

Blanchot, Maurice. 1981. *The Madness of the Day.* Barrytown, N.Y.: Station Hill.

______. 1982. *The Space of Literature.* Lincoln: University of Nebraska Press.

Borges, Jorge Luis. 1999. *Selected Poems.* New York: Viking.

Breton, André. (1928) 2002j. *Surrealism and Painting.* Boston: MFA Publications.

Caillois, Roger. (1935) 1984. "Mimicry and Legendary Psychasthenia." *October* 31:16–32.

Camus, Albert. (1942) 2012. *The Outsider.* Translated by Sandra Smith. London: Penguin Classics.

Coetzee, J. M. 1985. *Dusklands.* New York: Penguin.

Debord, Guy. (1967) 2014. *The Society of the Spectacle.* Berkeley: Bureau of Public Secrets.

Deleuze, Gilles, and Felix Guattari. 1994. *What Is Philosophy?* New York: Columbia University Press.

Derrida, Jacques. 1993. *Memoirs of the Blind: The Self-Portrait and Other Ruins*. Chicago: University of Chicago Press.

———. 1994. *Specters of Marx, the State of the Debt, the Work of Mourning, and the New International*. New York: Routledge.

———. 1998. *Archive Fever: A Freudian Impression*. Chicago: University of Chicago Press.

———. 2011. *The Beast and the Sovereign, Volume II*. Chicago: University of Chicago Press.

Dufau, Pierre Armand. 1876. *Souvenirs et impressions d'une jeune aveugle-née*. Paris: Didier et Cie.

Foucault, Michel. 1991. *Remarks on Marx: Conversations with Duccio Trombadori*. Translated by R. James Gold and James Cascaito. New York: Semiotext(e).

———. 2000. *Power*. New York: New Press.

Gracián, Baltasar. (1657) 1960. *El Criticón*. In *Obras Completas*, Edición de Arturo del Hoyo. Madrid: Aguilar.

Gray, Henry. 1918. *Anatomy of the Human Body*. 20th ed. Edited by Warren Lewis. Philadelphia: Lea and Febiger.

Harvey, David. 1979. "Monument and Myth." *Annals of the Association of American Geographers* 69:362–81.

Heidegger, Martin. (1927) 2010. *Being and Time: A Revised Edition of the Stambaugh Translation*. Albany: State University of New York Press.

———. (1962) 1972. *On Time and Being*. New York: Harper and Row.

Jay, Martin. 1993. *Downcast Eyes: The Denigration of Vision in Twentieth-Century French Thought*. Berkeley: University of California Press

Levinas, Emmanuel. 1969. *Totality and Infinity: An Essay on Exteriority*. Pittsburgh: Duquesne University Press.

Machado, A. (1917–24) 1988. *Proverbios y cantares*. In *Obras completas I*. Edición crítica de Oreste Macrì. Madrid: Espasa-Calpe/Fundación Antonio Machado.

Mitchell, W. J. T. 2015. *Image Science: Iconology, Visual Culture, and Media Aesthetics*. Chicago: University of Chicago Press.

Nancy, Jean-Luc. 2008. *Corpus*. New York: Fordham University Press.

Nietzsche, Frederick. (1878) 2010. "On the Baroque." In *Baroque New Worlds: Representation, Transculturation, Counterconquest*, edited by Lois Parkinson Zamora and Monika Kaup, 44–45. Durham, N.C.: Duke University Press.

———. (1887–88) 2014. *Beyond Good and Evil/On the Genealogy of Morality*. Vol. 8 of *The Complete Works of Friedrich Nietzsche*. Stanford: Stanford University Press.

Parker, Ian. 2004. "The Gift." *New Yorker*, August 2, 2004, 54–63.

Plato. 1968. *The Republic of Plato.* 2nd ed. Translated by Harold Bloom. New York: Basic.
Radiguet, Raymond. (1923) 2011. *The Devil in the Flesh.* London: Penguin.
Senden, M. von. 1960. *Space and Sight: The Perception of Space and Shape in the Congentially Blind before and after Operation.* Glencoe, Ill.: Free Press.
Sophocles. 1982. *The Three Theban Plays: Antigone, Oedipus the King, Oedipus at Colonus.* Translated by Robert Fagles. New York: Penguin.
Talbot, William Henry Fox. (1844–46) 1969. *The Pencil of Nature.* New York: Da Capo.
Wagenbach, Klaus. 1967. *Franz Kafka: Années de jeunesse.* Paris: Mercure.
Wordsworth, William. 2000. *The Major Works.* Oxford: Oxford University Press.

LITERATURE

Bataille, Georges. (1928) 1987. *Story of the Eye.* San Francisco: City Lights.
Baudelaire, Charles. (1869) 1970. *Paris Spleen.* New York: New Directions.
Beckett, Samuel. 1997. *The Complete Short Prose of Samuel Beckett, 1929–1989.* New York: Grove.
———. 2009. *Three Novels: Molloy, Malone Dies, The Unnamable.* New York: Grove.
Blanchot, Maurice. 1993. *The One Who Was Standing Apart from Me.* Barryton, N.Y.: Station Hill.
Breton, André. (1928) 1994. *Nadja.* New York: Grove.
Carson, Anne. 1998. *Autobiography of Red.* New York: Vintage.
Cervantes, Miguel De. (1605–15) 2003. *Don Quixote.* London: Penguin.
Coetzee, J. M. 1985 *Dusklands.* New York: Penguin.
Coover, Robert. 2000. *Pricksongs and Descants: Fictions.* New York: Grove Press
Cortázar, Julio. 1985. *Blow-Up: And Other Stories.* New York: Pantheon.
———. 1987. *Hopscotch.* New York: Pantheon.
DeLillo, Don. 1991. *Libra.* New York: Penguin.
Genet, Jean. 1967. *The Thief's Journal.* Harmondsworth, U.K.: Penguin.
Hamsun, Knut. 1996. *Hunger.* Edinburgh: Canongate.
Kafka, Franz. 2006. *Kafka's Selected Stories.* New York: Norton.
Lago, Eduardo. 2013. *Call Me Brooklyn.* Champaign: Dalkey Archive Press.
Lispector, Clarice. 2012. *Água viva.* New York: New Directions.
Michon, Pierre. 2008. *Small Lives.* New York: Archipelago.
Modiano, Patrick. 1999. *Dora Bruder.* Berkeley: University of California Press.
Nerval, Gérard de. (1855) 2001. *Aurélia.* Los Angeles: Green Integer.
Pessoa, Fernando. 2002. *The Book of Disquiet.* London: Penguin Classics.
Poe, Edgar Allen. 1983. *The Tell-Tale Heart.* New York: Bantam Classics.

Proust, Marcel. (1913) 2004. *Swann's Way: In Search of Lost Time*. Vol. 1. New York: Penguin.
Robbe-Grillet, Alain. 1959. *Jealousy: A Novel*. New York: Grove.
Sabato, Ernesto. (1961) 2017. *On Heroes and Tombs*. Boston: Verba Mundi.
Sebald, W. G. 1999. *The Rings of Saturn*. New York: New Directions.
———. 2001. *Austerlitz*. New York: Random House.
Woolf, Virginia. 1925. *Mrs Dalloway*. New York: Harcourt, Brace.

FILMS

Allen, Diana. 2007. *Still Life*. Cambridge, Mass.: Sensory Ethnography Labs.
Antonioni, Michelangelo. (1966) 2004. *Blowup*. Burbank, Calif.: Warner Home Video.
Baron, Rebecca. 1995. *The Idea of North*. Chicago: Video Data Bank.
———. 2005. *How Little We Know of Our Neighbors*. Chicago: Video Data Bank.
Castaing-Taylor, Lucien, and Véréna Paravel. 2012. *Leviathan*. New York: Cinema Guild.
Frampton, Hollis. 1971. *Nostalgia*. New York: American Federation of Arts.
Haneke, Michael. 2006. *Caché*. Culver City, Calif.: SONY.
Hitchcock, Alfred. (1954) 2008. *Rear Window*. Universal City, Calif.: Universal Pictures.
Marker, Chris. (1962/1983) 2007. *La jetée/Sans soleil*. Irvington, N.Y.: Criterion Collection.
O'Rourke, Dennis. 1987. *Cannibal Tours*. Los Angeles: Direct Cinema Ltd.
———. 2015. *The Good Woman of Bangkok*. San Francisco: Kanopy Streaming.
Port, Mattijs van der. 2016. *The Possibility of Spirits*. Amsterdam: University of Amsterdam.
Spray, Stephanie, and Pacho Velez. 2014. *Manakamana*. New York: Cinema Guild.

PHOTOGRAPHIC ART

Agee, James, and Walker Evans. (1941) 2001. *Let Us Now Praise Famous Men*. New York: Houghton Mifflin.
Berger, John, and Jean Mohr. 1981. *A Fortunate Man*. New York: Pantheon.
Calle, Sophie. 1988. *Suite Vénitienne*. Seattle: Bay.
———. 2009. *L'Hôtel*. Arles: Actes Sud.
———. 2011. *Blind*. Arles: Actes Sud.
Frank, Robert. (1958) 2008. *The Americans*. Washington, D.C.: National Gallery of Art.
Goldberg, Jim. 1995. *Raised by Wolves*. New York: Scalo.
Goldin, Nan. 2001. *The Ballad of Sexual Dependency*. New York: Aperture.
Sternfeld, Joel. 2012. *American Prospects*. New York: Distributed Art Publishers.

Winogrand, Garry, and Leo Rubinfien. 2013. *Garry Winogrand*. New Haven: San Francisco Museum of Modern Art.

ON PHOTOGRAPHY

Batchen, Geoffrey. 1997. *Burning with Desire: The Conception of Photography*. Cambridge: MIT Press.
Batchen, Geoffrey, ed. 2009. *Photography Degree Zero: Reflections on Roland Barthes's Camera Lucida*. Cambridge: MIT Press.
Barthes, Roland. 1981. *Camera Lucida*. New York: Farrar, Straus and Giroux.
Benjamin, Walter. (1931) 1999. "Little History of Photography." In *Selected Writings*, vol. 2, *1927–1934*, edited by Michael W. Jennings, Howard Eiland, and Gary Smith, 507–30. Cambridge: Harvard University Press.
Berger, John. 1991. *About Looking*. New York: Vintage International.
———. 1995. *Another Way of Telling*. New York: Vintage.
Burgin, Victor. 1982. *Thinking Photography*. London: Macmillan.
Cavell, Stanley. 2005. "What Photography Calls Thinking." In *Cavell on Film*, 115–33. Albany: State University of New York Press.
Damisch, Hubert. (1963) 1980. "Five Notes for a Phenomenology of the Photographic Image." In *Classic Essays on Photography*, edited by Alan Trachtenberg, 287–90. New Haven: Leete's Island.
Dyer, Geoff. 2005. *The Ongoing Moment*. New York: Pantheon.
Elkins, James. 2011. *What Photography Is*. New York: Routledge.
Flusser, Vilem. 2000. *Towards a Philosophy of Photography*. London: Reaktion.
Gross, Frederick. 2012. *Diane Arbus's 1960s: Auguries of Experience*. Minneapolis: University of Minnesota Press.
Kelsey, Robin Earle, and Blake Stimson. 2008. *The Meaning of Photography*. New Haven: Yale University Press.
Nelson, Maggie. 2112. *The Art of Cruelty: A Reckoning*. New York: Norton.
Papageorge, Tod. 2011. *Core Curriculum: Writings on Photography*. New York: Aperture.
Sekula, Allan. 1984. *Photography against the Grain: Essays and Photo Works, 1973–1983*. Halifax: Press of the Nova Scotia College of Art and Design.
Sontag, Susan. 1973. *On Photography*. New York: Picador.
———. 2004. *Regarding the Pain of Others*. New York: Picador.
Tagg, John. 1993. *The Burden of Representation: Essays on Photographies and Histories*. Minneapolis: University of Minnesota Press.
Wright, Christopher. 2013. *The Echo of Things*. Durham, N.C.: Duke University Press.

ANTHROPOLOGY AND PHOTOGRAPHY

Banks, Marcus, and Jay Ruby, eds. 2011. *Made to Be Seen: Perspectives on the History of Visual Anthropology*. Chicago: University of Chicago Press.

Bourgois, Philippe, and Jeff Schonberg. 2009. *Righteous Dopefiend*. Berkeley: University of California Press.

Desjarlais, Robert. 2015. "Seared with Reality: Phenomenology through Photography." In *Phenomenology and Anthropology: A Sense of Perspective*, edited by Kalpana Ram and Christopher Houston, 197–223. Bloomington: Indiana University Press.

Edwards, Elizabeth, ed. 1992. *Anthropology and Photography, 1860–1920*. New Haven: Yale University Press.

Pinney, Christopher. 2011. *Photography and Anthropology*. London: Reaktion.

Wright, Christopher. 2013. *The Echo of Things: The Lives of Photographs in the Solomon Islands*. Durham, N.C.: Duke University Press.

ETHNOGRAPHIC WRITING

Biehl, João. 2005. *Vita: Life in a Zone of Social Abandonment*. Photographs by Torben Eskerod. Berkeley: University of California Press.

Crapanzano, Vincent. 1980. *Tuhami, Portrait of a Moroccan*. Chicago: University of Chicago Press.

Deleuze, Gilles. 1977. "Nomad Thought." In *The New Nietzsche: Contemporary Styles of Interpretation*, edited by David B. Allison, 142–49. Cambridge: MIT Press.

Desjarlais, Robert. 2003. *Sensory Biographies: Lives and Deaths among Nepal's Yolmo Buddhists*. Berkeley: University of California Press.

———. 2016. *Subject to Death: Life and Loss in a Buddhist World*. Chicago: University of Chicago Press.

Garcia, Angela. 2010. *The Pastoral Clinic: Addiction and Dispossession along the Rio Grande*. Berkeley: University of California Press.

Jackson, Michael. 2015. *Harmattan: A Philosophical Fiction*. New York: Columbia University Press.

Leiris, Michel. 1981. *L'Afrique fantôme*. Paris: Gallimard.

Lévi-Strauss, Claude. 1992. *Tristes tropiques*. New York: Penguin.

Meyers, Todd. 2013. *The Clinic and Elsewhere: Addiction, Adolescents, and the Afterlife of Therapy*. Seattle: University of Washington Press.

Pandian, Anand, and Stuart McLean. 2017. *Crumpled Paper Boat: Experiments in Ethnographic Writing*. Durham, N.C.: Duke University Press.

Rabinow, Paul. 1977. *Reflections on Fieldwork in Morocco*. Berkeley: University of California Press.

Stewart, Kathleen. 2007. *Ordinary Affects*. Durham, N.C.: Duke University Press.

ON VISION, BLINDNESS, AND THE PHENOMENOLOGY OF PERCEPTION

Benjamin, Walter. 1969. *Illuminations: Essays and Reflections*. New York: Schocken.

Blanchot, Maurice. (1980) 1995. *The Writing of the Disaster.* Lincoln: University of Nebraska Press.

Classen, Constance. 1993. *Worlds of Sense: Exploring the Senses in History and across Cultures.* New York: Routledge.

Crary, Jonathan. 1999. *Suspensions of Perception: Attention, Spectacle, and Modern Culture.* Cambridge: MIT Press.

Derrida, Jacques. 1973. *Speech and Phenomena: And Other Essays in Husserl's Theory of Signs.* Evanston, Ill.: Northwestern University Press.

———. 2005. *On Touching—Jean-Luc Nancy.* Stanford: Stanford University Press.

Feldman, Allen. 1991. *Formations of Violence: The Narrative of the Body and Political Terror in Northern Ireland.* Chicago: University of Chicago Press.

———. 2015. *Archives of the Insensible: Of War, Photopolitics, and Dead Memory.* Chicago: University of Chicago Press.

Foucault, Michel. 1994. *The Birth of the Clinic: An Archaeology of Medical Perception.* New York: Vintage.

———. 1995. *Discipline and Punish.* New York: Vintage.

Garland-Thomson, Rosemarie. 2009. *Staring: How We Look.* Oxford: Oxford University Press.

Howes, David. 1991. *The Varieties of Sensory Experience: A Sourcebook in the Anthropology of the Senses.* Toronto: University of Toronto Press.

Hull, John. 2017. *Notes on Blindness: A Journey through the Dark.* London: Wellcome.

Jackson, Michael. 1989. *Paths toward a Clearing: Radical Empiricism and Ethnographic Inquiry.* Bloomington: Indiana University Press.

Merleau-Ponty, Maurice. (1945) 2012. *Phenomenology of Perception.* New York: Routledge.

———. 1969. *The Visible and the Invisible.* Chicago: Northwestern University Press.

Rancière, Jacques. 2006. *The Politics of Aesthetics: The Distribution of the Sensible.* New York: Continuum.

Schor, Naomi. 1999. "Blindness as Metaphor." *Differences: A Journal of Feminist Cultural Studies* 11, no. 2:76–105.

Schweik, Susan. 2010. *The Ugly Laws: Disability in Public.* New York: New York University Press.

Seremetakis, C. Nadia. 1991. *The Last Word: Women, Death, and Divination in Inner Mani.* Chicago: University of Chicago Press.

Seremetakis, C. Nadia, ed. 1996. *The Senses Still: Perception and Memory as Material Culture in Modernity.* Chicago: University of Chicago Press.

Stiegler, Bernard. 2008–10. *Technics and Time.* Vols. 1-3. Stanford: Stanford University Press.

Stoller, Paul. 1997. *Sensuous Scholarship*. Philadelphia: University of Pennsylvania Press.
Taussig, Michael. 1991. *The Nervous System*. New York: Routledge.
Throop, C. Jason. 2010. *Suffering and Sentiment: Exploring the Vicissitudes of Experience and Pain in Yap*. Berkeley: University of California Press.

ON IMAGES AND IMAGINATION

Adelfattah, Kilito. 2010. *The Clash of Images*. New York: New Directions.
Baxstrom, Richard, and Todd Meyers. 2015. *Realizing the Witch: Science, Cinema, and the Mastery of the Invisible*. New York: Fordham University Press.
Belting, Hans. 2014. *An Anthropology of Images: Picture, Medium, Body*. Princeton: Princeton University Press.
Berger, John. 2011. *Bento's Sketchbook*. New York: Pantheon.
Blanchot, Maurice. 1989. *The Space of Literature*. Lincoln: University of Nebraska Press.
Carbone, Mauro. 2015. *The Flesh of Images: Merleau-Ponty between Painting and Cinema*. Albany: State University of New York Press.
Clark, T. J. 2008. *The Sight of Death: An Experiment in Art Writing*. New Haven: Yale University Press.
Crapanzano, Vincent. 2003. *Imaginative Horizons: An Essay in Literary-Philosophical Anthropology*. Chicago: University of Chicago Press.
Deleuze, Gilles. 1986. *Cinema 1: The Movement-Image*. Minneapolis: University of Minnesota Press.
———. 1989. *Cinema 2: The Time-Image*. Minneapolis: University of Minnesota Press.
———. 2005. *Francis Bacon: The Logic of Sensation*. Minneapolis: University of Minnesota Press.
Didi-Huberman, Georges. 2009. *Confronting Images: Questioning the Ends of a Certain History of Art*. University Park: Pennsylvania State University Press.
———. 2009. "How to Open Your Eyes." In *Harun Farocki: Against What Against Whom*, edited by Antje Ehmann and Kodwo Eshun, 38–50. London: Koenig.
———. 2012. *Images in Spite of All: Four Photographs from Auschwitz*. Chicago: University of Chicago Press.
Goldstone, Brian. 2016. "Chains." *Guernica*, December 22, 2016. https://www.guernicamag.com.
Guibert, Hervé. 1996. *Ghost Image*. Los Angeles: Sun and Moon.
Jackson, Michael. 2008. "The Shock of the New: On Migrant Imaginaries and Critical Transitions." *Ethnos* 73:57–72.

______. 2016. *The Work of Art: Rethinking the Elementary Forms of Religious Life*. New York: Columbia University Press.
Mohaghegh, Jason, and Dejan Lukić. 2016. *Elemental Disappearances*. New York: Punctum.
Mitchell, W. J. T. 2006. *What Do Pictures Want? The Lives and Loves of Images*. Chicago: University of Chicago Press.
Pandian, Anand. 2015. *Reel World: An Anthropology of Creation*. Durham, N.C.: Duke University Press.
Romero, Andrés. 2015. "Image as Method: Conversation on Anthropology through the Image." *Somatosphere*, August 14, 2015. http://somatosphere.net/2015/08/image-as-method-conversations-on-anthropology-through-the-image.html
Spyer, Patricia, and Mary Steedly, eds. 2013. *Images That Move*. Albuquerque, N.M.: School for Advanced Research Press.
Stevenson, Lisa. 2014. *Life Beside Itself: Imagining Care in the Canadian Arctic*. Berkeley: University of California Press.
Stavrianakis, Anthony. 2016. "Thinking the Obvious: Determination and Indetermination in a Voluntary Death." *Terrain*, January 2016. http://terrain.revues.org
Sylvester, David. 1975. *Interviews with Francis Bacon*. New York: Thames and Hudson.
Taussig, Michael. 2011. *I Swear I Saw This: Drawings in Fieldwork Notebooks, Namely My Own*. Chicago: University of Chicago Press.
Taylor, Lucien. 1996. "Iconophobia: How Anthropology Lost It at the Movies." *Transition* 69:64–88.

ON BAROQUE VISION, LANGUAGE, AND AESTHETICS

Buci-Glucksmann, Christine. 2013. *The Madness of Vision: On Baroque Aesthetics*. Athens: Ohio University Press.
Deleuze, Gilles. 1992. *The Fold: Leibniz and the Baroque*. Minneapolis: University of Minnesota Press.
Law, John, and Evelyn Ruppert, eds. 2016. *Modes of Knowing: Resources from the Baroque*. Manchester, U.K.: Mattering.
Murray, Timothy. 2008. *Digital Baroque: New Media Art and Cinematic Folds*. Minneapolis: University of Minnesota Press.
Nietzsche, Frederick. (1878) 2010. "On the Baroque." In *Baroque New Worlds: Representation, Transculturation, Counterconquest*, edited by Lois Parkinson Zamora and Monika Kaup. Durham, N.C.: Duke University Press.
Port, Mattijs van de. 2011. *Ecstatic Encounters. Bahian Candomblé and the Quest for the Really Real*. Amsterdam: Amsterdam University Press.

Zamora, Lois Parkinson. 2006. *The Inordinate Eye: New World Baroque and Latin American Fiction*. Chicago: University of Chicago Press.

Zamora, Lois Parkinson, and Monika Kaup, eds. 2010. *Baroque New Worlds: Representation, Transculturation, Counterconquest*. Durham, N.C.: Duke University Press.

ON PHANTOMS, PHANTASM, SPECTRALITY, FABULATION

Benjamin, Walter. 1999. *The Arcades Project*. Cambridge: Belknap Press of Harvard University Press.

Buck-Morss, Susan. 1989. *The Dialectics of Seeing: Walter Benjamin and the Arcades Project*. Cambridge: MIT Press.

Deleuze, Gilles. 2011. With Claire Parnet. *Gilles Deleuze from A to Z*. DVD. Cambridge, Mass.: Semiotext(e).

Deleuze, Gilles, and Felix Guattari. 1987. *A Thousand Plateaus: Capitalism and Schizophrenia*. Minneapolis: University of Minnesota Press.

Derrida, Jacques. 1992. *Given Time: 1. Counterfeit Money*. Chicago: University of Chicago Press.

———. 1994. *Specters of Marx: The State of the Debt, the Work of Mourning, and the New International*. New York: Routledge.

Derrida, Jacques, and Bernard Stiegler. 2007. *Echographies of Television*. Malden, Mass.: Polity.

Didi-Huberman, Georges. 2009. *The Surviving Image: Phantoms of Time and Time of Phantoms: Aby Warburg's History of Art*. University Park: Pennsylvania State University Press.

Dubord, Guy. 2014. *Society of the Spectacle*. Berkeley, Calif.: Bureau of Public Secrets.

Flaxman, Gregory. 2012. *Gilles Deleuze and the Fabulation of Philosophy*. Minneapolis: University of Minnesota Press.

Good, Byron. 2015. "Haunted by Aceh: Specters of Violence in Post-Suhara Indonesia." In *Genocide and Mass Violence: Memory, Symptom, and Recovery*, edited by Devon Hinton and Alexander Hinton, 58–82. Cambridge: Cambridge University Press.

Gordon, Avery. 2008. *Ghostly Matters: Haunting and the Sociological Imagination*, 2nd ed. Minneapolis: University of Minnesota Press.

Husserl, Edmund. 2005. *Phantasy, Image Consciousness, and Memory, 1898–1925*. Dordrecht: Springer.

Klein, Melanie. 2012. *Envy and Gratitude and Other Works, 1946–1963*. New York: Free Press.

Klossowski, Pierre. 1997. *Nietzsche and the Vicious Circle*. Chicago: University of Chicago Press.

———. 2007. "Nietzsche, Polytheism and Parody," In *Such a Deathly Desire*, 99–122. Albany: State University of New York.

Lukić, Dejan. 2014. *Hostage Spaces of the Contemporary Islamicate World: Phantom Territoriality*. London: Bloomsbury Academic.

McLean, Stuart. 2017. *Fictionalizing Anthropology: Encounters and Fabulations at the Edges of the Human*. Minneapolis: University of Minnesota Press.

Nass, Michael. 2014. *The End of the World and Other Teachable Moments: Jacques Derrida's Final Seminar*. New York: Fordham University Press.

Pilar Blanco, Maria del, and Esther Peeren, eds. 2013. *The Spectralities Reader: Ghosts and Haunting in Contemporary Cultural Theory*. London: Bloomsbury Academic.

Segal, Hanna. 1997. "Phantasy and Reality." In *The Contemporary Kleinians of London*, edited by Roy Schafer, 71–95. Madison: International University Press.

Sprinker, Michael, ed. 2008. *Ghostly Demarcations: A Symposium on Jacques Derrida's Specters of Marx*. New York: Verso.

Zigon, Jarrett. 2015. "What Is a Situation? An Assemblic Ethnography of the Drug War." *Cultural Anthropology* 30:501–24.

Žižek, Slavoj. 2009. *The Plague of Fantasies*. London: Verso.

———. 2014. *Event: A Philosophical Journey through a Concept*. New York: Melville House.

AND SPIDERS

Deleuze, Gilles. 2000. *Proust and Signs*. Minneapolis: University of Minnesota Press.

Deligny, Fernand. 2015. *The Arachnean and Other Texts*. Minneapolis: Univocal.

Lukić, Dejan. 2016. "Putting-Into-Orbit." Essay accompanying solo exhibition of Tomás Saraceno, *163,000 Light Years*, June 30–November 11, 2016. Museo de Arte Contemporáneo de Monterrey: MARCO. Monterrey, Mexico.

Raffles, Hugh. 2010. *Insectopedia*. New York: Pantheon.

Saraceno, Tomás. n.d. "Hybrid Webs," "How to Entangle the Universe in a Spider Web," and other projects. http://tomassaraceno.com.

Lightning Source UK Ltd.
Milton Keynes UK
UKHW041240101219
355098UK00013B/400/P

9 780823 281114